CONGRATULATIONS

Songwriter To The Stars

by Bill Martin

First Printing: 2017

Published by: Dujio

ISBN 978-1-5272-1281-7

FOREWORD

"To merely observe that Bill Martin has written a few songs is like saying that Ken Dodd tells the odd joke or Picasso painted one or two teapots. It kind of misses the point. Songs of all shape and size have poured from him. Some disappear without trace but some have lasted long enough to remind us he has won five Ivor Novellos, three ASCAP Awards and a reputation as one of the most prolific songwriters of his time plus as indefatigable a raconteur about the world of music as you would imagine - providing you had never met Sammy Cahn.

Like Sammy he has a great zest for his job and for living. His is a story of joy – a life set to music.

His website tells all there is to know of him – www.billmartinsongwriter.com.

'Nuff said. Read on..."

- Sir Michael Parkinson -

Dedication

Dedicated to my four children Meran, Alison, Angus and
Melanie who all believed in my dreams that I would become
a major songwriter and last but not least to Jan who has
been my steadying influence and has made me laugh
through my ups and downs.

Acknowledgements

To Spencer Leigh, a brilliant book writer and Merseyside DJ who was the first to talk to me and inspire me to write a book.

To my friend Stuart Cheek (Cheeky) who helped me put the ideas together.

To my friends of yesterday, songwriters Sammy Cahn and John Lennon who always told me to eventually write my life story and Brad Clark who put the book together and is my technical guru/editor.

My thanks to you all.

CONGRATULATIONS
Songwriter To The Stars

by Bill Martin

INTRODUCTION

Tin Pan Alley is the name given to the collection of music publishers and songwriters in the area of Manhattan at West 28th, between 5th and 6th Avenue and is usually dated to the mid 1880s. The origins of the term are unclear but the most likely account is that it was a derogatory reference to the sound of many pianos resembling the banging of tin pans. In the 1910s, the term Tin Pan Alley also started being used to describe London's Denmark Street because of the large number of music shops and publishers there. Denmark Street, named after Prince George of Denmark in the 17th century, runs from Charing Cross to St. Giles and is no more than about 500 yards long but it still holds the name Tin Pan Alley today.

Over the years, the street came under threat from development for office space when a great developer named Harry Hyams, who had a unique way of getting planning permission for high rise buildings, constructed Centrepoint. However, it remained unused for many years but he knew the value of the building would rise so he left it empty, thus managing to avoid paying any rates. In the meantime, he decided to buy the surrounding properties including Denmark Street, with the aim of building another Centrepoint and all the music publishers (who had cheap rents) suddenly left when Hyams started charging them much more. Thankfully Hyams was refused planning permission because the council didn't like his tactics with the original Centrepoint. However, as far as the songwriters and publishers were concerned, the damage was done and they are now spread all across London. More recently, construction of Crossrail has introduced different challenges for the street and its future still remains unclear. However, a campaign was mounted and English Heritage have now given Grade II listed status to eight buildings in the street.

As part of this, in April 2014, I was invited, along with several other ex-occupants of Tin Pan Alley, to attend the unveiling of a blue plaque commemorating its significance as the focal point of the British music industry. The plaque, at no. 9 where The Giaconda cafe was, reads 'This street was 'Tin Pan Alley' 1911-1992. Home of the British Publishers and Songwriters and their meeting place The Giaconda.

Denmark Street was where I started in the music business and wrote my biggest hits but the story starts in Govan, Glasgow.

Chapter 1 - No Mean City

I. Scotland, Glasgow and Govan

I wasn't born Bill Martin. I was born William Wylie Macpherson and I grew up as Wylie Macpherson. All my old, dear friends call me Wylie. I did think of calling this book, Who Is Bill Martin Anyway? by Wylie Macpherson. I'm Scottish, I'm part of a small nation and even though I changed my name to be in the music business, (as did many people back then, take Adam Faith (born Terry Nelhams-Wright), Cliff Richard (Harry Webb), Matt Monro (Terence Parsons) and Elton John (Reg Dwight), I'm very proud of being Wylie Macpherson, but the name 'Bill Martin' brought me luck.

I didn't have a traditional Scottish upbringing with kilts and all that, but I was very aware of being Scottish. I still feel that way and I like to wear the full highland regalia from time to time.

On the other hand, the famous Scottish music hall entertainer, Sir Harry Lauder never made any impression on me. He was a stage Scotsman with his tam-o'-shanter, kilt, sporran and twisted walking-stick. He sang 'Roamin' In The Gloamin'', 'I Love a Lassie' and 'A Wee Deoch-an-Doris' and wrote most of his songs but I feel embarrassed when I hear them as it gives listeners wrong ideas about Scotland. I can't speak for those in the north of Scotland who may have liked him, but I know he didn't appeal to folk like me who lived in Govan, Glasgow. In the main, his appeal was to people who'd left Scotland, the ex-pats who were living around the world, often in Canada or Australia.

Although my father was a very good musician, I was never very keen on him playing the accordion for the same reason, and that TV series with Andy Stewart, The White Heather Club, did nothing for me. I couldn't be bothered with Jimmy Shand and his Band.

We didn't like the English, but not in a derogative or vicious sense. If we played them at football, we always wanted to win and we never read English football results. We were only interested in Scottish teams.

Where I grew up, everybody had a Scottish accent. Some Scottish people speak so broadly that they cannot be understood by the English. I never wanted to lose my accent but I did want to speak more clearly. As a result, I am understood anywhere in the world whereas most of those who come from the poor districts in Scotland are not, as they never got the chance.

I'm very proud of coming from Scotland and being raised in Glasgow. You're going to hear some stories of hardship but the human spirit is a wonderful thing and everybody had a good sense of humour. Billy Connolly is exceptional but growing up around him, there were a thousand people in Glasgow who could have become stand-up comedians. You could go into any bar or shipyard and hear some funny stories or witty observations. Billy Connolly may not agree with all I say but he would agree with that.

A lot of readers may be surprised to learn that the IRA didn't set off any explosives in Glasgow or indeed, in the whole of Scotland, but it doesn't surprise me. Scotland is too sectarian. If Protestants had been bombed in Scotland, they would have taken it out on the Catholics in Scotland, not on the Catholics in Northern Ireland. That's why Scotland never wanted to get involved in the conflict as, once it started, it would have been a bloodbath but on the whole, only a tiny minority cause trouble.

You may recall the would-be Muslim bombers at Glasgow airport. That same day the Muslims who lived in Glasgow marched in Sauchiehall Street with signs saying, "It wasn't us." There has been no more trouble since.

There's a good joke about the bomber at Glasgow airport. He had been arrested and he said, "I had been promised 72 virgins", and the policeman replied, "Then why did you come to Glasgow?"

In 1983, I was invited by the Lord Provost of Glasgow, Dr Michael Kelly, to write a song for the city. The previous one had been 'All The World's Coming To Glasgow' in 1938, which was to celebrate the Empire Exhibition at Bellahouston Park on the south side of Glasgow. That song was appallingly kitsch with an anti-French sentiment so I didn't want to write anything like that. I wanted to write something that had the style of 'I Left My Heart In San Francisco' but at the same time I knew that something like that wouldn't be right for Glasgow. I called it 'No Mean City' and it tells everybody what a great place Glasgow is. Unfortunately, the Provost at the time didn't like the title, but I am still hopeful that Tony Bennett will record it one day as it is perfect for him.

No Mean City

No Mean City the city I adore
The shipyards and there's more
The river Clyde just flows with pride.

No Mean City it greets you with a smile
And when that laughter rings the city really swings.
      Let yourself feel like a millionaire promenade in George's
Square.

No Mean City the city I adore
There's no place I love more than Glasgow town.

No Mean City it steals your heart and soul
Then gives it back in gold,
Different class and bold as brass.

No Mean City it waits to shake your hand
You'll never end the day without a friend.
      They tell me it's true but then, I always knew a welcome
will always be found.

No Mean City the city I adore,
There's no place I love more than Glasgow town.

Meet me at eight don't let me be late for the show
Take in the lights see all the sights
Wherever you go.

No Mean City there's mischief in those eyes
They're witty and they're wise
You'll have good times even when you're down.

No Mean City the city I adore
There's no place I love more than hanging around
I'm boxing clever whatever weather I found
No Mean City that's Glasgow town.

© Bill Martin

II. Govan life

My father's parents came from the Isle of Skye and the name Macpherson means "son of a parson". My grandfather, Alistair Macpherson, was a poet but he couldn't make a living from it and he came to Govan, a shipbuilding part of Glasgow, to find work in 1900. In 1918 he wrote an epic poem in both English and Gaelic that was published in book form as "Welcome to Alexander Somerled Angus, the son of the heir of MacDonald, Prince of the Western Isles, Chief of Clan Colla, Lord of the Race of the Clan." That's the title! Some of my lyric writing skills may have come from him but my love of short catchy titles must have come from somewhere else. He had some standing as a poet as his work was sometimes submitted to Queen Victoria in the early part of her reign.

I read my grandfather's English poems when I was a small boy and they led me to the dictionary. I wanted to find out what they were about. He was obviously a learned man and you can tell from reading the poems that he was also a nice man. From these poems, I picked up that you don't have to rhyme all the time.

He met his wife, Jeanne, my grandmother on my father's side, on the Isle of Skye. She was a piano teacher. That's where the music comes from. She gradually went blind but she was the driving force behind the family. She could make a few shillings stretch out to feed and clothe the whole family. Everybody loved her and she was very musical.

My father, Ian Macpherson, was born in Govan in 1904. My grandmother wanted my father to have piano lessons. He complained when the teacher hit him over the knuckles with a ruler if he hadn't played the scales properly. My granny dismissed the tutor, and that was the end of my dad's formal training. Granny didn't teach him herself as she preferred to make money by teaching others.

As it happens, my father didn't need any lessons. He was a natural, vamping along to the hits of the day and to the new generation of American jazz which was swinging its way into Scotland. He never played in a dance band but a piano was a magnet to him. He would play at the Salvation Army Hall and the Pierce Institute in Govan for tea dances and also to entertain his friends.

My father had a brother and a sister. Uncle Colin was a refined man with a clipped moustache, who went to India and Africa , whilst Auntie Lucy was a very sedate lady. Both were very decent and genteel people. The real characters, however, were on my mother's side.

My mother, Letitia Wylie, known as Letty, was also born in Govan in 1906. Her parents had come from Northern Ireland but the prospects looked better in Govan and they moved there. Letty was the third oldest in a family of seven sisters and four brothers so she was part of a very large family. She worked as a tailoress after leaving school and then in mid-1920s worked as a housekeeper in England for the wealthy.   She moved back to Govan and met my father.

The oldest of Letty's six sisters was Auntie Maggie, who lived in Fife. Then came Auntie Betty, who was disfigured because she had a hot water pot poured over her in a dreadful accident in the kitchen when she was young. She couldn't make money in Glasgow and she went to America. She became the catalyst for the sisters going back and forth to America. Auntie Agnes also settled in New York, while Auntie Sadie and Auntie May remained in Scotland and Auntie Marion went to England.

The seven sisters all lived until their 90s and beyond, but the four brothers drank heavily and died early deaths. They were all Wylies, this was my mother's family name, and Uncle Bobby, in particular, was a tough guy who was always fighting the Hudson family in Govan. His father told him to get out of Glasgow and move to London if he wanted to fight. And that's what he did. I recently met Joe Storrie, a taxi driver who'd known him and said that he had fought his way from King's Cross to the Elephant and Castle and had the greatest punch of anybody he'd seen. He found himself in an altercation one day in a pub and once said to the other chap, "Come outside !" As he walked out, a bus knocked him down and that was the end of Uncle Bobby. He died later that night as a result of heart failure and shock.

Uncle Sammy went to New York to make some money because his sisters were there but never made it. During the crossing, he fell off the boat, drunk, and was never found again.

Uncle Alex was 35 and a handsome man with jet black hair. One night, in the early 1950´s he was singing an Al Jolson song outside my parents' door in the tenement, when, probably thanks to one drink too many, he slipped and fell down the concrete stairs, breaking his neck instantly.

Uncle Hughie, the youngest brother, did get to New York and he became the chief of security for the United Nations building. He never had to pay tax and then he passed the job on to my cousin, Alistair, who retired from the role only a few years ago. Uncle Hughie never married and he worked in Manhattan, though he lived in Brooklyn as he didn't like Manhattan. When he retired at 60, he had a great pension. He stood at the door of the wine bar and said, "Right, you bums, everything is paid for. I'm not going to come back to Manhattan so you'll never see me again." They took him outside and said, "Hughie, this is for you." It was a big limo with three ladies of the night inside, all scantily dressed. He stepped back and fell down a trapdoor that led to the wine cellar, broke his neck and died later that night of a heart attack.

My mother always said that my father had nice blue eyes. He was a great laugh and she was very pleased that he could play the piano. They were married on 29th December 1933, when my father was 29 and my mother 27. After the wedding they were too late to have their photographs taken so they had to go to the studio the next day. The photographer told them, "This is no laughing matter. You are not really married until the photographs are taken." Maybe that's why they look so miserable in their wedding photographs.

My parents lived at 7 Taransay Street, Govan, right by the Fairfield shipyard. The house was a 'two-up, the first', which meant that it was the first flat on the second floor of a four storey red sandstone tenement built in the 1870s.

Their first child, my brother, Ian Alistair, was born on 25 January 1935. He says that he remembers everything from nine months of age, which is ridiculous. Still, if you meet him, he can give you all the details about knowing everything he saw out of his pram when he was 10 months, according to him.

I was born on 9 November 1938, the same day that the Nazis started their onslaught against the Jews. That night, known as Kristallnacht, many Jews were murdered and the Nazis destroyed synagogues and Jewish businesses.

On a much lighter note, my birth on 9 November 1938 coincides with the start of the Beano, Britain's best-loved comic which was published by D C Thomson & Co in Dundee. Some people might liken me to Dennis the Menace, but I was a Bash Street Kid who ended up meeting

Lord Snooty and his Pals in real life. It was also the date of the first appearance of the comic hero Superman.

Unlike my brother who was born in a hospital, I was born at home, which was normal for the second child in those days. My father went to get the midwife and 'Auntie' Jeannie stayed behind. She and Uncle Jack were our neighbours and not really an aunt and uncle. I popped out and Jeannie cut the cord. My father came running back and said that the midwife would be five minutes. Jeannie said, "It's too late. The baby's here." My mother held me up and said, "Let's call it a day." As my son-in-law John said, years later, I could have ended up as Monday, Tuesday, Thursday or Friday...who knows !

We only had two rooms at home. My parents slept in the back room which included the kitchen and a recess for my parents' bed. I was born in the front room or 'the hole in the wall', a little alcove where my brother and I would be tucked in snugly at nights. Amazingly, our room also had a piano. God knows how it fitted. We shared a lavatory with the rest of the tenement, probably totalling 30 people. The key hole grew bigger every day through use until eventually you could peer in and tell people to hurry up.

My brother, who was nearly four when I was born, wasn't impressed by my appearance into the world. He'd been given a toy tank and was playing happily with it on the floor when the midwife approached with me in her arms.

"Oh, you've got a lovely wee brother," she apparently said.

He slapped me and said, "Take him away! I don't want him!"

I suspect that my big brother has been saying that ever since, although we've had plenty of laughs along the way.

You could say that I was really born in a shipyard as the Fairfield shipyard literally was across the street. There were no big walls: you were just looking at the cranes. If you walked ten yards or so, you would be in the shipyard. There were 100,000 people working in the Glasgow shipyards at that time. Famous ships such as The Queen Mary and The Queen Elizabeth were built there.

From the front room, you could peer over the shipyard across the River Clyde to the granary at Partick and beyond that to the Campsie Fells, a sweeping, undulating vista of hills. On a very clear day, you could see the top of Loch Lomond, but you'd have to crane your neck and hang out the window with binoculars. I'm sounding idyllic now but you could hear the clatter and the crash of the shipyard from early morning until late at night.

There were trams in the street and everything was hustle and bustle. The noise could be colossal. When people spoke to you, they barked at you and often leaned into you at the same time. I've got a loud voice, I know that, and it can be a drawback, but it comes from living in Govan. The majority of people were self-respecting and hard-working, but there were some very tough, hard people who didn't give a damn. From the 1930´s through the 1950´s, every Friday and Saturday night saw lots of fights and even more laughs.

Two streets up from us was the main street with all its pubs, called the Govan Road. There were parks beyond that. There was an area known as 50 Pitches; it was 50 football pitches and everybody played there on a Saturday or after school, but never on a Sunday. Sport wasn't allowed on a Sunday. Nothing was allowed in Scotland on a Sunday!

Glasgow was a key city in the Second World War. The country needed ships to survive: it needed warships to fight and merchant vessels to join the Atlantic convoy. The upper Clyde was booming with life and intense activity, which made it a target for the Luftwaffe. London was the Nazis' main target but other British cities including Glasgow were also prime targets.

It was not the best of times to be bringing up a young family. There was talk of sending us somewhere in the country but my mother wanted us to stay together. Govan and its residents were second class citizens compared to London. We had to be there for the war effort and I can't recall anyone being evacuated. My brother played games with shrapnel and stuff that had fallen from German planes. I don't know how we survived but the community spirit was great.

My father was in a reserved occupation working in the shipyards during the war and so we were all together as a family. The air raids came regularly but I was too young to be scared and somehow I thought that we would be safe. Every family was assigned a specific shop in which to shelter so, when the sirens went off, my mother would gather up coats and blankets and we would grab some food and we'd all head down the stairs to go into the cellar at Jack's the Baker in Govan Road, our designated shelter. Throughout this time, my mum and dad's music kept us going and I think that, on the whole, that has made me optimistic.

It was either late 1941 or early 1942 and, although I know it was nothing personal where Hitler's Luftwaffe were concerned, I do remember being frightened by the noise as the German pilots dropped bombs on the shipyards. I was taken from my bed to the shelter and I was sitting on a chair in my pyjamas and a sweater. The minister from the Govan Parish Church arrived. My dad started playing his accordion and my mum and the minister sang 'Indian Love Call', the song that starts, "When I'm Calling You", which was made famous by Nelson Eddy and Jeanette McDonald. I can hear my mother's pure and crystal clear singing to this day. During the War, my father left his accordion in the cellar so that he could entertain all those taking shelter.

One night the Germans came to Govan and they must have had the map upside down because they bombed the wrong side and hit the Singer Sewing Machine premises although to be fair to the Luftwaffe, they had stopped making sewing machines and were making ammunition. As they dropped their bombs over the residential part of Clydebank, you could see the fire for miles and we thought it was the end of the world. As a result of that night, 500 civilians were killed.

One night the Germans dropped a landmine with a parachute and it got tangled in a large crane outside our tenement We could see the bomb swaying on cords from the front window. It took the bomb disposal squad several hours to make it safe and the crowd that had gathered nearby gave a huge cheer when it was safely defused – no health and safety back then.

We often took refuge where the dustbins were kept in little stone buildings called middens. Once, when a number of the children were gathered there during a bombing raid, I said to my mother, "Are you going to get me out of here? There are black things all over me?" She said I was talking rubbish. All the wee boys that were asleep were covered in mice, they were just running across us, and she got me out. Because of the shipyards, the whole of Govan was infected with mice. The vermin crawled out of the skirting board in the flat and scurried across the floor as we were eating. We had to make sure that we didn't leave any crumbs or they might jump on the chairs. At night, you could hear them scuttling about behind the walls. I was terrified of mice and to this day, I still hate them.

I got to know John Ebenezer Brown, the minister for the Church of Scotland, very well. He was a kindly man with a shock of white hair and a booming voice. John Brown himself was to become the father of one of our Prime Ministers, Gordon Brown. Gordon was born in 1951, not in Govan, and he was largely brought up in a manse in Kirkcaldy.

I still have a book I received from the minister in 1947 for regular attendance at the Young Worshippers League. Apart from saying you had attended Church all year it was a little booklet of Classics, designed to encourage us to read. Mine was an abridged version of Treasure Island and I recently bought and read the whole book which was fantastic. Then every year from then till I was 18, I got a book or a Bible for perfect attendance. I recently became friendly with Gordon Brown and decided to give him the abridged version of the books for his two wee boys.

After sweating and toiling in the shipyards, the folks of Govan liked nothing better than a few bottles of Indian Pale Ale with a sherry or gin and lemon for the ladies with a sing-song and a bit of dancing. Friday nights were okay, but because most men worked Saturday morning shifts, Saturday nights were electric.

The music was so important and the piano and the accordion were very important instruments in Govan. I don't remember anyone playing the bagpipes when I was small. My father was the best around and he would always play the piano on Saturday nights at Mr Hamilton's. Mr Hamilton was the coalman. I thought he was the great American singer, Al Jolson because he was black during the day and white at night. There was no such thing as political correctness to a wee Govan boy in the 1940's. Mr Hamilton had a better piano and a better house. He had carpet and we had linoleum. I would be taken along even when I was only two or three. It was a boozy atmosphere with cigarettes and evenings full of songs.

'The Hokey Cokey' with all its actions amused us young children and was very popular at VE Day parties in May 1945. Years later, I would meet the man who wrote it, Jimmy Kennedy, and he features in my story.

Most tenements in Govan had a piano of sorts – some more playable than others as people couldn't afford to tune them – and my father was always expected to give the partygoers a tune, but he never needed encouragement. He could play some nice chords too and his wide finger span helped him to play well. If the flat didn't have a piano, he would take along his accordion.

He had a fine partner in my mother Letty, who was a good singer. I can see her with her hand on Dad's shoulder as he played the piano, a cigarette hanging out of his mouth and a broad smile on his face. The room would be full of folk and they would stop and listen when my mother sang. Her voice would soar through the house and I was very proud of her.

On a Saturday or Sunday morning, I learned how to read the mood of the house by what my dad was playing on the piano. If I heard 'Who's Sorry Now', I'd have to be careful. I didn't want a slap in the face as a consequence of their disagreement. On the other hand, if I heard 'If You Knew Susie', I knew that the day was going to be lively and fun. My mum might hug me and say, "Your dad and I had a great time last night." which meant a bit of kissing and cuddling!

Nothing much happened in Govan on a Sunday. You went to church. There were no pubs open. That's why they all got plastered on Saturday night. You went for walks but the place was empty. You were brought up to go to church on a Sunday and who says that that is not the best way? It is wrong that the high street shops open on Sundays. There is no such thing as a Sunday these days. I'm not religious at all now but that was a totally wrong thing to do. There is no light and shade in anyone's life today. There once was tranquility on a Sunday. That said, I would go to St Mary's, the parish church, and hear Gordon Brown's father with his booming voice, so there was not much tranquility there either.

There were plenty of nephews and nieces around. I attended Sunday school, and while children never went to funerals, weddings and christenings were always grand family occasions. Although Govan folk didn't have much money, they always knew how to dress up and the Sunday best was collars and ties, the best suit and the hair slicked back flat, while the ladies wore dresses, coats and hats. Sometimes there were bawling babies at the service, waiting to be christened.

One of my mother's friends was having her daughter christened.

"And what will I name this baby?" said the minister, Mr John Brown.

"Spindonna," replied her father.

"I name this baby, Spindonna," said the minister.

"Naw," said her father, "it's pinned on her,"

There was a safety pin on her gown with a wee piece of paper that said her name was Annie.

There were gales of laughter in the church at that, which was very different from the sombre Church of Scotland ways at the time.

As the girl grew up, she was known to us all as Spindonna. I met her some years later, in the late 60´s and said, "Hi", Annie.

She said, "Don't call me that, I'm Annette and I'm marrying Joe soon."

I said, "Do you mean Joe the Hungarian?" Joe Kurstanez had come from Hungary and his parents had changed their name to Kuerten. "You can't marry him with a name like that. You'll be known as Annette Curtain."

"Oh, stop it, Billy," she said.

"Well," I said, "I´m going to call you Spindonna."

My father worked in the shipyards and served his apprenticeship in Alexander Stephenson and Sons as a copper and tinsmith and then worked as a store clerk in the engineering part of the business.

When money was tight, my mum worked part-time in a local bakery (and our aforementioned air raid shelter) known as Jack's. She helped make the pies, rolls and buns and she left the house very early each morning, around 5am. The Buchanans lived in our tenement on the ground floor and their oldest daughter used to come up in the morning and get Ian and I dressed for school.

I had started school at five and went to Fairfield Primary School in Fairfield Street and later to Govan High School. I wasn't too well in the early years at school and until I was 15, my mother was concerned about my health. I was often too sick to go to school and stayed at home where mum would make sure I drank plenty of fluid and tell me stories. I'd listen to big band music on our large valve Philips radio which had a warm, booming tone.

My brother recalls that I was quiet and not very well as a child. I was peely-wally (that's pale skinned) and as skinny as a rake. It wasn't until years later when I was heading to South Africa to play football that I had an X-ray and they discovered a scar on my lung which suggested that I'd had tuberculosis as a kid. No one had noticed but there was a lot of sickness around with all the dust and grime and the smoke from the home fires as well as what was coming from the shipyards. We lived in unhealthy conditions but we were always told that we had to go to school no matter how ill we were feeling.

We all ate together in the kitchen. There wasn't a lot of variety in the menu: bread and dripping, fried eggs and if we were lucky, some bacon.

These days, people have daily baths but not even the dockyard workers had daily baths. They would simply wash their faces and hands. We had a bath once a week in a tin tub in front of the fire range. As I said, there was a toilet on the landing, shared by the families. That's about 30 people, so you'd be lucky to get in, and you learnt how to hold your wee. We couldn't afford the luxury of toilet paper. We tore strips off the Scottish Daily Express or any newspaper to make do. As a result, the toilets were often blocked because the paper wasn't absorbent.

I only went into Glasgow itself when I was getting older. It was an adventure to go into the big shops. My parents would take me to the pet department in Lewis's and tell me it was Glasgow Zoo! We didn't have any pets and I can't remember many being around: some people owned dogs, but not many, and no cats.

Govan is a very important part of my psyche. In 2010, I went to the Centenary of my school, Govan High, and the speakers were the headmaster, myself, Sir Alex Ferguson and Alex Salmond, the first minister of Scotland. It was a great thrill. I told this tale of an only son coming downstairs and saying to his parents, "I'm not going to school today, nobody likes me." The mother says, "You've got to go to school." "Mummy, I'm not going. Everybody hates me." The father puts down his newspaper and says, "Charles, you're going to school today because you're 45 and you're the headmaster." Alex Salmond loved that and I thought, "I've lost that joke."

The headmaster said that it was very important to give the pupils some encouragement. Their parents had lived on benefits and their parents before them so there were three generations of the unemployed in Govan all on the dole. Instead of German and History, they are now teaching woodwork, metalwork, hairdressing and motor mechanics. It is not normal schooling and it is more to get people off the dole.

A lot of people have given up hope and I might still have been living in Govan, but for one thing, determination.

There has also been the added problem of drugs. Drugs came in the 70s and they caused a massive problem in Glasgow and Scotland as a whole. Glasgow has a terrible reputation for that now, but Glasgow is not as bad as London as it doesn't have that gun culture. Yet.

It was my uncle Colin who said "Once you leave Govan, you'll never come back." He was always travelling and he often went to India. He called himself Ceemac and he drew cartoons. When I went to South Africa to live, the last words he said to me were, "You'll never come back to live in Glasgow, never mind visit Govan, but Govan will never leave you."

I think Uncle Colin was right as he had seen the determination in me. You have got to aim for something and nobody's going to criticise you if you fail. A lot of people in Govan didn't even venture into England and still don´t.

In 2011, Govan High included Manchester United's manager, Sir Alex Ferguson, plus three really intelligent men, and me in their first six entrants for their Hall of Fame. The others were world renowned paediatrician, Professor Frank Sharp, Willie Jones who runs Gleneagles and Sir Robert Easton, Chairman of Yarrow Shipbuilders although Bob sadly died before the ceremony. I said to Professor Sharp, a very brainy man and DUX (cleverest) of the school, "Frank, it was great to be in the same class as you when I was 12." He laughed, shook my hand and said, "We were in the same class for five minutes Bill, until you were assessed."

Alex Salmond is exceptionally bright but he doesn't go to the same gym as me! He is very personable and I have never known anybody who cares so much for Scotland. I've met lots of ministers and politicians, and I am sure he is genuine. He has stayed true to Scotland but may yet come to London.

III. Moving to Priesthill

After the war, Glasgow had to come to terms with a massive housing problem – the slum tenements in the Gorbals and Govan were to be pulled down and thousands of families were being sent to new homes.

When they built these new developments like Priesthill and Easterhouse, they didn't include pubs, restaurants, shops and community centres and so there was nothing for anybody to do. There was nowhere to walk and people had to take buses to go anywhere. It was bound to lead to trouble. The kids were bored out of their minds but they didn't have the knife culture that they have now. They had the bottle culture: they would break a bottle and fight. The singer Frankie Vaughan, who did so much to encourage Boys' Clubs, even came to Easterhouse to get them to turn in their weapons but they never did.

We were on the council's list for a new home. Priesthill was a brand new housing scheme on the south side of Glasgow and only five blocks had been built by the time we arrived. Eventually, it would become a large district of Glasgow with thousands of families but then it was still a green place with nearby fields and parkland. The area surrounding a huge water tank was a popular playground and there was a superb hill for sledging during the winter.

We moved to our brand new home in Priesthill in 1948, although I still went to school in Govan and my Mother kept going back for years as she missed her Govan friends and her sisters. It was a massive improvement over Taransay Street. Our home was a three bedroom apartment with a kitchen, a lounge and joy of joys, a bathroom with a toilet. It was luxury for all of us.

Not only that, with concrete floors, concrete skirting and metal door frames, there were no mice. We felt we weren't lacking for anything. My brother and I were millionaires when it came to the love we received from our mum and dad. We didn't get all the things we wanted, but we got everything we needed. One Christmas we both got bikes and we were able to cycle round the district. This gave us a wonderful sense of freedom, but my mother didn't like the new home because she missed her friends in Govan.

We had a big radiogram and I used to listen to March Of Dimes, which was an American programme on AFN after the War, so I listened to that from about 1948. We didn't get a television until 1958.

In the 1950s I would listen to Radio Luxembourg. My father, though, preferred The Billy Cotton Band Show on BBC Radio and I always thought that was nonsense, you know with "Wakey! Wakey!" and all that. Max Bygraves was on the radio with Peter Brough and his ventriloquist's dummy, Archie Andrews, in Educating Archie. A ventriloquist on radio, give me a break! How did he get away with that? Later on, he appeared on TV and people could see his lips moving and that was the end of Peter Brough´s career.

My father had a job as a builder's clerk and he had to go and see someone at the top of a tenement block that was being repaired. His eyes weren't that good and he slipped and missed his step. He fell 60 feet and was unconscious for three days. We were very worried about him, but he came round and made a good recovery. When he was on the mend, my mother wanted him to put a picture on the wall. He got up rather shakily and climbed the ladder to hammer in the nail. He was unsteady and fell off, landing on the box of nails. Some of them were sticking in his head when he tried to get up. After three months, he started working again. He got a job as a store clerk for the gas board, but after that accident, he didn't bother to do much else in life, except for playing the piano, going to parties and having a cigarette or a bet or a wee dram!

After we moved out of Govan, my own health began to improve and by the time I was 14 or 15, I'd developed my strength, thanks in part to my brother who was four years older and taught me the exercises he´d learned in the RAF. I never was a hooligan and I was never in a gang. I was happy just playing football with my school pals.

Living in Govan had been pretty bleak. I can't remember any sunny days at all, and Priesthill wasn't much better. As I remember it, it was always cold and often freezing. Maybe that's why I'm so fit, because when I woke up in the winter, there was always ice on the inside of the window.

As I said earlier, the school I went to was Govan High. You were hampered from the day you started because you were put in a box. Your future was mapped out if you were born in a tenement. There were only three ways out of the shipyards: the forces, going into the arts perhaps by acting, or become a footballer.

The clever kids were known as dux of the school and the girl that I would marry was dux at her school. She was very clever. I didn't have the opportunity really, but perhaps I didn't have the interest. Like me, Alex Ferguson was at Govan High, while Billy Connolly was at the Catholic school. You can't say that Billy Connolly, Alex Ferguson and I are not clever, we could have done anything. Who knows what we would have achieved if any of us had gone to university, although I guess we haven't done too badly.

Billy Connolly was always different. He lived in Partick on the other side of the River Clyde, opposite Govan and we were on nodding terms. His mother had run away and he was brought up in one of those houses which have four homes in a little block, and it was a nice, sandy building. He was loud and tall and always different. He joined the Territorial Army and he would be dressed like that. He would be a cyclist and be dressed as a cyclist. He went to extremes with everything he did. He was the first person that I saw wearing a long coat. He was like a Teddy Boy but he had style.

There were four rows in the classes. Some of the front row became academics, whilst Frank Sharp became one of top paediatricians in Great Britain. The second row was for the boys who became accountants. The third row was for guys like me who had no idea what we wanted to do. The fourth row was for all the loonies, pressing each other's pimples and things like that and they were not interested in anything at all. There was a history and music teacher called Miss Reynard and at the time I never knew why they called her Foxy. She was about 30 and very attractive and she would do a round of the sequential song "Step we gaily on we go" and when it got to the fourth row, where the dopey boys sat, nothing would happen. She'd say, "Pay attention". She'd start again and this time when it got to the fourth row, somebody would sing the old song, "Oh, you can roll a silver dollar down upon the ground." They would never sing the same song as us.

My school record was not great and I could never have been an academic. I loved history but I couldn't be bothered with maths and English. I loved to know about the world and I was good at geography.

All of us, the clever ones and the dunces, were all in the same class and that is where the Scottish system of education was clever. You knew that if you didn't pay attention, you'd be in the yard working as a labourer, so it encouraged the smart ones to work harder.

When I was growing up in Govan, the one big gang was the Razor Gang and they had bits of razor blades under their lapels. When they got in a fight, somebody would grab one of them to head-butt them and their hands would be ripped to shreds. You didn't mess about with these guys.

We were okay in Govan because the other gangs were frightened to come near us. Also, Govan was such a tough place that you never knew who was in the gang. There were 100,000 shipyard workers and they were all tough guys, and all the Govan Razor Gang had good parents who worked hard. There were street fights, one on ones, but you didn't have gangs walking around and frightening the ladies.

The minister, John Brown, had asked me to join the Life Boys and the Boys' Brigade. He said, "Listen, Billy, I want you to believe in God until you're 18. After that, you're old enough to fight for your country and you can believe what you want." I joined the Boys' Brigade and was given a Bible for perfect attendance every year till I was 18. My parents didn't plaster religion into me and religion is something that I have never been able to accept. I don't see how there can be all these different gods and all the hatred in the world and now I am not religious at all.

My brother Ian and I were the first ones to sign up for the new Boys' Brigade at Priesthill. He had been in the Life Boys and I had just started going to the 213 Boys' Brigade at St Mary's Church at Govan Cross. We now joined the 203 Boys' Brigade at Pollok, run by Captain Lennox, and then one of the demobbed guys, Jim Shaw, took over on a temporary basis but ended up doing it for the next 25 years. I've always admired his devotion. The Boys' Brigades were a critical part of my life because of the pipe band and the football matches on Saturday afternoon.

The Boys' Brigades were terrific: you had gymnastics and you had the discipline of cleaning your uniform and the like. It was fun and you looked forward to a couple of nights a week in the club as we were treated like a Boys Club.

Ian played the bagpipes in the Boys' Brigade and eventually became a teacher of the instrument and a pipe major. I had a set of drumsticks and would practice rudimentary paradiddles on a block of wood before I was given a real snare drum. One of my proudest moments was marching with the pipe band while my brother, already well regarded, was leading the pipers from the front. My brother joined the Kinning Park Pipe Band which won a national medal at the Highland Games. I was always striving to catch up with his Boys' Brigade badges. If he gained a semaphore or an athletics badge, I tried to do it as well. The sleeves of my jacket were covered in triangular badges, but somehow Ian always had another new one to add to his jacket. Of course, he had more badges than me as he was four years ahead of me.

I can demonstrate its importance to me as I still have my badges hanging on the wall in the study at my house in Portugal. I've the Queen's Badge and lots of silver ones for signalling and fireman and ambulance duties. In the end, I got them all, same as my brother.

As a family, we went away every year during the Glasgow Fair – the two weeks' holiday in July when the whole of Glasgow would go off in search of fun and sunshine. Sometimes it was a trip with my parents to a guest house in Blackpool or down to Stevenson on the Ayrshire coast for a month when my father would come for the weekend. It had miles of sand dunes and it was a healthy place for running about as well as for meeting new friends. Then from the age of 12, I went to the Boys' Brigade summer camps in Ballantrae where all we seemed to do were marching drills, learning to play in the pipe band and play football.

The Boys' Brigade was an important part of my life as I met the men like Jim Shaw and Hawthorn Stewart who taught me the importance of discipline. That even included how to dress and how to clean your shoes and all that was very good for me. To this day, my shoes are always freshly polished. I was in the BB until I was 18, which is the age you usually left although my brother stayed until he was 21.

There was a big difference between us when we started work. Ian was very clever and he was the apprentice of the year at Alexander Stephens and Son and served his time as a joiner. He was bright and very capable and the shipyard singled him out and sent him to Gordonstoun public school for six months' tuition. He survived their regime of cold showers and meagre meals. Ian was a great prospect, picking up prizes at night school and college.

In his final year as an apprentice, he worked on the SS Olympia, one of the last great transatlantic liners to be built on the Clyde. He worked in the furniture shop making its luxurious fittings and fixtures. It was meticulously fitted by Glasgow tradesmen who took great pride in their work. The ship is now preserved as an icon in Greece. Most of the kitchens in Govan ended up with shining slabs of Wayright, a kind of formica which was used in the liners but mysteriously disappeared in large quantities from the yard!

From about 1954, my mother was going over to work in America because the pay was better there and two of her sisters lived and worked in New York. She worked for a Mr McKay, who had one of those Gatsby style, high-society mansions with a ballroom. He had made his fortune from sandpaper and she was his sewing mistress. She would work for him and then come back home with the dollars. She'd change the money into sterling and she kept us going. She'd also work as a sewing mistress in Crookston Hospital in Glasgow. She was an amazing person.

On one occasion, Louis Armstrong came to play at Mr McKay's mansion in the USA and he needed a button on his tuxedo. As my mother was sewing it on, he said, "When were you born, Letty?" and she said "You don't ask a lady that." He said, "I didn't mean it that way. I don't know what year I was born. I don't even know the date, so I just tell everybody, I was born on July 4, 1900." He asked everybody he met to sign his book with their date of birth. She looked at the book and saw Frank Sinatra in there. They keep it in some museum now and I think my mum signed it.

My father ended up working a very simple life for the gas board, being a clerk for little money. He gambled what he had. On October 16 1957, my father won £1,876, which was a huge sum. My mother took the £1,800 and gave him the £76 and that's when she bought a whole pile of things for the house.

We would always ask my father, "How did you get on today?" and he might say, "I backed a horse, it won at 16/1," "Really? You must've made a fortune?" "No, I doubled it for the next race, and the horse fell."

Although I might nowadays put bets on at the races, I've never gambled and I've never smoked cigarettes because of my father, who did both. My mother was the boss. She used to say to us, "Don't let me catch you smoking or I will bang your heads together." Once, my brother was smoking a cigar when he was 33 years old and my mother said, "What's that?" He said, "It's a cigar." I don't think she really knew what they were. So I started to smoke cigars, moving onto Cubans later on —then gave them up when I was 60.

Jumping forward to 2011, my wife Jan and I went to Cuba on a trip organised by Ranald McDonald, the owner of Boisdale´s Restaurant group. Jan had broken her leg so I bought myself a business class ticket but such was her determination not to miss out on the trip, that, at the last minute, she booked a flight for herself. However, all that was available was economy class.

In the business section, there was an empty seat next to me so I thought that, once we´d taken off, I´d try and get Jan moved forward. However, just as we about to depart, a lady rushed on and took the seat and asked me whether I would move so that she could sit next to her friend, who was also in Business class. I refused at it would have meant that I ended up with a window seat and I much prefer the aisle. Besides, she wasn´t much of a babe (I guess my political correctness still falls short). Then her friend, a very good looking lady, approached me saying that the seat was for her. I said I didn´t care who it was for, I was staying put.

Meanwhile, Jan got herself upgraded and the two women, having now persuaded another passenger to change seats, sat behind us, talking about how unchivalrous I was. When we arrived with the rest of the Boisdale party I realised that the two women were part of our group and that the good looking one was Nancy Dell´Olio so I had to turn on the charm to recover the situation. Whatever you may read about Nancy, I found her to be great fun and sexy. Sadly, the other woman, Annie Gunn, a successful PR executive and agent, died in 2014 at the tender age of 47. We had built bridges to the extent that she was going to be my agent for this book.

Back to Govan, we didn't have a lot of money but family love and trust was everywhere and I had no option but to leave school at 15. I had to work and bring money home to my mother and I went to work in the shipyards. I was a terrible apprentice, I felt useless and I knew it wasn't for me.

My dad persuaded the personnel manager, Alan Blacklaws, originally from Edinburgh and a former goalkeeper for St Mirren, to give me a start. He had seen my brother's huge potential with a saw, plane, hammer and chisel and thought I might be the same. I wasn't. I was a day-dreamer who found it hard to concentrate.

The work didn't hold my interest. For three years, I was an apprentice in the same shipyard as my dad and my brother. I was paid 18 shillings 11 pence for a 44 hour week. Yes, less than £1 a week! In 1956, a journeyman's wage at 21 was 10 guineas a week.

The pubs by the shipyards may have had names like the Govan Arms, but the shipyard workers never used them. I remember them as seven pubs and they were nicknamed Numbers 1,2,3,4,5,6,7, and the workers used to come out of the shipyards and make for them. All the pubs closed at 9 o'clock and you might be in Number 6 and hear someone say, "Have you seen Charlie?" They'd be told, "I don't think he made it past Number 2." The women were not allowed in pubs, so they used to all hang around outside, which led to fighting. The women were wondering: "Where the hell is my husband, spending all of our money?" On a Saturday night, the workers might take their wives out.

Before he became the greatest football manager ever, Alex Ferguson served his apprenticeship as a toolmaker in Remington Rand and played football professionally, then later had a pub called Fergie's. Everybody put things on the slate until the following Friday when they'd come in with their wages. The only time he was caught out was with a Norwegian sailor, who got free drinks because he was only there for a week and then going back to Norway. He never paid for his week's drinking! He thought it was Scottish hospitality but many years later, he read Sir Alex´s book and realised he had owned this pub and he offered to send the money. Alex laughed and declined the offer due to the Norwegian´s honesty.

The yards were very well organised. They couldn't have 100,000 men starting at seven o'clock so they staggered your starting and finishing times. I started at ten to eight and then lunch would come at ten past 12, and every shipyard had different times.

The shipyards were compartmentalised. I was an apprentice marine engineer in the engineering department and I liked walking. Billy Connolly was a welder and my brother was a joiner. You weren't allowed to go for walks but I used to do it and I would be daydreaming trying to write songs. I would get bollockings all the time. They knew I couldn't have taken 15 minutes to go to the loo.

Working there was a struggle for me but I loved the Glasgow patter and sense of humour. There was always plenty of joking and laughing. My brother was much smarter than me when it came to practical work and so it proved to be during our apprenticeships.

The foreman came up to me once as I had made a mistake over a spigot and a flange and the work on the ship was ruined. I saw him coming towards me and his face was blue, He said, "You stupid fucker. How many 'thous' in an inch?" I was a third year apprentice and I said, "I don't know. There must be millions." There are a thousand and I got the red card and thrown out of the shipyard. The big gates closed to me. The shipyard's production had suffered because of my stupidity.

I was thrown out at 3pm and nobody left the shipyard at 3pm. I was wandering about with big steel toe-capped boots and a boiler suit. I trudged back to Priesthill and my mother said, "What are you doing here?" I had to tell her I'd been sacked and she said, "What are you going to do now?"

My mother asked what had happened but she knew that I wasn't cut out to be a shipyard worked. I persevered and my brother got me into G&J Weirs at Cathcart, a pump company that is still very famous. They took me with the proviso that I would have to work night shifts. My dad told me to buckle down and work hard and I did complete my apprenticeship as a marine engineer in December 1959.

I became fairly proficient but I was glad to be on the night shift. It was during a dinner break that I heard Bobby Darin's 'Dream Lover' on the radio. The lyrics were tight and modern and the record blended rocking music with snappy words. This struck me like a bolt of lightning. This was my kind of rock music and I knew then that I could make it as a songwriter. Bobby Darin was a cross between Frankie Laine and the rock singers. It was exactly what I was looking for. I remember when he had out 'Multiplication' that I wrote something called 'Simplification'. Also, I still have a letter from July 1958 in which Bob Kingston, MD of Southern Music, a Tin Pan Alley music publisher, turned down a song of mine, 'Oh, Mary Mary' so at least I was in there swinging the bat.

Most of the people who worked in the shipyard came from Govan, although there would be a few from outside. The officers and the directors lived in posh places. They all wore suits and ties. When I left Govan and the shipyards, I swore that I would never wear overalls again. I had worn dirty overalls from the age of 15 to the age of 21, and once I left, I never wore them again.

Billy Connolly thought the same way. He was a welder in the same shipyard. The rain was pouring down and he said, "I am thinking of packing it in and joining a folk group." This old guy looked up at him with the rain dripping off his nose and he said, "You'll have a better life than this, son. You should do it." And he did. You have to gamble. I have no time for people who say that they never had the opportunity. I say, 'Kill or cure' and get on with it. If a decision goes against you, it goes against you, but at least you've tried.

In 2010, there was a funeral for the union leader, Jimmy Reid and I couldn't go because I was in the Norwegian fjords on a cruise ship giving my music talks. He was the militant who had taken over Glasgow shipyards. Billy Connolly gave a eulogy as did Sir Alex Ferguson and they painted a picture of the past. One hundred thousand people worked in those shipyards and now there's none.

Chapter 2 - Music, Music, Music

I. Tales Of The Empire

Although I was born and raised in the hard-drinking, God-fearing, fist-fighting community of Govan, I knew, right from the start, that a love of music and songs would dominate my life.

In working class Govan before I was born, there had been popular operatic arias, Neapolitan and Viennese waltzes and Scottish songs, and then, bang, along came American jazz and Al Jolson. Al Jolson was an early example of a superstar and when he said in the first talkie, The Jazz Singer in 1927, "You ain't seen nothing yet", he was right. My dad took me to The Jolson Story in 1946 with Larry Parks as Jolson. I knew right away that 'California Here I Come' was a brilliant song and it has a lyric that still makes me tingle.

Al Jolson made so much money that he retired at 50, but, like most performers, he found the bug of performing was just too strong. He made a comeback but he died in 1950 at the age of 64. These days he is regarded as politically incorrect because he blacked up but if you look at photographs of the thousands who lined the streets in Los Angeles for his funeral, there are plenty of black people around so they can't have objected to what he was doing.

In the 1930s, Bing Crosby became an even bigger star than Al Jolson. People used to argue over which one was the better actor or singer. Bing had a stream of great songs – he was the happy-go-lucky, smooth crooner. We all sang 'Pennies From Heaven' and waited expectantly for his new

Road films with Bob Hope to be shown in Govan. It wasn't like today where films are screened everywhere at the same time: you had to wait several weeks for a film to reach the provinces. I especially loved Fred Astaire and Ginger Rogers and the Irving Berlin musicals.

The Road movies were utterly captivating. Their blend of knockabout humour, witty one-liners, top songs from Hollywood songwriters and a love story was pure escapism for many of us living in grey and grimy surroundings. They contained some great spoofs, often poking fun at successful films of the period so that many of the jokes may not be apparent today. The Road To Morocco came out in 1942 but it was regularly rerun in our cinema. Bing had asked Johnny Burke to write a song that said "I love you" without actually using those words and the result was the wonderful 'Moonlight Becomes You', which is now a standard. The Road To Morocco was a satirical take on the Arabian Nights with Bing, Bob and the gorgeous Dorothy Lamour and, unusually for a silly comedy, it was nominated for two Oscars. I never imagined that I would get to meet two of Bing and Frank Sinatra's main songwriters, Sammy Cahn and Jimmy Van Heusen, and that I would become friendly with Bob Hope, playing golf with him and having dinner at his house.

Following on from the Road films, we had those daft comedies from Dean Martin and Jerry Lewis like The Caddy and Artists And Models. I used to love them. Dean wasn't just a stooge: he was a very good comedian too. I'd even say that he was a better comedian than Jerry Lewis. Dean had many hits songs including 'Memories are Made of This', 'Return To Me' and 'Volare'. The difference between Dean and Frank was the captivatingly lazy atmosphere Dean created whenever he sang. Dean never changed his manager – or his style - and as a result, he died a very rich man.

I was in another world watching the MGM musicals with the likes of Fred Astaire and Bing Crosby and I always used to look at who'd written the songs. I´d stay in the cinema to read the credits and still do to this day: it's fascinating. A singer as well as a dancer, Fred Astaire had a remarkable talent for interpreting songs and just about all the great songwriters wanted to give him their work.

On a more serious theme, I loved Frank Sinatra in The Man With The Golden Arm, but I didn't really understand it at the time as it was all about drug-taking. There was a great score in that film, composed by Elmer Bernstein. I went to see The Joker Is Wild which included 'All The Way' and that is one of the best songs ever, written by Sammy Cahn and Jimmy Van Heusen. Another film I remember loving is Sweet Smell Of Success with Burt Lancaster and Tony Curtis, but then I loved Tony Curtis in just about anything. Years later, in the latter part of his life, I was fortunate enough to meet him in The Beverly Hills Hotel and I must confess that I was mesmerised by his wig which was somewhat ironic as, in the 50s, lads would walk into barber shops and ask for 'A Tony Curtis'. I guess you had to hope that the barber didn't think he'd starred in the King and I.

My mum enjoyed taking me to the pictures as Govan was well endowed with cinemas. There was the Lyceum, a large modern place on Govan Road, the Plaza, the Vogue which held 2,500 people and was Art Deco, and the Elder, which was the fleapit. My earliest trips were to see children's films such as Snow White And The Seven Dwarfs, Bambi, Dumbo and The Wizard Of Oz.

In the Elder, you were itching to get in and scratching to get out. There were divan seats in the balcony. Guys and their girlfriends used to get up to mischief there. I'm sure that more than a few Glaswegians were conceived in the back row. It was noisy and anarchic with a hazy atmosphere as everybody smoked. The guys in the balcony would undo their trouser buttons and pee over the balcony. The people in the stalls would get drenched and shout back "Why don't you shake it all about". Obviously, my mother wasn't with me when I went there, but that's the way the Govan was. At times, there was plenty of wanton hooliganism and extremely coarse behaviour.

There was a feeling of violence in Govan, a kind of fear that something could suddenly erupt. I didn't want to be cocky because these guys took no prisoners and so I just watched myself and became street-smart. That's why Alex Ferguson's street-smart: you were taught how to use your wits as opposed to being an academic. The academic boys would be living in Shawlands and lovely districts but we were in the flat-cap brigade in tenements.

My mother took me to the Glasgow Empire every Thursday night – maybe it was the cheap night! Actually, my parents knew the famous manager of the Empire, Charles Horsley, as he knew my dad was a piano player who was great at parties. The theatre was part of the Moss Empires chain and I saw everybody: Laurel and Hardy, Frank Sinatra, Johnnie Ray, Frankie Laine, Guy Mitchell and many more. How's that for a list of legends?

Guy Mitchell was revered in Scotland: there's a line in 'She Wears Red Feathers' that goes "She lives on just cokie nuts," and I still say 'cokie nuts' instead of 'coconuts'. There is also the wonderful line, "Six baboons got out bassoons and played 'Here Comes The Bride'". I was intrigued that one guy, Bob Merrill, had written most of Guy Mitchell's hits including 'She Wears Red Feathers' and 'Feet Up!' In the end, Guy Mitchell was too flippant, too cowboyish for me. He could sing ballads, but in my view, nobody could sing ballads better than Frankie Laine and Johnnie Ray. Bob Merrill went on to write Funny Girl with Jule Styne and included such great songs as 'People' and 'Don't Rain On My Parade.' He'd already written smash pop hits such as

'How Much Is That Doggie In The Window', 'Honeycomb' and 'Mambo Italiano.' In later life he suffered from depression and he was found dead in his car in Culver City, having taken his own life with a pistol.

Frankie Laine's voice was out of this world and fans would queue for hours to see him. Frankie Laine was my ultimate hero. He was a good songwriter too. He wrote a great song 'We'll Be Together Again', which Sinatra recorded after he split from Ava Gardner. I used to go backstage and I met Frankie Laine when I was 14. I was impressed that he took the time to talk to me and I joined his fan club. I still think Franke Laine's records are great and his 'Answer Me' was surely, in my opinion, the inspiration for Paul McCartney's 'Yesterday'. Just play them back to back and you´ll hear for yourself that it´s the same cadence. .

These guys were larger-than-life performers and Johnnie Ray was sensational when he sang 'Such a Night' and 'Cry'. I never knew whether it was an act or real as he would cry on stage. You could see the tears falling down. We thought he was going to collapse from emotion and he was defiantly moving away from the more refined performances of Bing Crosby and the Ink-Spots. Even Elvis tried to emulate him with his version of 'Such A Night.'

I saw Frank Sinatra at the Glasgow Empire in 1953 when he, comparatively speaking, was down and out. He had lost his way as Frankie Laine, Johnnie Ray and Guy Mitchell had taken over, and it was just before he made his big comeback with the war film, From Here To Eternity. He'd committed himself to a tour of Great Britain and the theatre, which seated 2,000, was half-empty. He was as skinny as the microphone. His voice was at its best, but there was a big black crack painted on the floor on the stage. He walked on and jumped over the crack and said, "You nearly lost me there" but, although he could sing, he didn't have the timing for jokes. Sinatra was singing very tortured, very slow ballads, all aimed at the actress Ava Gardner, who wasn't there. He had left his wife Nancy for Ava and even though they married, their relationship was very quarrelsome. The press had been very critical of their behaviour and by 1953, Frank had lost his direction. He didn't know what he was doing and he didn't care. Through Johnny Mercer (the co owner of Capital Records and writer of so many classics such as ´Moon River´and ´Autumn Leaves') he regained his standing. This was due to the fact that Mercer signed him to Capitol and released all those wonderful albums such as ´Come Fly With Me´, ´Come Dance With Me´and ´Songs For Swinging Lovers.´ I especially remember him singing 'Try A Little Tenderness'. Bing Crosby had recorded an excellent version but Frank took the song to another level, and the Glasgow Empire crowd loved it.

Years later in the 70s I was taken to a bar opposite the famous Brill Building (from where many famous songwriters worked) in New York by Stanley Mills, a member of ASCAP (American Songwriters, Composers, Authors and Publishers). An old guy was playing piano in the corner of this saloon and a man at the bar shouted "Hey Stumpy, get off the piano". I looked at the piano player and he had no fingers on his left hand (I was told he´d lost them when serving in the Navy in WW2) so when he was playing, he just hit the chords with the fist of his left hand and his right hand played beautifully.

The man at the bar shouted "Hey Stumpy, get off the piano" a further 3 times. Stumpy finally stood up and flattened the guy with one punch. As he returned to the piano, I asked Stanley who Stumpy was. His reply was "Harry Woods, an old songwriter."   "What did he write?" I asked.   Stanley said "Try A Little Tenderness !"

Sinatra would get songs from Jule Styne and Sammy Cahn. They knew how to write for Sinatra and when Ava Gardner left him, he said to Jule Styne, "If you don't stay with me, I will kill myself." He stayed with him for nine months and then Frank said, "I'm over her, you can leave." Jule made one mistake – Esquire magazine asked him for an interview. Songwriters don't get many invitations for big interviews and so he said yes. He said in the interview that staying with Sinatra had been like living in a shrine to Ava Gardner. There were photographs of her everywhere. One night Sinatra tore up a big photograph of her and they spent the next few hours finding every piece of the photograph and putting it back together.

Sammy Cahn had written great songs with Jule Styne including 'Five Minutes More' and 'Saturday Night Is The Loneliest Night Of The Week' in 1944 and I can hear Sinatra doing it: it had exquisite timing. But now, as far as Sinatra was concerned, Jule Styne was dead for giving the interview. There was no in-between with Frank. That fallout notwithstanding, Jule Styne had a great career writing with Bob Merrill. It was years before Sinatra spoke to him again.

As soon as Sinatra saw the interview, he telephoned Sammy Cahn and said, "You no longer write with Julie. You write with Jimmy Van Heusen from now on." And that's what happened. It turned out to be a good decision as Sammy Cahn and Jimmy Van Heusen became a great songwriting team. They wrote songs for the albums, 'Come Dance With Me' and 'Come Fly With Me' which were so clever.

Jimmy Van Heusen was sex mad, drink mad and Sinatra mad, in that order, and before that, he was sex mad, drink mad and Bing Crosby mad. He lived next door to Bing and then he lived next door to Sinatra. Sinatra would say, "We are going out tonight" and Jimmy had to find the girls. I liked Jimmy Van Heusen. He was a fantastic piano player and he admitted that he was a whore for his songs. He thought I was terrific because Sammy Cahn didn't drink and I did.   Jimmy, much like his great pal Sinatra, preferred

Jack Daniels and it found very amusing that me, being a Scotsman, drank Gin and Tonic.

Frank Sinatra had been taught three things by the band leader Tommy Dorsey: first, how to hold your breath because he couldn't work out how Tommy Dorsey could play the trombone so effectively. Dorsey told him, "Watch me when I'm playing and you'll see I open the corner of my mouth very slightly and breath in but you can't do that as a singer. He told Sinatra to swim under water and learn how to build up the capacity of his lungs. Dorsey also taught him how to hold his liquor and how to hold a grudge. Just look at that feud between Tommy and his brother Jimmy. Frank Sinatra excelled in grudges: nobody held a grudge better than Sinatra.

The Glasgow Empire was a legendary theatre where stars were born – and sometimes throttled at birth. If you were no good, they threw bottles and Dr Henry Farmer's pit orchestra had netting over it. The sax player once ended up with beer dripping down his head and his instrument soaked.

In 1957, I went there with my mother to see Mario Lanza and she thought he was so handsome. He sang 'Be My Love' and 'The Loveliest Night Of The Year' so beautifully. Then after one song, a Glaswegian shouted, "Hey, Mario, give us 'Temptation'." Lanza never bothered to reply and the orchestra broke into another of his fine songs. After the huge applause at the end, the man repeated his request, "Hey, Mario, give us 'Temptation'." Once again it was ignored. He did another song and the man shouted again, "Come on, let's have 'Temptation'." Mario Lanza responded, "But I don't know 'Temptation'. It is not one of my songs." The voice shouted, "It's my mother's favourite song. You've got to sing it." "Sorry," said Mario, "I don't know the song so I can't do it." "Okay," said the heckler, "Then show us your cock!" Everyone fell about laughing and the heckler wasn't even thrown out.

The poor English comics were guaranteed a hard time. When Des O'Connor was a young man, he arrived to perform at the Glasgow Empire, and I was there. As soon as the baying crowd heard the first few syllables of his accent, the place erupted and the audience threw bottles at him. Des fainted on stage in front of everyone. The conductor asked if he was all right; "Excuse me son, but is this part of the act?" "I'm just pretending so they can take me off," he whispered. So Des was dragged off stage and taken to his dressing-room and the doctor was called, who declared him fit and healthy. "I don't think I can go back on," said Des, "My stomach's not right." "Let me put it this way," said the manager, Charles Horsley, "I'll be telling Mr Moss about this incident and saying the doctor cannot find anything wrong with you. If you don't come to the theatre tomorrow night and finish the rest of the week, then your show business career will be over." Des weighed it up and he went back out the next night and had more bottles thrown at him. By Friday, the audiences had stopped throwing bottles and were beginning to laugh. That week at the Glasgow Empire made his career.

It wasn't easy for Mike and Bernie Winters. Mike was the smooth-talking straight man and he came out saying, "Hello Glasgow, how are you tonight?" This was met with abuse and when his brother looked out of the curtain, someone shouted, "Oh fuck, there's two of them." They got a torrent of bottles thrown at them and even though they became immensely popular, they never returned to the Empire.

II. One, Two, Three O'Clock, Four O'Clock, Rock!

As the 1950s kicked in, life in post-war Britain was changing. There was still austerity, the remnants of rationing and bombed-out wastelands in Glasgow, but from

America, a new breed of young person was now arriving; the teenager. I was one of the most willing converts. I was becoming interested in fashionable clothes and shoes. I've always liked to look and feel good, but in Glasgow, I set out to be a trendsetter.

The film that made the biggest impression on us teenagers was Rock Around The Clock with Bill Haley. Bill Haley's record had previously been used in Blackboard Jungle, a classroom drama which remains contemporary. Glenn Ford was very good in that but Sidney Poitier at the age of 30 was a little too old to be playing a schoolboy! I liked Rebel Without A Cause which had a great cast. Everything was right about that film. It seemed so true to life with James Dean playing a rebellious teenager.

When my mother was in America, I met a guy in Scotland who had a motor bike he was throwing out and he said, "Take it before my son wants it." Even though I got it for free, I wasn't sure that I could afford it as I would have to pay tax and insurance. I did take it - it was a Triumph, a good little motorbike. I would go down to the countryside. I wanted to be James Dean, but I was always cautious. Nobody wore helmets in those days. I wasn't part of a gang but I felt I was part of the scene with that motorbike and I was very proud of my black leather jacket. It was an American pilot's jacket that my mother had brought back from the States. Years later when my son Angus wanted a scooter or motorbike, Jan and I bribed him with the offer of a car when he passed his driving test. I have never told him that I once had a bike !

My mother also came back from America once with the first Elvis Presley record I'd heard. She said that nobody liked him in America, but that would only be amongst the people she was with. People at my golf club would say that today about Amy Winehouse because she wasn't their cup of tea, but she was a great singer.

I met Amy in Le Sport Hotel in St Lucia when I was having lunch with some friends. She was tiny with a big hairdo, a bigger bust and, when I spoke to her, her eyes were bright as she was there to dry out and stay off drugs. She was bubbly and had two massive bodyguards with her. I introduced myself and told her I was a songwriter and mentioned a few of my songs. I said your Mummy and Granny would know my songs and when I mentioned ´Puppet On A String´, she knew it as her Grandmother had the record.

I said I´d send her management a slow version of "Puppet" that had been recorded by Sandie Shaw. Amy said she´d love to hear it and, who knows, maybe record it. Whether she received it, I am unaware and now I´ll never know because, as the world knows, she died on July 26th 2011, less than a year after our meeting. Amy was like the American singers, Billie Holliday and Sarah Vaughan, yet she was also unique.

The BBC radio stations never played a lot of popular music in the 50s and it was very difficult to get to hear the new rock'n'roll records. You heard more of Pat Boone on Family Favourites, than you did Elvis Presley - Pat Boone was on there every bloody week! He was safe and you seldom got Elvis, and even a great record like Gene Vincent's 'Be-Bop-A-Lula' never made the Top Ten, probably because not enough people heard it due to lack of air play. You could go to record stores and listen to records in the listening booths, but if they sensed you wouldn't be buying anything, they'd ask you to leave.

I loved the music of Bill Haley and his Comets, Chuck Berry, the Everly Brothers, Little Richard and Elvis Presley. The first record I ever bought was Chuck Berry's 'School Day'. John Lennon said, "If the name rock'n'roll hadn't have been coined, they could have named it 'Chuck Berry'." Chuck was that good and he was the best rock'n'roll lyricist. His pianist, Johnnie Johnson, helped him write those songs but it took him many years to establish his financial rights, finally obtaining a 50/50 split. They put Johnnie Johnson in The Rock And Roll Hall Of Fame recently because he had helped Chuck with the melodies.

I've got a picture of myself with Chuck Berry in London and I said it was a great pleasure to meet him. I said, "You're the Cole Porter of rock'n'roll," and he thought that was terrific. He always referred to himself 'the Cole Porter of rock'n'roll'. I do think that these guys had a huge influence on the Beatles, on all of us.

I didn't buy many records but I would listen to as many as I could at Lewis's a Glasgow department store. I bought the occasional Elvis and I bought Carl Perkins' 'Blue Suede Shoes'. The best introduction to any record anywhere is Little Richard's 'Tutti Frutti' with its "Awopbopaloobop Alopbamboom." It's nonsense but it grips you immediately. That's good advice for songwriters: grab the public's attention as soon as you can. I loved the Platters, who sang great ballads with a beat, and I bought a Pat Boone song, 'I'll Be Home'. I pretended that I had bought it for my mother but I had really bought it for myself.

I went to dance halls in Glasgow: the Locarno, the F & F and the Barrowland were all great. I met a girl called Senga at the Barrowland, and Senga was Agnes backwards. She was a very attractive girl, who was the dux of her school. I knew she was a Catholic but that didn't bother me. I was dancing with her and she told me that she lived in the Gorbals which was a very tough area. We had a date and I went to pick her up. I started to limp when I got to the Gorbals and I walked that way to her house. She saw me coming and said, "Why are you limping? Have you hurt your leg?" I said, "Nobody's going to trouble me if they see I've got a limp." She said, "You stupid fool. They'll kick the shit out of you because they'll know you can't run away." That was the end of that. I didn't go back there again.

The Protestants and the Catholics didn't fall out in Scotland but you always had people saying, "Oh, she's a Catholic." There was no nastiness. You would ask a girl at a dance what school she went to and if she said 'St Aloysius' or 'St Gerard', you knew that she was a Catholic so you had better not continue your chat. It was unusual for Catholics and Protestants to marry. In those days, you'd ask what school she went to before you asked for her name. If it was Govan High, then you had to be a Protestant.

Rock'n'roll was taking off and Glasgow was embracing the new sound. All this great music was happening, so Saturday became the best day of the week. I'd play football in the afternoon and go dancing in the evening. I'd started going out with a shy young girl called Margaret Howe. She was very sweet and attractive and we got along really well. We first met when I was 14 but didn't start going out till a little later.

Frankie Vaughan was one of the first British artists to impress me, but he wasn't really rock'n'roll. Tommy Steele was a good performer but he didn't have the conviction to do rock'n'roll properly. It was very funny when Alex Harvey, a Govan lad with a very tough upbringing, was publicised as Scotland's Tommy Steele. I had seen him as a Teddy Boy and he could have eaten Tommy Steele alive. It set him back really as he wasn't Scotland's Tommy Steele at all but a sensational rocker. Scotland's Eddie Cochran would have been better, although he didn't have Eddie's astonishingly good looks. Alex was the first one from Scotland who showed us that we could do it like the Americans. He finally had a hit as The Sensational Alex Harvey Band with a cover of "Delilah" before dying aged just 46 from a massive heart attack. Incidentally, somewhere along the way, he and I were distant cousins.

Lonnie Donegan, also born in Glasgow, was known as the King of Skiffle, but his influence was far more wide-reaching even though he said he hated rock'n'roll. He influenced everybody. I know Cliff Richard rated him very highly even though their styles were very different, and the Beatles had started as a skiffle band because of Lonnie.

I went with my mates to the Isle of Man in 1957. I wanted to form a pop group and we called ourselves the Casuals. There was Frankie Quinn, Jim Thompson and James Thorburn and we would try and harmonise. Only one of us could harmonise properly so I knew it was going to be a flop. I could carry a tune but the others were messing about. That Isle of Man holiday was the first real sunshine that I can remember. I certainly hadn't seen suncream before.

Cliff Richard's 'Move It!' was a great rock'n'roll record and 'Living Doll' was a great pop song. 'Move It !' was the first pop song I'd heard that could compete with the American songs, and I was surprised that Elvis never covered it. I'd love to have heard him sing it.

'Living Doll' composer Lionel Bart later said that his song was based on ad he saw for a blow-up doll, but we didn't think of anything like that when we heard it in 1959. It sounds obvious now.

Funnily enough, I never rated Cliff as an actor. Maybe it was the parts he was given but he was a great singer. Elvis, on the other hand, could have been a great actor and I loved what he did in King Creole and Jailhouse Rock. I didn't go to any of his movies after that as they had silly plots and even sillier songs.

I paid no attention to his later movies and I didn't know that Elvis had recorded a song called 'Puppet On A String' in a film called Girl Happy in 1965. I've heard it since and it was rubbish. I would never have borrowed anybody else's song title: nobody did back then, but now that is done all the time by some of today's songwriters.

I loved it when the rock'n'roll stars revived oldies that I knew. Fats Domino did 'Blueberry Hill' in his wonderfully rich voice, Gene Vincent did 'Over The Rainbow' rather plaintively and Freddie Cannon hollered 'Way Down Yonder In New Orleans'. In 1959 Emile Ford and the Checkmates went to the top with 'What Do You Want to Make Those Eyes at Me For', an oldie that my dad had played a lot. Alan Hawkshaw was the organist on that record and years later, I asked him to play on the demo (demonstration record) for 'Puppet On A String'. He was an excellent organ player and he became rich through writing the theme music for Countdown as well as several other TV themes.

III. Songwriting ambitions

Our piano stool was overflowing with sheet music that was either bought on a Saturday afternoon or else borrowed from musical friends. People were swapping sheet music the whole time and everybody would be writing down lyrics. From an early age I would study sheet music just as a bookie would check the form of racehorses. I noted the names and addresses of the publishers and noticed that they were all in London. If I was to become a songwriter, I would have to move to London.

I recall my father singing the songs of Flanagan and Allen, who were both in the Crazy Gang. They included 'Run Rabbit Run', 'We're Going To Hang Out Our Washing On The Siegfried Line' and 'Underneath The Arches'. However, his preference was for American songwriters, and that's the way I went too.

My all-time favourite lyric is Cole Porter's 'I've Got You Under My Skin'. It is a song that gets to you if you are truly in love with somebody. You would walk across coals for them and sacrifice anything, as the song says. Frank Sinatra's recording with Nelson Riddle builds up to a great crescendo, like you wouldn't believe. It is a fabulous arrangement. What could be better than having Frank Sinatra, Nelson Riddle and Cole Porter on the same record? And it is their finest hour.

There is a little trombone solo on that record by Milt Bernhart. Sinatra would never say "How did I sound?" when he made a record. He knew he sounded great. He would say "Let's hear it." If he said, "I'll be back," you knew there were problems. You had to check your charts. This day, the band had all applauded when he sang 'I've Got You Under My Skin', but Frank said, "I'll be back." His chauffeur took him to a fruit and veg shop and he bought two full boxes of oranges, brought them back and walked up to Milt Bernhart and he said, "When it comes to the trombone solo, stand on these because you're the star of the show."

Frank Sinatra's own songwriting was terrible – 'Mr Success' is juvenile and 'I'm A Fool To Want You' wallows in self-pity. Bobby Darin was often compared to Sinatra – often by Darin himself, who said, "If I'm great now, what will I be like when I'm Sinatra's age." He didn't have the depth of voice or the phrasing that Sinatra had, but he was a much better songwriter. If he'd applied himself, Bobby Darin could have been one of the greatest songwriters as he could write in so many styles. In the end, we never found out how great Bobby Darin could be as he died when he was much too young. He died in 1973 when he was only thirty-seven.

Apart from the piano, the radio was my gateway to the changing sounds of popular music. I would tune in to Radio Luxembourg on 208 metres to hear The Adventures Of Dan Dare or Dr Kildare, but it was Pete Murray's late night Top 20 that I was desperate to hear. At first, it was just the sheet music charts but then the music papers such as the New

Musical Express came along with their record sales chart in 1952. I would jot down the Top 20 every week in an exercise book and the titles of the songs and the names of the artists were magical to me. I'd try and predict who might make it to the top and increasingly, I was right. I was learning the ingredients for a catchy pop song.

I was more interested in this than school work although I did stick with reading and writing. The popular music of the day was more fascinating and relevant to me than what was happening in Korea or India or the emerging Cold War. I wasn't a big reader but now I am catching up on the classics and and loving them. On my latest cruise to Australia and New Zealand, I saw the house that Robert Louis Stevenson built in Samoa. What a house! It was incredible – a huge house in huge grounds. To think he wrote Treasure Island when he was 29, the same age I was when I wrote 'Puppet on a String'. I know what I would have preferred to have written!

The first song I wrote was 'Angels in the Sky' when I was ten. The Crew-Cuts later recorded a song called 'Angels In The Sky' but it wasn't mine. My next song was 'Walking All The Way To Heaven' and I thought; "I can do this but I've got to get out of the God thing, writing about angels and Heaven."

I didn't want to write rock'n'roll songs as I preferred arrangements that were fuller than guitar and drums. I wanted to write something like 'Till The End Of Time', which was a big hit for Perry Como in 1945. It was written by Buddy Kaye with a little help from Chopin, and Buddy was to play an important part in my life in the 60s when he helped me secure my first major publishing deal. I was paid £30 a week, which was a lot of money in those days. It should also be noted that Buddy wrote such classics pop songs as Dusty Springfield's "In The Middle Of Nowhere" and "All Cried Out," "Speedy Gonzales," which was a hit for

Pat Boone and many more, including the theme tune to TV's I Dream Of Jeannie.

Looking back, I can see it was very beneficial that I was catholic in my tastes and saw that there was as much good in show tunes and standards as there was in rock'n'roll. Because I loved novelty songs, it got my brain thinking and I knew I didn't want to write clichéd songs that rhymed 'moon' with 'June'.

The best novelty songs sounded so easy and I'd wonder, "Why didn't I think of that?" Lita Roza's 'How Much Is That Doggie In The Window' was a terrific piece of songwriting. She hated the song but it was really because she wanted to be taken seriously as a singer. Billy Cotton's 'I've Got A Lovely Bunch Of Coconuts' was a great fairground song. Billy even looked like a fairground barker. Lonnie Donegan's 'Puttin' On The Style' was brilliant and it was a song that begged you to write your own verses. I also loved Lonnie's 'Does Your Chewing Gum Lose Its Flavour On The Bedpost Overnight?' What an ingenious title. Lonnie was the skiffle king and it's been overlooked that he was also the king of comedy songs. He had a great sense of humour and he could perform comedy songs in a very distinctive voice. He was also an influence for the Beatles as John Lennon formed a skiffle group called The Quarrymen with a young Paul McCartney.

There were scores of novelty songs in the early 50s and they continued in the rock'n'roll era. I loved Sheb Wooley with 'Purple People Eater', Barry Mann with 'Who Put The Bomp' and later, Bernard Cribbins with 'Right, Said Fred'. I also learnt that records do not have to be long: you can make your point and then leave. One of my favourite records is 'The Letter' by the Box Tops which is less than two minutes long. Adam Faith's 'What Do You Want' is all over in 90 seconds! In fact, we were trained to write songs that lasted less than 3 minutes as the BBC refused to play anything longer.

I studied the names of songwriters and I marvelled at Bob Merrill who wrote so many novelty hits for Guy Mitchell as well as the 'How Much Is That Doggie in the Window'. Look at the versatility of Terry Gilkyson who wrote 'Memories Are Made Of This' and 'The Bare Necessities' from The Jungle Book. In addition, Terry sang with the American group, The Easy Riders, who sang backing on the Dean Martin version of the song.

I also loved musicals and the great songs were not necessarily sung by great singers. Look at My Fair Lady. The lyricist Alan Jay Lerner was walking round Hyde Park with Rex Harrison. They had both been married several times and Rex said, "Alan, if we had only been gay, life would have been so much easier for us - and cheaper." That's where Alan got the inspiration to write 'A Hymn To Him' which has the opening line `Why can´t a woman be more like a man'. Alan gave Rex Harrison songs that he didn't have to sing, but his contribution would go along perfectly alongside the melody. It was brilliant.

Richard Rodgers was my favourite Broadway composer. His first lyricist Lorenz Hart could not write anything until he had a melody so Richard Rodgers had to write the melodies for 'Where Or When' and 'Manhattan' and then Lorenz Hart would walk about with these melodies in his head and write the lyrics. Richard Rodgers was impatient and often went out looking for him. He once shut Lorenz Hart in a lavatory to get him to write lyrics to three melodies that he´d given him.   Lorenz proceeded to write on lavatory paper, the words to ´Bewitched, Bothered and Bewildered´, Where Or When´ and ´My Funny Valentine´.

Richard Rodgers' melodies for the Rodgers and Hart songs flowed like jazz. Lorenz Hart wrote some very clever words to fit the melodies. Unfortunately, Hart was an alcoholic and he died aged just 46. His next partner, Oscar Hammerstein, was different. Oscar liked to write the lyrics first and then Rodgers would write the melodies. The Rodgers and Hammerstein songs are rather stilted because of that. 'Do-Re-Mi' sounds regimented, as pointed out by Stephen Sondheim who said, that Oscar Hammerstein wasn´t the greatest lyricist. Whatever Sondheim says, Oscar was an incredible lyricist. ´Cockeyed Optimist' is a work of genius and I will stand on a 6ft 7inch Stephen Sondheim's coffee-table, look him right in the eye, and tell him that.

In 1975 I was lucky enough to meet Richard Rodgers at the Sherry Netherland Hotel in New York although sadly his jaw cancer was noticeable. We spoke about Lorenz and Oscar and he realised I knew about songs. I asked him if any of the lyrics that the two of them had given him had made him cry and he said, "When Oscar gave me 'You'll Never Walk Alone' for Carousel, I cried." He told me that nobody had ever asked him that question before. He wasn't fond of people playing around with his melodies and after Peggy Lee recorded her version of 'Lover' with a dramatically different arrangement from that originally conceived by him, Rodgers said "I don't know why Peggy picked on me, she could have fucked up Silent Night." The doo-wop version of the Rodgers and Hart song 'Blue Moon' by The Marcels in 1961 angered Rodgers so much that he took out full page newspaper ads urging people not to buy it. He failed and it went to number one both sides of the Atlantic.

I was a lead drummer in a pipe band when I was 12 and my brother was a lead piper. I never played the drums at home as they were kept at the Boys' Brigade headquarters. I went marching around the streets and then we went to the camps. I never wanted to be a drummer but I've got the timing.

My brother played the piano and bagpipes and when my mother was told by a gypsy in Blackpool, "One of your sons is going to be very famous in the music business", she assumed it would be my brother. She was also told that we would both live to a great age and neither of us would die in an accident. My brother got everything. Once he got a xylophone: imagine a xylophone in a sitting room on a council estate. I knew that he would not progress musically. I went through jazz and Frank Sinatra and when he came back from the forces, he was still into jazz. He never got rock'n'roll at all: he preferred Ella Fitzgerald to Chuck Berry. He couldn't begin to understand how I could write songs.

Ian was the top boy in the Boys'Brigade. I was never close to him and he was never close to me. When my mother was away in 1956, he went into the RAF. I was alone with my father so I was a lonely little guy, but it was great because he was playing all those songs on the piano.

I did take some piano lessons as a child and I got to Grade 8 of my London Royal Academy of Music, which is quite good. I liked learning the scales, and I can do them to this day. The teacher said, "What is it you want to do with the piano?" I said, "I want to be a songwriter." She said, "You've got a natural gift for melody. You shouldn't inhibit it by playing the piano. Let your melodies flow in your head, because the melodies should crystallise there." Some years later, the great Henry Mancini also told me that. He got 'Moon River' worked out in his head before he played it and he wrote many of his great melodies like ´The Pink Panther Theme´ and ´Days Of Wine and Roses´ in London at the Mayfair Hotel in London. In fact Hank (as he was known) wrote all his great melodies in the Mayfair Hotel because he liked the house piano.

61

He was a lovely man who even offered to write the wedding march for my wife Jan and I at our ceremony in 1972. Jan, however, wanted ´A Whiter Shade Of Pale` which is based on Bach´s Air On A G String.

That's why some great piano players like Rick Wakeman don't write too many big pop songs. The keyboard is inhibiting them and they make the songs too complicated. Les Reed, the great songwriter, arranger and my good friend whose catalogue includes 'Delilah', 'The Last Waltz' and 'There´s A Kind Of Hush', warms up by playing Rachmaninov. He has to be going for half an hour before you can get him to simplify things. When you hear his songs, you sing the arrangements as well – just sing his 'Delilah' to yourself and you'll see what I mean. I wanted to be a pop songwriter and I know no great musician could have written 'Shang-A-Lang' for the Bay City Rollers but more about them later.

On the subject of 'Delilah', Les Reed wrote the music whilst Barry Mason, another good friend of mine, wrote the lyrics. Barry tells the story of the time he went to the bar at the BBC and had to answer the call of nature. He was pointing Percy at the Porcelain when the guy at the urinal beside him, a well known (and unpopular) BBC Radio producer starting whistling 'Delilah' which was riding high in the charts at the time. Barry said to the guy "I wrote that song". The producer replied "I thought Les Reed wrote it" Barry said "Les wrote the melody and I wrote the lyrics". "Well, I'm not whistling the fucking lyrics am I" came the response.

However, for the time being, this desire to be a songwriter had to be kept secret. It wasn't a manly thing to be doing in Govan and I didn't feel that I could tell it to anybody and I certainly didn't want to play them my songs. I had an ability to play football and I hoped I could do something professionally.

Chapter 3 - Team Spirit

I. Football

I was a good footballer. My brother Ian recalls that I was known as 'The Animal'. He says that I was a strong left half (midfield player) with a hard shot but I was lacking in finesse. That might be so, but I certainly loved the game and turned out for Pollok Hawthorn, a juvenile football team in Glasgow and we won many honours. Ian was called for national service as an airframe mechanic in the Royal Air Force and also trained as a body-builder.

My dad was a proud Glasgow Rangers supporter and both Ian and I followed his lead. Just down the road in Govan was Ibrox Park, the home of Glasgow Rangers. In 1946 I was carried in to see Rangers play Moscow Dynamo and there were about 100,000 people watching the match. It was only a shilling to watch the football. Unlike today, you could be a fan of a top football team and it wouldn't cost you very much to support them.

Ian and I were fanatical 'Gers fans from the earliest days and when we weren't playing ourselves, we trooped down to Ibrox to watch their great players. 'Follow, Follow' was the Rangers' signature tune although I have to admit that the Celtic song 'It's a Grand Old Team To Play For' is much better.

I've been so glad to have met great footballers and I've always found that they liked music. Matt Busby told me that he loved Rod Stewart and songs like 'I Belong To Glasgow', and the thrill of my songwriting lifetime so far was writing and recording 'Back Home' for the England World Cup

Squad of 1970, which gave me another Number 1 and a gold record.

I met Bill Shankly, the Scotsman who transformed Liverpool FC. He was terrific and I don't think he realised he was so funny. In that respect, he was more like an Irishman than a Scotsman. He signed Ron Yeats, big centre-half from Scotland and he said to the press, "Come in and walk round my centre half" instead of "Come in and interview him." He knew about motivation and so did Alex Ferguson and Tommy Docherty. They were immense characters and I loved players like George Graham, Willie Waddell, Geoff Hurst, Bobby Moore and Alan Ball, Ally McCoist, Denis Law, Paddy Crerand, Willie Morgan, Franny Lee who all became great friends.

I got on well with Terry Venables, who was a good singer and had sung with Joe Loss. I've known him since 1965. Like me, he liked being in Denmark Street and being around songwriters. He created the TV crime series, Hazell, and he is a great pundit/commentator too. He has now ventured into the hotel business, buying and running, with his wife, Yvette, a boutique hotel near Alicante called La Escondida. A man of many talents.

I knew Alex Ferguson at Govan High School. He is two years younger than me and you didn't pal up with people who were younger than you. The only reason I knew him was because he was a good footballer. We said hello to each other and we were in the Boys' Brigade. He was playing at the best level and I was below that but we played for the same school. Alex went to Queen's Park right away – that was in 1958 - and I went to Blantyre Celtic, which was a good team, and then he got signed to Dunfermline and then Rangers. He was a very good player but when he married a Catholic girl, Cathy, that was his career with Rangers virtually finished due to the bigotry in Scotland. He could have been the Rangers' manager (he was also briefly

Scotland's manager after the death of the great Jock Stein) but he hated the bigotry as any sensible person would. Still, he is now recognised as the greatest football manager of all-time and arguments from Sean Connery fans aside, I think he is the world's most famous Scotsman.

Alex never worked in the shipyards in Govan, he worked in Remington Rand but he became the shop steward for all the apprentices. If we – that is, Billy Connolly and me - were going out on strike, it was Alex Ferguson who took us out. Alex knew how to win an argument and he was a top man. He maintains a good dignity in defeat too.

Alex Ferguson is never late for anything. He is dedicated and was always first in the training ground. He was always very loyal to his players but also very hard – he certainly knows when to hold and when to fold. He can call your bluff which is probably why he is an excellent Kalooki player.

I played with Bobby Collins when he was with Pollok. He was a tiny little man, yet very aggressive, and a phenomenal footballer. He said to me, "You're tough and strong but I am not sure you'll make it. You have a good left foot but you don't have a good footballing brain. I hope you have something else." I wanted to tell him, "I write songs, you little bastard, I'll be bigger than you," but I didn't want to tell anybody that. In later life Bobby Collins drove a taxi in Leeds and then got Alzheimer's Disease, so it was a very sad ending for a fabulous footballer, when he died in 2014. All the other players like Jackie Charlton and Billy Bremner revered him.

When Bobby Collins played for the Rangers' arch-rivals Celtic, I couldn't admit I liked him. When he went on to play with Don Revie's Leeds United, I could come clean. He was 5 foot 4 inches and a brilliant little pocket battleship of a player. I modelled my game on his. They called him the

General and he ran that Leeds United team. Those guys he played with will tell you that he was the main guy.

Footballers are a different breed today. They get obscene money. It's easy to say that if you're not making it yourself but the top footballers get even more than rock bands. Look at the scandals surrounding players like Wayne Rooney. He paid a prostitute and he thought that nobody would find out. It's naïve to think that money can cover everything. There is a song, 'Money Is The Root Of All Evil' and if he went with a prostitute, she was not just doing it for £1,200 but for the payment from the newspapers. These footballers don't realise that they are being set up. If you're getting £6m a year for playing and another £30m from endorsements, you must be stupid if you think that everybody is going to stay quiet. There are leeches all round. They want some money and five minutes of fame, no matter what's it's for. When this used to happen in Hollywood in the golden years, the studios were able to cover it up with a network of press officers and connections.

Alex hated all this publicity around Wayne Rooney and Ryan Giggs. He is a great family man and he had Ryan as a role model footballer until he was in headlines for non-footballing reasons. Giggs has been decorated more times than any other footballer and he won everything that's possible, including the BBC's Sports Personality. Hopefully he'll now have a successful career in management which would bring him the knighthood he deserves.

Alex was able to control his footballers' drinking life and their gambling life but he has no control over their bedroom life. He used to find out where the players were and he would march them out of the pub. He could even have controlled George Best. He would have told him, "Nobody's bigger than the club and I will get rid of you unless you change your ways." In my opinion his greatest strength is his man management. He was able to adjust from the days of the famous 'hairdryer' and kicking over tea urns to dealing with the more sensitive players of today who have agents agitating for a move. It is no surprise to me that he is now in great demand on the lecture circuit, including a prestigious engagement at Harvard. He is some motivator.

The players of the past would have their fun by going to restaurants, buying cars and playing golf tournaments. Look at Franny Lee – that is Francis Lee from Manchester City. He was paid £20 a week for playing and then he went into business and made toilet rolls. He eventually sold the business for £8.35m. He also has a patent for creating those black and white signs that you see as you are turning a bend in a car. He was very astute. The majority of today's big earners don't think like that as they are earning so much money while they are playing so don't have the incentive.

When he was a lad, Kenny Dalglish lived near the Ibrox stadium and his wall was full of Rangers players, he supported them but they never signed him because of the bigotry in Glasgow between Catholics and Protestants. He went to Celtic and he became one of the greatest strikers ever.

I first met Kenny in 1970 when he was a shy boy and he can still give that impression, although he is very witty and a very caustic wit when he wants to be. I got to know him in 1974 when we produced the record 'Easy Easy' for the Scottish World Cup Squad. He has never lost his funny Glasgow accent and he is a very sincere and loyal family man. He was a phenomenal player winning many trophies with Liverpool including the European Cup and the Double as player-manager. As a manager he won the Premiership with Blackburn and it was a shame that things didn't quite work out when he returned to manage Liverpool although a lot of people forget that it was Kenny who signed Luis Suarez. He knows what he is doing and he is a lovely guy and his dignity during the period of the Hillsborough disaster and since has been admirable. In addition Kenny and his wife, Marina, raise a lot of money for charity.

I thought Liverpool would benefit from having a manager who speaks English, as they do with Brendan Rogers, but I was wrong. That said, Jurgen Klopp speaks excellent English and seems to have what it takes. There is no business in the world where you would have management who don't speak the language of the workers. You wouldn't bring a Russian foreman into an English car factory to discuss components. What is going on is just bizarre. I totally disagree with foreign managers in football and I think there are too many foreign players. The game has got out of hand financially, but that's Rupert Murdoch for you. That is why football hardly shuts down in the summer. Sky wouldn't allow them to close because of the viewing figures.

II. Getting married

In 1958, my mother gave me some money and I went to London for two weeks to try and sell myself as a songwriter. I knew the publishers' addresses and I tried to find Denmark Street but I was also told that the Music Publishers and Songwriters were in a place called Tin Pan Alley which, of course, I couldn't find either. The holiday underlined what I already thought. I would have to come to London and make it as a songwriter. As I had limited money, I stayed with one of my mother's sisters, Auntie Marion, in Romford, Essex. I may just as well have stayed in Blackpool as I had to take the train every day into London. I did find Chappell's Music Publisher in Bond Street. They looked after the likes of Cole Porter, Irving Berlin and Rodgers and Hammerstein and employed one name I'd heard of, Jimmy Henney, who later became a music pundit on TV. I asked to see him without success but his assistant, Terry Oates, kindly did and politely told me how to get to Tin Pin Alley as my songs weren't for them. It was too late to go then though as I was catching the train back to Glasgow.

I thanked him and also, after that, sent him a Christmas Card every year and he became a good friend when I made the grade in later years. Terry and his wife Mandy built a large music publishing company called Eaton Music. It is still around to this day but alas Terry died 3 years ago with a who's who of the music business at his funeral.

So, the two weeks had drawn to a close and I had searched everywhere but Tin Pan Alley being only a tiny street, when I asked people, no-one knew where it was until Terry Oates told me on my final day in London. You must remember that this was 1958 and I had no street map so I went back to Glasgow with my tail between my legs.

There was one prospect on the horizon that was not too alluring. I might have to do National Service and I didn't think I was cut out for square bashing. I could appreciate the need for defending your country but I couldn't see the need for it at the time. I was caught in music, just like John Lennon and those other boys who left for Hamburg. As luck would have it, the Government was talking about ending conscription but that didn't happen until the end of 1960.

I didn't think that I would learn anything worthwhile in the forces and it wouldn't help me as a songwriter. I even thought it might take away the feelings that I had for music and for songwriting. I might not be able to listen to the radio and so I didn't want to be in the army. I thought my best bet was to get out of the country but where ?

I had finished my apprenticeship and I saw an opportunity of working in South Africa and playing football at the same time. My mother borrowed the money from her sister, my Auntie Sadie, so I could go to South Africa.

I'd been good at football since I was 12 - not great but good enough to get into the junior team and then into the senior teams. I'd been playing for Blantyre Celtic and I nearly signed for Partick Thistle, but I broke my arm when I was supposed to have a trial. Perhaps it was no great loss as Billy Connolly told me that he thought the name of the team was Partick Thistle Nil.

When I first met Margaret Howe, she was like a young Elizabeth Taylor. I was 14 and she was 15 and I thought she was a stunning girl with a great figure. I used to chat her up when she lived in the older part of Priesthill, my council estate after Govan. Mag, as I called her, lived in Househillmuir, just down the road. I used to stand under a lamppost and I would look up into her kitchen to see her. It gave me inspiration for writing songs. She thought that I was too young for her at first but we started going out when I was 16. We would go to the pictures and we became an item. I would stand outside her house every night. Her father, who was a taxi driver, used to call me Hugo as in "You go to.... F*ck!"

Her mother had died and she looked after her father until he died. She had a twin sister May and two brothers, Ian and Jim, but I said, "Why don't we start our own life together?" I told her my plan, which I admit sounds crazy now. I told her that we should go to South Africa. I would escape the call-up and we could come back with some money and head to London where I would become a songwriter. She thought that was stupid but she went along with it.

I had a false tooth because the dentists near the shipyards in Govan would be pulling your teeth out all the time as they got more money for that than for fillings. I lost my false tooth the night before I got married. I was also getting married with a broken wrist which had happened in a football match the previous Saturday.

In January 1960 we had a tiny church wedding and the reception was held in my bedroom in Priesthill with all the furniture moved into the main room. There were about 25 people there and Mag looked beautiful. Neither of us had slept with anyone else before. I don't regret my marriage at all, but something was telling me that I was too young for this commitment.

Chapter 4 - South Africa

It was such a cheap flight to South Africa in 1960 that we had to go all over the place from one airport to another to get there. The first stop was in Madrid. I remember writing to my brother and telling him that the hotel rooms had little foot baths. I thought the bidet was for my feet. Then we got to the next country and I saw the skull-and-crossbones everywhere – I didn't realise that was a sign for danger in electricity boxes – and the next day it was Agadir in Morocco where they had just had some earthquakes. Then it was Egypt and Nigeria and it took us days to get to South Africa. When we finally reached our destination of Johannesburg, I already knew I had made the wrong decision. I'd felt that I had to get out of Glasgow but now I wanted to leave South Africa before I'd even set foot in the country.

When I arrived in Johannesburg, I found that most of the white people were Jewish. There were a lot of Christians in South Africa, but the main businesses were run by people who were Jewish. All the diamond business and the schmutter trade, which is what they called the rag trade, were Jewish. Nothing wrong with that: it was just a culture shock for me. When I left Govan, I didn't know any Jewish people.

Also, I'd never met any black people. There were a few people from Pakistan selling household goods door-to-door in Govan but that was it. This was all new to me. If you travelled in the bus, there were seats at the front for 'whites only'. I couldn't understand it and to this day, I can't understand why different races can't get along.

But something was very definitely happening in South Africa. The British Prime Minister, Harold Macmillan came out and addressed the South African parliament in February 1960. He made that famous speech about the wind of change. He said, "The wind of change is blowing through this continent, and whether we like it or not, this growth of national consciousness is a political fact. We must all accept it as a fact, and our national policies must take account of it."

I went to Africa with a wife, very little money and a broken wrist. I tried to get a job with my hand stuck in my pocket. One potential employer said, "What's wrong with your hand?" I said, "I'd broken my scaphoid but the plaster comes off tonight." He gave me the job and I took the plaster off myself. That is why I can't turn my left wrist back very far and it's another example of my impulsive behaviour.

I was employed as an engineer but I was no more an engineer than a bus conductor. I was sent to Sharpeville and I was at Sharpeville when the massacre occurred on 21 March 1960. I was sent to a city called Vereeniging, which is close to the township of Sharpeville. The streets were like streets from a Western movie for the whites, both for the whites and the blacks. There were wooden shacks on either side, which were shops and houses but only for white people whilst we were in the only hotel.

The police stations were known as 'locations' – the one in Sharpeville was a compound with a big wired fence and the police had Land Rovers and Gatling guns. We saw this huge mass of black people walking towards the location. I had never seen so many black people together. They were angry with the police for some reason: I'm not sure how it started. They marched up to the fence and when they reached it, they shook it violently. I was working near the site on a pylon and I was watching it happen.

A young policeman went out and told them to move away. They took no notice and continued to protest. He had a Gatling gun on the top of a Land Rover and he sprayed them with bullets. They panicked and ran. That led to a chain reaction in which 66 Africans were killed and 200 injured. It was carnage but the South African government at the time said that they had crushed a rebellion. It became such a significant event in 1960 that March 21 is now called Human Rights Day in South Africa.

I got back to the hotel and a young 23 year old Englishman with a very beautiful wife said they were going to drive back to England in his Austin Mini Clubman that night. He thought this was like the end of the world and he had to get out. He was driving back through Africa and I'd love to know whatever happened to him.

I felt that way too. I thought a huge race war was about to happen and we didn't want to be caught in it. We decided to leave Vereeniging that night. Mag and I left – we had no possessions to speak of – and we went to Johannesburg and we moved into a beautiful district called Hillbrow. It was classy then but now it is a no-go area. It is the biggest drugs area in Johannesburg. When you are driving through, you daren't stop at the lights as you could be shot as it is mostly Nigerians living there.

I had cut off my plaster on my hand so that I could get a job in Vereeniging and I had lasted two days. I went to Johannesburg and got accepted as a midfield player for Johannesburg Rangers FC and when my father was asked, he loved to say I played for Rangers, implying it was Glasgow Rangers. No one ever asked him for further details! I had made the grade as a professional soccer player but I wasn't really good enough. It is like writing a song but knowing that Elvis would never record it. I wasn't good enough as a soccer player but I have never lost my love for the game.

It was supposed to be an all white team but Percy Owen looked dubiously suntanned. In 1963, he was to achieve a club record of 41 goals in the season, but sadly he was killed in the troubles.

The legendary Blackpool, Stoke and England player, Stanley Matthews came out to play some exhibition football matches. He was 45 then but he was still playing for Blackpool. I played against him and nearly injured him. His manager came in at half time and said to me, "Don't you ever touch him again. They are not here to see you, you smelly piece of shit. They have come to see Stanley Matthews. Stanley is going to play this game, waltz about and score the winning goal and you keep well away from him." Everyone was taking the mickey out of me after that. Boy, could Stanley play.

In addition, I got a job at Garlicks selling office equipment. I was given a car and I didn't know how to drive. One guy in the football team told me that his brother conducted driving tests. I said, "I've never driven before." He said, "Tell him you've driven and I will come and pick up the car with you." They gave me a little van and he showed me what to do. Then I met his brother and we went to this compound, which was full of rubber obstacles. I had to show them how to park and I was knocking things down. His brother said, "I'll take you out on the road now." He said that we would go down to a township where the black people were, and of course he hated black people. As we were driving along, he said, "Ah, you nearly got him." I got my licence and crashed the car within a week!

South Africa is a beautiful country but it had been consumed by hatred. It wasn't just that the blacks were separated from the whites. It was that they were subjected to cruelty and injustice. The whites were using them as slave labour too and they lived in poverty without electricity and running water: they would work ridiculous hours in factories for very little reward. I was very disturbed all the time I was there.

Another racial incident occurred when I was with friends in the Witwatersrand Stadium. There were three of us and we wanted to hear Hendrik Verwoerd, the Prime Minister of South Africa. He was known as the Architect of Apartheid. I wanted to see if he was an orator like Hitler who had some hold over the country, but we never heard him speak. There was a big crowd and one of my friends had a camera.

At Witwatersrand Stadium, when his would-be assassin, David Pratt said "Dr Verwoerd", he turned, his head went up and the bullet went through his cheeks. My friend took the famous shot of the blood coming out of Dr Verwoerd's face and sold it to the Rand Daily Mail. They thought he had been assassinated but he wasn't. About six years later, Dr Verwoerd was stabbed and killed in the House of Assembly. This was yet another incident that made me think, "What am I doing here?"

Nelson Mandela was all over the papers and he was named as one of the ringleaders of this racial war. At the time, he was called a terrorist because he was blowing things up. He was arrested and locked up but I knew that arresting one man wasn't going to calm the tensions. Mandela was a giant in height but it would be sometime before he became a giant in history.

I was in Kenya with the football team when Tom Mboya, right hand man to President Kenyatta, was killed. I am not a politician but I knew it wasn't right to have all these millions of black people being curtailed by a few white people.

I first met the famous record producer, Mickie Most, in South Africa. He wasn't a big-shot then, although he was to become the UK's number one record producer (along with Sir George Martin who, of course, famously produced the Beatles' music). I knew of Mickie as he had made some records as the Most Brothers for Decca in the UK. He came out to South Africa as he wanted to marry a local girl, Chrissie, who came from a wealthy family which had made its money from fruit. Her parents said that she was only 16 and he couldn't marry her until she was 18. They said that if he came out to South Africa and stayed for two years, they would know that his intentions were honourable.

When I discovered he was in town, I used to nip round to the studio with my songs. He would see me coming and duck out the back door. He used to say, "That noisy Scotsman thinks he can write songs and he can't." I accept that the songs may have been rubbish but he didn't give me a chance.

When I got back to England and had some songs accepted, I bumped into Mickie in Denmark Street and he said, "Oh, I used to see you in South Africa." I said I was now here and he said, "Congratulations" which is a good title for a song. To be honest, the minute he saw me in the Regent Sound Studio, he was off again. Years later, he released the records that Phil Coulter and I made with Kenny, which included 'The Bump'. After the success of 'The Bump', we became great friends and he was a decent guy as he never once asked for a percentage of the music publishing for himself.

In order to earn enough money to get out, I had to save as much as I could and earn extra whenever possible. I was playing football professionally in South Africa and working as a salesman. I would sell office equipment after training. Mag was very worried about the situation as well and was all for going back. She was making money by working as a

PA. Being clever and bright, she was very good at it. We saved every penny and that's how we got back.

I had short hair like Steve McQueen and I always had great ties and shirts, so I looked a wee bit different. I liked those American ties with a little pin. This guy asked me if I wanted to be a male model and he said that it was easy money. They wanted me in a swimming costume for £100, and they would take my front, back and sides. I signed a piece of paper so they had all the rights. I first saw one of the photos in a medical journal, but they appeared everywhere. They had painted black spots on my body and the caption was, "This man has fungus because he doesn't use this." I had signed away my rights and there was nothing I could do. Everybody thought I had fungus. I went to a party where my picture was plastered on the wall with a note that said, "Watch him. That's the guy who has fungus."

I said that I would never do that again and the guy from the agency said, "No, it's okay. I've got a terrific idea." Coca-Cola is taking down that big billboard ad on the road from Hillbrow into Johannesburg, and you'll be on the replacement. I said, "Are you going to paint anything on my body?" He said, "No, no, I promise you. You're going to be dressed as a guardsman with a sword and there will be three other guys too." I thought this would be fantastic as, coming down that hill, I would be able to see my face for miles. I thought I'd be able to live with this but it turned that I was the smelly one who hadn't used the deodorant.

Once again, I told the guy that I wasn't happy about this and he said, "Look, I will give you an ad with a beautiful girl." I said, "What am I doing?" He said, "Nothing. You're just having a cup of tea. There are no snags at all." They only got a girl who was well over six foot and I am much smaller. They got a ladder for me to take the cup of tea up to her, and it said, "Even small men can deliver the best tea." It looked like I was a dwarf, but I did get the money so we were able to come back.

When I was in South Africa, my whole life was in a quandary and all I could think about was songs. I'm sure my predicament inspired 'That's The Only Way'. I sent that song over to London and it was accepted through the post by Paul Rich who worked for Freddie Bienstock, and Freddie was Elvis Presley's publisher. Paul Rich had been a band singer like Dick James (who became the Beatles' publisher) and when the big bands finished, they went into publishing and Paul worked for Progressive Music. The big singers at the time were Adam Faith and Cliff Richard, and he thought 'That's The Only Way' would suit Adam Faith:

"You for me, can't you see,
That's the only way."

I was ecstatic as I had got my first song accepted and I knew I had to get to London as quickly as possible and make things happen.

Looking back, I can see that being in South Africa wasn't a complete wash-out. In fact, my two years in South Africa were like a finishing school for me. It broadened my mind and I had made my Scottish accent more palatable to outsiders. I found out that I knew how to sell, even if it was only office equipment. I acquired a better dress sense. I had dressed neatly in Glasgow but there was something of the spiv about me. Now I was more like a gentleman and I had good manners. My mother was very impressed and I also gave her back the £200 she had lent me.

I made some friends in South Africa especially one Scots guy, John Rowley, whom I'm still in touch with. Another friend, John Bidwell, was eaten by a crocodile. His dog got attacked and the crocodile pulled the animal under to drown him. John was fighting the crocodile but he didn't realise that another one was coming up behind him.

We had had some equally tense moments. I have a great photograph of Mag and I standing on top of Victoria Falls, and a canoeist had taken us out there. I can't believe we did that. We were standing on a stone overlooking the falls and watching the canoeist fighting the currents. What if he had had an accident or fallen overboard? How would we have survived? I get cold shivers every time I think about it. When you're 21, you don't think like that, but I knew I had to return to my sort of civilisation.

One music highlight was to be part of a massive crowd In Eloff-President Street in Johannesburg. The crowd were there for one of the biggest pop groups Cliff Richard and the Shadows in 1961 and, as it was pre The Beatles, they were a world wide success. I tried to meet Cliff and The Shads at their hotel – no chance! Who'd have thought that this Scots guy standing in the crowd would years later get Cliff back to number 1 for the first time in three years with 'Congratulations' and that Bruce Welch and Brian Bennett of The Shadows would become great friends.

Chapter 5 - Partners

I. Entering Solomon's Temple

Mag and I arrived back in the UK in October 1962 and once again, we had no money as I had to pay for the flight and I felt I had to pay back my mother. I knew that my chances of success would be stifled if I returned to Glasgow.

I wanted to settle in London as quickly as possible as I was determined to become a professional songwriter. I believe that you need confidence but I am not big-headed. I have confidence in what I can do and I have tremendous drive and I always wanted to succeed.

I knew I would be able to see Freddie Bienstock as he had accepted 'That's The Only Way'. Adam Faith did record the song but it was never released. It is probably still in EMI's vaults somewhere.

I met Adam Faith at the Ivy three weeks before he died in 2003. He had been an actor for years but now he was thinking of going on the road singing his hits as in the 60s. He didn't want to put a band together due to the cost and I said, "Why don't you go to EMI and get your backing tracks? And, while you're about it, get my backing track for 'That's The Only Way' and do that one too." He might have taken my advice, but then he died of a heart attack, allegedly whilst shagging a young bird in a Stoke-on-Trent hotel room. I can think of worse ways to go !

You get used to songs not being released. Songwriting is a series of disappointments. You write something that you think is great and then you're disappointed because nobody else does, but when you write something that everybody likes, it is the best feeling ever. It is even better now, 50 years later, when a perfect stranger knows something I wrote all those years ago.

As I could sell office equipment, I got a job with a company doing what I had been doing in South Africa. I soon found that I couldn't be bothered with that and I found a new job with Saxa Salt. My hair was black and white so I looked like a cruet set. I was very fortunate in that a car came with the job and even luckier to discover that my driving licence from South Africa was an international one and so I was allowed to drive in the UK without taking a further test.

As it turned out, I couldn't have been a salt salesman at a better time as the snow really came down that winter of 1962/3. It was a terrible winter for everybody except salt salesmen. I was in huge demand. I was supplying Tesco, which had just started, and I would arrange to get the salt out on the roads for the councils. I'd be very busy in the mornings and then I would head to Denmark Street for lunch as my ambition was to get to know as many publishers and songwriters as possible.

One side of Denmark Street was music publishers' offices and the other side had the Tin Pan Alley club and a coffee bar, La Gioconda. Denmark Street housed every major publisher except Chappell's, who, as I said earlier, were in New Bond Street.

This may be an opportune time to explain music publishing to those not in the industry. A music publisher signs your song to a contract, making the song a copyright. The music publisher collects 100% of the revenue, and gives the songwriter 50%. When the song goes abroad, say to a German music publisher, he takes 50%, sends 50% to the original publisher who then gives 50% of that to the songwriter - that is why I became a music publisher as well as a songwriter.

One of the key publishers, TRO-Essex, run by David Platz, was directly above Regent Sound Studio in Denmark Street where a lot of demonstration records were made. He heard the tunes being recorded in the studio as the walls were so thin. If he heard something he liked, he would give them a publishing contract. That's how he got the Rolling Stones' publishing. It was as simple as that. David Platz was a great negotiator and he hardly had to move from his office to make a fortune.

David Platz was a survivor of Auschwitz and he had started his music publishing career with 'Rock Island Line,' a hit for Lonnie Donegan in 1956. He was financed by Howie Richmond of The Richmond Organisation (TRO), who had their own successes with 'Music, Music, Music' and 'Fly Me To The Moon'. David Platz was to sign the Rolling Stones, The Who, The Move, Procol Harum and many more.

The Beatles' record producer, George Martin told Brian Epstein that the best publisher was David Platz but he had a lot on his plate. "If I were you," he said, "I would go and see Dick James." George himself wrote music and 'Niagara' had been published by Dick James. The Beatles first single, 'Love Me Do' had gone to Ardmore and Beechwood but that was an old-time EMI music publishing company that showed little interest in the Beatles. Dick James was hungry and he gave them the standard contract for the time. I'm told that the Beatles earned £800 from publishing royalties when 'Love Me Do' became a Top 20 hit.

When I first heard 'Love Me Do', there was an explosion in my head. Here were four British guys who were sounding better than the Everly Brothers. I knew that the wind of change was about to hit the UK music business.

At lunchtime, you either went to La Gioconda where you would meet sensible music publishers like Dick James, David Platz or Cyril Gee, the hustlers who were always looking for new songs and new writers, or the Tin Pan Alley Club and the local pub, The White Hart, where the song pluggers would get so drunk that nothing would happen in the afternoon. I realised that it would be better to build up everything myself and establish my own career.

Here's an example. Leslie Osborne had the job of placing theme tunes. If the tune got rejected, Leslie would say, "May I play you one of mine?" They would say, "Come on, Leslie, let's go for a pint instead." In 1985, the BBC wanted a theme for their new soap, EastEnders and he thought, "Here's an opportunity." He was well into his sixties by then and he played something of his to the BBC and they said, "That's lovely, Leslie, who wrote it?" He knew he shouldn't say himself so he said, " A young musician called Simon May." He went back to the Music Publisher and he said, "Right, Simon, you have just written the EastEnders theme tune and it's written with me." They then worked on it together. A negotiation took place and Leslie kept his percentage but his name was taken off the credits after a few years.

There was a couple that looked after Leslie and stayed near him in Brighton and when he was dying, he offered them his house. They said, "No, thank you, we would rather have the royalties from the EastEnders theme," and they allegedly own half that theme now. The PRS apparently got the house for their members' fund.

There were a lot of Cyrils at the top of the music publishing business – Cyril Simons, Cyril Shane and Cyril Gee. I felt my name, Wylie Macpherson, was too Scottish. When I went to Denmark Street, I thought it wouldn't work and Cyril Gee at Mills Music said, "Change it. Ten letters are lucky for songwriters." I said, "Why's that?" and he said, "Cole Porter, Lorenz Hart, Lionel Bart, Chuck Berry."

Although he wasn't around then, there would soon be John Lennon. So I became Bill Martin (because Dean Martin was my favourite singer). It wasn't until I had written 'Puppet On A String' that I realised he had forgotten to tell me about Oscar Hammerstein, Burt Bacharach and George Gershwin. I could have stayed Wylie Macpherson.

Cyril Gee was a good businessman but he didn't know anything about hit songs. Before Roger Greenaway went in with his songwriting partner Roger Cook for a contract, I said, "Ask for a £500 advance." Roger said, "We'll never get that." Cyril did give them £500 each and Roger gave me a very welcome £50 and a bottle of Scotch. They weren't known at the time but they went on to write 'I'd Like To Teach The World To Sing' and one of my favourite 60s songs, 'You've Got Your Troubles'.

When I came to Tin Pan Alley, the first guy who befriended me was Tony Hiller, who was a general manager at Mills Music. He was always trying to latch onto songwriters to help and maybe write songs with them. He was enthusiastic and he was very, very funny. He knew I was skint and he would take me to his house and feed me. Tony Hiller befriended everybody and that's why everybody likes him. He was, in the past, in a very good singing act with his brother, Irving called, would you believe, the Hiller Brothers.

On the other hand, Tony's wife, Moira, was always moaning at him and giving him a hard time. They had a little dog called Major, a Yorkshire terrier, which used to run across the room and jump on your leg and start shagging you. She would go, "Major, stop that!" and Tony would say, "That's the closest you'll ever get to a shag in this house."

In April 1976, the day after he won Eurovision with 'Save Your Kisses For Me', Tony went back home and packed his bags. His wife said, "Where do you think you're going?" and he said, "I'm leaving. I've had enough of you. Keep the house, keep the lot, I'm off." He walked out. He gave her everything, got his hair permed, got his teeth done and there he was, the manager and songwriter for Brotherhood of Man.

When I was coming back to the UK in 1962, I asked my pals in South Africa where I should live in London. They said "Peckham", winding me up as there were more black people there than in Johannesburg, We lived in Peckham (long before Del-Boy and Rodney of the tv series "Only Fools and Horses") for a month and then moved a few miles away to Lewisham.

I worked from Monday to Friday and played football on Saturday mornings. Just before my first song was published in 1963, I dropped into Fred Compton and Bernie Ecclestone's motorcycle showroom in Lewisham to look at the BSAs and Nortons. Bernie Ecclestone, a very cocky little guy, said to me, "What are you doing in here?" I said I was looking at the bikes and he said, "You're not going to buy a bike." I said, "How do you know?" He said, "I just do. I know you're not a buyer, so don't come back." That wasn't very nice, but he didn't want to watch customers who weren't going to buy anything. The following week I returned and he threw me out. Years later Bernie Ecclestone would come back into my life.

As I said, shortly after I came to London, I heard the Beatles' first single, 'Love Me Do', and from then on, I was a huge fan and was to follow everything that they did. I had loved the songs of the early 50s and the rock'n'roll era but my heart soared when I heard 'Love Me Do'. It was so different and I still think it is one of the Beatles' best songs. That harmonica was so haunting and the record had a different feel to anything else from British artists. I knew then and there that they would change the music business.

I saw the Beatles at the Odeon Cinema in Lewisham in March 1963. They were on tour with the Americans Tommy Roe and Chris Montez, but it is the Beatles that I remember. I was 24 and probably the oldest person there. It was brilliant how it all worked.

John Lennon had a great personality and their look, with the left-handed guitarist, Paul McCartney was great. The band was so tight and I knew they were going to be enormous.

Elvis Presley's manager, Colonel Tom Parker and the Beatles' manager, Brian Epstein had much in common: they were both bad managers! One was a crook and the other was incompetent. They had the biggest artists in the world: the Beatles more so than Elvis because they changed the world with their dress sense and their personalities and regional accents. Elvis changed the music world.

Brian Epstein was a very nice man but not tough enough to deal with the sharks. He may have thought he was friendly with the publisher, Dick James, but Dick was one of the sharks. For example, John Lennon and Paul McCartney never received decent money from their sales in Europe, but I was probably the first songwriter to work out how it should be done. In the end, when Northern Songs was bought by ATV, they changed the royalty system and the earnings split in favour of, and to placate, Lennon and McCartney.

I was in Tin Pan Alley at the time of the Beatles in 1963, hanging about with their music publisher, Dick James, and a little guy I knew, Mitch Murray. Dick James had been born Richard Vapnick and Mitch Murray was Lionel Michael Stitcher, so there was nothing unusual about changing your name.

Mitch Murray had written 'How Do You Do It', a Number 1 for another of Brian Epstein's acts, Gerry and the Pacemakers. Actually, the Beatles had turned down 'How Do You Do It' because they had wanted to write their own songs and they only made a half-hearted attempt at recording it. It was passed over to Gerry and the Pacemakers who cut a terrific version..

Mitch Murray wrote a follow-up in the same vein, 'I Like It', and I thought I would try my luck with 'Do It Now', a song I'd written, which had the same brand of cheeky innuendo. Dick said, "I really like it and it's going to be Gerry's next record."

Unfortunately for me, Gerry Marsden had other ideas and wanted to try something different. He recorded 'You'll Never Walk Alone' with great success and I can't knock him for it. It was his third Number 1 and Rodgers and Hammerstein's first football anthem (in so far as the likes of Liverpool and Celtic supporters treat it a song for the terraces) but I believe he would have done almost as well with 'Do It Now'. That illustrates a golden rule of songwriting. Anybody can write a song but you have to get the record.

As well as the Beatles and Gerry and the Pacemakers, Brian Epstein was signing anyone and everyone in Liverpool with talent. He was impressed with an 18-year-old lad, Tommy Quickly, and his first single combined Lennon and McCartney's 'Tip Of My Tongue' with Mitch Murray's 'Heaven Only Knows'. I can see why Lennon and McCartney gave that one away and Brian Epstein wanted something stronger for his second single. Brian liked 'Do It Now' but he felt the title wasn't right for Tommy's audience of young and innocent schoolgirls so I changed it to 'Kiss Me Now', but I always felt that 'Do It Now' was better.

'Kiss Me Now' came out on 22 November 1963, the day that President Kennedy was shot. Who wanted to buy a happy-go-lucky pop song after that? Still, we did get some radio play and an appearance on Thank Your Lucky Stars. I heard someone whistling it which was a great thrill.

I remember sitting in Dick James' office at the end of 1963. While I was there, Dick got a phone call from Brian Epstein who was in America, to say the Beatles had broken through to number 1 in the U.S. charts with 'I Want To Hold Your Hand'. Dick was giving him some other sales figures – Gerry and the Pacemakers had sold a million with 'You'll Never Walk Alone', and so on. Dick went through the list of Epstein's artists and finally he said, "Tommy Quickly's been on all these shows with 'Kiss Me Now' but we've only sold a couple of hundred copies." I think my Mother bought every one.

Years later, I would go to Liverpool and see the reconstruction of the Cavern and The Beatles Story at the Albert Dock. I was very impressed and it was a thrill to see an old poster for Tommy Quickly appearing with the Beatles.

Tommy Quickly's next single, 'Prove It', was written by Gerry Marsden and that didn't sell either. In the end, Tommy Quickly's failure had nothing to do with his talent. He was okay as a performer, but Brian Epstein had too many artists on his books. Looking back, I would like to have written for more of his artists. Billy J Kramer had a lovely voice and as I'm sure I could have come up with something suitable, I don't know why I didn't try.

Most of the songwriters I know, like Roger Greenaway and Les Reed, wanted to be performers but I knew I couldn't be and my ambition was to spend my life in music and be as good a songwriter as possible. I couldn't be an Irving Berlin but I was going to try. I also knew more about the songs of the past than anyone I'd met and I was sure that would help me. My friends probably thought I was nuts.

I knew that a lot of songwriters worked in teams – Richard Rodgers and Lorenz Hart, Richard Rodgers and Oscar Hammerstein, George and Ira Gershwin, Sammy Cahn and Jimmy Van Heusen, John Lennon and Paul McCartney, and Burt Bacharach and Hal David – and I liked the idea of having a partner.

I met another songwriter, Tommy Scott a Scotsman, who also thought that we would make a good team. I went to his manager, Phil Solomon, and he said, "As long as Tommy says you're good, that's fine by me."

Everybody was wary of Phil Solomon because he was a tough negotiator and a slow payer with royalties. In his favour, he had a great knack for finding talent and the Irish trio, the Bachelors were the cornerstone of his fortune. He also had the Viscounts, Them with Van Morrison, and very soon, Tom Jones, The Viscounts and Tom left soon afterwards though with, one of the Viscounts, Gordon Mills, becoming Tom's great manager.

Phil Solomon loved me because I could translate what Van Morrison was saying. Someone would ask Van, "Where's the band?" and he would say, "Er, tharoverthar", which would mean, "There, they're over there", but nobody understood that. He clipped everything. The Belfast accent is like the Glasgow one, they shorten all the words too, so I had no trouble understanding him. In my opinion, Van is the best soul singer to come out of Great Britain and a terrific songwriter.

Tommy Scott was a good hustler and if I owe anything to anybody, I owe it to him. He taught me how to sell a song and he introduced me to so many people. He taught me how to hang about with music publishers. He was brilliant and he would say, "Even if you've only got the B-side, it's still great because you will get the same royalties when the record is sold."

Tom Jones was born in Pontypridd as Thomas Woodward. When he first came to London, he was billed as Tommy Scott with the Senators and my songwriting friend, Tommy Scott said, "We can't have that" and made him change the name. Actually, my Tommy Scott was really Tommy Kilpatrick, so you can see how confusing all this was. Incidentally, Billy Joel's real name is William Martin Joel, and he did call himself 'Bill Martin' for a short time until someone pointed out that there was a number 1 songwriter in the UK with that name !

Tom Woodward agreed to change his name and he became Tom Jones, which tied in with the release of the Albert Finney film and so was excellent publicity. I was also in and out of Regent Sound and one day, Gordon Mills came into the studio: he had the session after us and he was doing a new song he had written for Sandie Shaw. Tom Jones was doing the demo and at the end of the session, I heard Tom say to Gordon, "I'm going to knock you out, boyo, if I can't have this song for myself." Gordon said that he had promised it to Sandie Shaw and there was nothing he could do about it. The song was 'It's Not Unusual' written by Gordon Mills and Les Reed. Sandie felt that the demo was so good that she couldn't improve upon it and she let Tom have it. It became his first Number 1.

I couldn't go from Lewisham every day to London and work at Saxa Salt as it was taking up too much time. I had to find somewhere nearer. Tommy Scott had a girlfriend, Jo Wright, and Jo's father owned three houses in Old Church Street, which is off King's Road, Chelsea. Jo would later marry, becoming Jo Gurnett, and successfully managed the careers of Kenny Everett and Terry Wogan. I was shown a house, number 34, that belonged to Thomas Carlyle, the

Scottish writer who had inspired Charles Dickens. That sounded a good omen to me. Mag and I got the ground floor and the basement for £10 a week. It's still there and it's a beautiful house.

We didn't have any children then and I wasn't interested in married life. I was obsessed by songwriting and that's all I wanted to do. I left Saxa Salt at the beginning of 1964 to concentrate on songwriting. Mag wanted children and won out. Meran, which is a lovely Scottish name that Mag chose, was born in 1965 and then, in 1967, along came Alison, another good Scottish name. There were wonderful little girls and still are very beautiful as they get older.

In August 1964, Phil Solomon, the music publisher, agent and manager, offered me £30 a week working with his company, One Four Two Music. He wanted me to write with Tommy Scott but also to undertake general office duties and to place some of his other songs with various artists. I would also be earning songwriting royalties and the first £20 a week would be deducted from those royalties.

Phil's father had had a big business in Ireland, Solomon's Record Store, and Phil's brother, Mervyn, had founded Emerald Records, also in Ireland. The distribution was through Decca in England and that is how Phil became very close to Dick Rowe at Decca. He put the Bachelors, Them and Twinkle with Decca.

Tommy and I wrote songs for the Bachelors and we wrote the B-sides of two very big hits, 'I Wouldn't Trade You For The World' and 'No Arms Can Ever Hold You'. You won't have heard of our songs, 'Beneath The Willow Tree' and 'Oh, Samuel Don't Die', but they did very nicely for us. We should have got a lot of money for them but more of that later.

As I explained earlier, publishers would send you a contract that was 50/50, that is, they would keep £50 of every £100 earned and the songwriters would get the rest. However, there were a lot of tricks and so it was never a proper 50/50 split. For example, they might publish the song abroad, keep 50% of that and send 25% back to the UK for the songwriters. They did it to the Beatles and everybody.

Roughly speaking, the songwriters earned £5 from every 1,000 records sold, so if a record sold 250,000 copies and I wrote it with Tommy Scott, I would be entitled to £625. On top of that there would be additional amounts for performances and radio plays. Historically, the rates were always higher for sheet music than records because publishers had originally thought that sheet music was more important than records.

In fact, Tommy and I were writing B-sides and album tracks all over the place. We even wrote one for Van Morrison. Everyone could see that Van was very talented, but I did think that the rest his band, Them, were rubbish. He didn't stick with Them for long. Maybe he was frustrated.

If you see clips of the Bachelors, they are all smiles, but it was an act as, allegedly, they never really got on together. I wasn't surprised when the two brothers, Con and Dec Cluskey, sacked John Stokes. The matter even went to court with the brothers claiming that he sang "like a drowning rat" and that his voice had been overdubbed on records without his knowledge. My then songwriting partner, Phil Coulter got involved in that court case but I, very wisely I think, stayed out of it. When the matter was settled, John Stokes said that he would rather listen to drowning rats than the new Bachelors on stage.

Some of the songs I wrote with Tommy Scott have a third name on them, Gregory Scott, but there was no such person: it was Dick Rowe from the Bachelors' record company, Decca, getting in on the act. Dick didn't write any of the songs but Phil Solomon said it was part of the deal, we had to do that, and Dick was using a pseudonym because he didn't want his bosses at Decca to know as he would violating his contract. I must have put his son, Richard, through public school, and this is when I realised that I would have to be tough to make it in this business.

Dick was infamous for having turned down the Beatles with the line, "Guitar groups are on the way out, Mr Epstein", but in truth, it was not Dick Rowe who turned down the Beatles, but his assistant, Mike Smith, who preferred another new band, Brian Poole and the Tremeloes, a band from Essex managed by Peter Walsh. Rumour at the time had it that Peter Walsh handed Mike Smith a brown envelope to sign The Tremeloes.

Although he was meant to be looking after our interests, Phil Solomon was a man who took care of himself. He had three sets of books – one for the artists, one for the taxman and one for himself – and that's one way to make a fortune for yourself.

Right from the beginning, I wanted an association with something Scottish but not of the Andy Stewart, Kenneth McKellar and Moira Anderson variety. I wanted something at the sharp end. I found the Beatstalkers in a small ballroom in Glasgow and I wrote 'Mr. Disappointed' for them, which is like an Otis Redding song. It was a good record, but they were let down by their management who were weak and had no business knowledge of the worldwide music industry.

Few of the managers knew how to handle an act properly. If a record company gave a band £1,000 advance, the manager was supposed to take 10% or whatever his cut was, but it was very tempting to keep all the money and say, "I am going to be doing this with it." That's why so many of the bands were skint. They didn't get anything.

As well as the Beatstalkers, I had the Boston Dexters from Edinburgh who were sensational and had Tam White as a front man. Dick James was going to publish my song, 'There It Is' ("There it is, That funny feeling from me to you.") and I thought it would suit the Boston Dexters. I went round to see the very gay record producer, Joe Meek, at the studio in his flat at 304 Holloway Road. He didn't take to me but he liked the picture of the band. I thought that Joe might fancy the bass player, wee Allan Coventry, and that got them through the door. However, when he saw them, it was Tam he wanted. Tam White had a gruff voice – he was a stonemason and he spoke as if he was made out of granite. For the couple of hours, Joe Meek chased Tam White round the studio. He was trying to kiss him and Tam wanted to knock him out. Joe was saying, "We'll put you in this little room and I'll work with you on the song." We were thrown out as he wouldn't oblige, but the Boston Dexters got signed to EMI.

Their mistake was to sing my songs. I am a pop songwriter and although I knew that Tam had a great bluesy voice, I am not the type of guy to write the blues. I had written "I've got something to tell you, baby, something to tell you now." It was rubbish and Tam said, "I'm gonna kill the guy who wrote this song." I was standing next to them in the studio and I thought, "I'd better not say it was me." The Boston Dexters was one of the best groups to come from Scotland and I wrote three songs for them and ruined their career. I am still great friends with wee Allan and his beautiful wife Vivi - the bass was bigger than him! – and I was very sorry when Tam died in June 2010.

In 1966, I wrote 'Messrs Lindsay, Parker and Flynn' for Lee Drummond who had been in the Boston Dexters. It was about the music business and would have been perfect for

Roger Miller, who'd done 'King Of The Road'. There's a touch of the Lovin' Spoonful about it too. The single was a hit in various counties and I remember the German publisher loving it. It's a good lyric:

"I was really small time
Till I met this fellow who really knew the score,
Swore I was the greatest of all time.
I said, 'Uh, uh, tell me more.'
He said, 'With your kind of face,
You could go any place you want to.
But first we had better call in
Messrs Lindsay, Parker and Flynn."

Tommy Scott wasn't that great a songwriter but he was a good producer and he made 'Terry', which was a very successful and controversial hit for Twinkle about a motorcyclist who got killed. I would watch Tommy at work and I was learning all the time. I was excited to be there and I would even get the odd session fee, collecting £9 a time for my efforts. I banged the tambourine on Them's 'Baby Please Don't Go', 'Here Comes The Night' and 'Gloria', and I've still got the tambourine. More to the point, I got to know session musicians like Jimmy Page and John Paul Jones, who became part of Led Zeppelin. I was a ligger really, whilst they were proper musicians. Both of them were to play on the demo and Jimmy on the actual record of 'Congratulations', although they are not too keen to tell people as they became members of the biggest arena rock band ever.

Tommy Scott introduced me to the American songwriter, Buddy Kaye. Buddy had written 'Speedy Gonzales' for Pat Boone and together they had written 'Boys Cry', a Top 10 hit for Eden Kane. He later wrote 'In The Middle Of Nowhere' for Dusty Springfield. I went to see him at the Cumberland Hotel at Marble Arch. He said, "I know what it's like when you are a struggling songwriter and recently married. I've got a couple of presents for you." He gave me two little marmalade pots that he had obviously taken from the breakfast table at the hotel.

I was realising that Tommy Scott wasn't as talented as me as a songwriter and I wanted a different partner. Tommy was also as pushy as me and there isn't room for two pushy guys in a team. Buddy Kaye introduced me to Phil Coulter and I knew we would get on together.

Phil Coulter had been brought over by Phil Solomon to arrange for the Bachelors, and he was very shy. He was a very good piano player and could also play the guitar, while Tommy just played the guitar. We did get on together and Buddy, Phil and I wrote 'A Train Full Of Sunshine' but Phil Solomon did nothing with it.

I have been trying to get 'A Train Full Of Sunshine' back as it's a good song but Phil Solomon sold his catalogue to Freddie Bienstock, and Freddie wouldn't give you a virus as he was a real mean guy as far as songs were concerned. The publishing industry is full of people who make the wrong decisions out of spite.

I didn't want to stay with Phil Solomon as I needed to broaden my career. He really had a show business stable – he managed the comedian Frank Carson, if that is possible - and I wanted to be with the publishers. Tommy Scott felt that he couldn't leave Phil Solomon so I started writing with Phil Coulter.

Phil Coulter wasn't sure about leaving Phil Solomon. He was married with a child and he was worried about the potential insecurity of a new job. I said that I would arrange for a guarantee for three years, which I did for 1966, 1967 and 1968. I said to Phil, "If you don't take the gamble now, you will never write pop hits. You'll never get more than £50 a week from Solomon."

I talked Phil into leaving but he never even came to the meeting (nothing unusual there as he seldom turned up for meetings) with our new music publishers, Jimmy Phillips and his brother, Bill. They accepted us on Buddy Kaye's recommendation and we were offered £30 a week each, starting on New Year's Eve 1965. That was decent money and as it turned out, we were one of the last songwriting teams to be put under contract in Tin Pan Alley because the world was changing and groups were writing their own material.

Phil Solomon told me that if I left him, my career would be over but I knew he couldn't have done anything to stop me. He was bluffing and nobody could frighten me. My Govan upbringing held me in good stead. What was he going to do? Kill me? As soon as my contract was up with him, I was off, but I wasn't clever enough or rich enough to sue him for my past royalties as he dodged about so much.

I left Phil Solomon after a year, knowing that he owed me a lot of money, particularly from those songs for the Bachelors. I kept asking him to settle with me and I even took legal advice. I thought of auditing his books, but which books would he have shown us? I knew that he owed me a lot but in March 1970, Phil sent me a cheque for £1.12.8d (£1.63) and I was so insulted that I never cashed it. However, I framed it to remind me to never let it happen again. By then, I had had a lot of success and I couldn't be bothered to pursue it any further but I am annoyed that he was allowed to get away with it.

Solomon never said anything about our win with 'Puppet On A String' and never congratulated us. Years later, when he was dying, he said to Phil Coulter that we had written

'Puppet On A String' and 'Congratulations' when we were with him, which is total bollocks. We had left him in 1965.

In the 1970s, we were checking in with Phil Solomon at the Carlton Hotel in Cannes as the famous Annual Music Business festival, MIDEM, is held there. He spoke impeccably quietly and he had good manners. His wife, Dorothy, who was good looking was talking to someone else while he signed in. He never raised his voice but he said, "What do you mean – you don't have my suite? Get me the manager." The receptionist said, "That will make no difference because he will just say what I say." The manager came out and he said, "I trust my staff completely. If they say there is no booking, there is no booking."

Phil said, "If I don't get a room, I shall start stripping off here." The manager said, "It makes no difference what you do."

Phil took off his collar and his tie, and then his trousers and he was in his boxer shorts, socks and suspenders. The manager said, "Monsieur, you are just making a fool of yourself. Nothing will change. There is no room in the hotel."

Phil said, "Dorothy, start stripping."

Dorothy said, "What?"

He said, "I would like you to start taking your clothes off. Just in your own time while you're talking."

Dorothy took her jacket and her skirt.

He said, "Dorothy, take off your stockings." So she took off her stockings but kept the high heels.

Just then a Japanese delegation came in and Solomon spoke to them. He introduced Dorothy to them and then said, "Dorothy, bra off." She said, "Philip!" He then takes off his singlet.

The manager said, "Stop this" and Phil said, "I will if you will give me the key to my suite. Otherwise, by the time you have rung the police, I will have taken off my underpants and Dorothy will have taken off her panties. I will be suing you."

The manager then said, "It just so happens that we have a suite that is available." Phil says, "Dorothy, put your clothes on" and we all applauded.

I am pretty sure that the hotel had been given a back hander to give Phil's suite to somebody else. Some concierge pocketed 1,000 francs and Phil Solomon had been dropped. But you didn't do that with Phil. He was very dramatic, a brilliant salesman and a brilliant manipulator. He could have kept all his stars but it was in his nature to bend the rules in his favour and was too strong for artistic people, leaving you the feeling that you'd been cheated.

When Nijinsky won the Derby in 1970 I happened to be at the Derby in top hat and tails standing next to Soloman, Phil said to me, "Bill, have you got one million pounds on you?" I said, "I beg your pardon." He said, "I want to buy Nijinsky. It will be worth it, it will be good value." He didn't buy the horse, but that's how Phil thought.

Phil Solomon died in 2011 at the age of 86. He was a one-off and despite our disagreements, I enjoyed his company. He was full of ideas and he never thought small. He told me I had the ability to sell and then taught me how to close a deal.

II. An Englishman, An Irishman and A Scotsman

Jimmy Phillips had been working in and around Denmark Street since 1919. He had worked for the publisher, Lawrence Wright and he made a lot of American songs popular here such as 'The Peanut Vendor', Stormy Weather' and 'On The Sunny Side Of The Street'. He even published 'The Teddy Bear's Picnic'. He started an agency with Leslie MacDonnell, later the managing director of Moss Empires, and they discovered the bandleader Joe Loss.

Jimmy married his secretary Irene Dunford in 1928 and they had two sons, Peter and Robin. In 1933, Jimmy ran the Peter Maurice Music Company and he signed up great writers like Jimmy Kennedy, Michael Carr and Eric Maschwitz. He owned and published wonderful songs like 'Isle Of Capri', 'South Of The Border' 'These Foolish Things' and 'A Nightingale Sang In Berkeley Square'.

Talking of secretaries, it was in 1966 at Keith Prowse Music that I set eyes on a tall blonde girl with an amazing pair of blue eyes, Jan Olley. She was the secretary to one of the executives and, although she then left, I was to meet her a few years later.

Eric Maschwitz was The Director General for the BBC and was a songwriter who wrote classics like 'A Nightingale Sang in Berkley Square'. I am also convinced 'These Foolish Things' is one of his lyrics under another name. The BBC told Eric he had to stop writing songs as it looked bad that he, as the Head of the BBC, would be playing his own songs. What did he do - he wrote a play, Goodnight Vienna. In 1960, he visited Prime Minister Harold Macmillan in Bromley on BBC business when, whilst being driven back in the rain, he saw a sign at the Odeon Lewisham, saying Goodnight Vienna. He told his chauffeur to stop the car and he went up to the doorman who was standing under a brolly as it was pouring, and said, "I'm Eric Maschwitz and I wrote that play. How is it going?" The doorman said, "It is doing as well as a play called Goodnight Lewisham would be doing on a rainy night in Vienna. There are only two people in there."

Jimmy Phillips was known as Honest John Turner as he used to put that name on songs that he hadn't written. Geoffrey Parsons usually did most of the work but Jimmy is listed amongst the composers on 'Smile' (which has Charlie Chaplin's melody), 'Poppa Piccolino'. Oh, My Papa'. and even the wartime classic, 'Lili Marlene'. Still, it was Jimmy who recognised that this German song should have English words. Jimmy also published the first British song to top the US hit parade, 'The Gypsy', written by Billy Reid in 1946 and recorded by the Ink Spots.

In 1958, Keith Prowse Music and Peter Maurice Music merged to make KPM Music and Jimmy Phillips became managing director with a large staff, (including his sons, Peter and Robin, both lovely, helpful guys who definitely assisted Bill and Phil, making us songwriters a lot of money from our music), so he was one of the most important men in Denmark Street. As if that wasn't enough, Jimmy was responsible for starting the New Musical Express which included the charts and was a very important paper in the music business in the 60s and 70s.

Jimmy Phillips had signed Lionel Bart when he was writing hits for Tommy Steele and other British pop stars. Lionel's contract was up in 1960 and he left Jimmy and KPM Music and announced four weeks later that he had written Oliver! Jimmy Phillips said that it was impossible for him to write that in four weeks so he must have written it while under contract. He sued him and Lionel went to Max Bygraves to help him out. Max had had a big hit with the title song from Lionel's show 'Fings Ain't What They Used To Be' so they knew one another. Lionel sold the music publishing rights of Oliver! to Max for £850 which he promptly spent on a house in Reece Mews in Fulham and later sold him the film rights to Oliver! for £45,000.

Jimmy Phillips sued Lionel and Max did a deal with David Platz of Essex Music (a proper music publisher) leaving him with a small percentage of Oliver and Platz in turn did a deal with Jimmy Phillips bringing the case to a close. As a result, Max got a good slice of Oliver! whereas Lionel made some misjudgments and lost his share.

Later on, Lionel Bart invested his own money in a musical about Robin Hood called Twang! but nobody went to see it. By the 1980s, he was living in a council flat in Islington. Then Cameron Mackintosh kindly gave him a percentage of Oliver! when he restaged it at the London Palladium. He didn't have to do that and it was really an exceptionally generous thing to do.

There hadn't been many British writers who could compete with the Americans, but Jimmy Kennedy and Michael Carr could match the best of them. Jimmy Kennedy was a reserved Irishman and he has a statue in Londonderry looking over the Atlantic Ocean acknowledging that he wrote 'Red Sails In The Sunset'.

Jimmy Kennedy had an ability to read upside down. He could read letters and see contracts so it was very useful. During the war, he saw a letter to Jimmy Phillips telling him to get his kids to America.

Jimmy Kennedy said, "Am I your top songwriter, Jimmy?"

He said, "Of course you are."

Jimmy Kennedy said, "Then why can't my kids go to America?"

So Jimmy Phillips arranged for Jimmy Kennedy's wife and children to go America. His wife fell in love with the captain of the ship and he never saw her again.

Jimmy Kennedy kept every penny he ever made but his partner, Michael Carr, was always skint. He was a flamboyant songwriter from Yorkshire. One Friday evening, Michael came into Mills Music reception with a white face and I happened to be there at the time. He fell to the floor and said, "I'm dying. Get hold of Jimmy Phillips."

I said, "Michael, you're in the wrong office. KPM is next door."

He got up, walked out, went next door and did the same routine. I walked in. The receptionist said, "Michael Carr is dying", and Michael winked at me. I said, "You'd better get hold of Jimmy."

Jimmy came out and said, "What do you want, Michael?"

"I'm dying, Jimmy."

Jimmy said, "Would £100 keep you alive for the weekend?"

"That would be great, Jimmy."

Jimmy said, "Here you are. Now, wipe all that flour off your face and get to the pub."

Michael Carr's heyday had been in the 1930s but he kept going into the 1960s. He would say, "Ideas just come to me. I could write another hit song tomorrow." He wrote 'Kon-Tiki' for the Shadows in 1961 and 'One, Two, Three, O'Leary' with Barry Mason for Des O'Connor in 1968. I envy Barry for that as it would have been a great experience to have written something with the man who wrote 'South Of The Border'.

Jimmy Phillips saw Phil and I as an odd couple like Jimmy Kennedy and Michael Carr, though I've never collapsed on the floor with flour on my face and begged for money. But we were an unusual combination – a quiet Irish Catholic and a noisy Scottish Protestant. Taken together, the three of us were an Englishman, an Irishman and a Scotsman. Jimmy Phillips was an immense talent but he hadn't moved with the times and that was why he wanted us.

Phil Coulter was born in Derry on 19 February 1942. He was the son of a Catholic detective in the Royal Ulster Constabulary, which would have been very unusual at the time. His father played the fiddle and his mother the piano, and he studied at Queen's University in Dublin and the Royal Academy of Music. He had a BA in music, which certainly impressed me, and is also a Doctor of Philosophy, which impresses me even more. Early in 1964, he had had some success in Ireland with his song, 'Foolin' Time' for Butch Moore and the Capitol Showband.

Later on, Phil and I wrote another song for Butch Moore, 'Good Thing Goin'', which was recorded with two of the most famous session singers, Sue and Sunny. That was in 1968 and then about ten years later, we had a surprise as Phil's instrumental version became a Northern Soul hit.

Many of the partnerships of the past combined a lyricist with a musician – Sammy Cahn and Jimmy Van Heusen, Dorothy Fields and Jimmy McHugh – but John Lennon and Paul McCartney had an unusual partnership in that both could write words and music. Lennon was the better lyricist and McCartney the better melodist, but there are plenty of examples of Lennon writing good melodies and McCartney good words.

Both Phil and I could both write words and music independently and so we could both write songs alone. Phil was by far the better musician but I had more of the ideas and was a great motivator. I might give Phil a title and an idea and a bit of a melody, and he would do the rest.

It has sometimes been assumed that Phil did the writing and I did the selling. Phil has even called me his "business manager" but that's rubbish. You don't give a business manager 50%: you give him 10%, so of course I wrote the songs with him.

Left to himself, Phil could be lazy so I had to keep us going. On the other hand, he had the patience to finish a lyric or a melody whereas I would get fed up and want to do something else. On the whole, our partnership worked very well and brought out the best in both of us.

You can't be part of a team unless you can freely criticise the other's work without offence. It has to be constructive criticism, so it is rather like a marriage. As you might expect, the tendency is to write bad rather than good songs. At the start, we used to discipline ourselves to write five to ten songs a week and some of them were frighteningly bad, but they were stepping-stones as we were finding out how to work together. I had a simple criterion when we'd finished a song: "If I can't remember this in a couple of day's time, then nobody else will."

"John Lennon and Paul McCartney" sounds much better than "Paul McCartney and John Lennon", although it probably doesn't to Paul McCartney. It's the same with "John and Paul" as opposed to "Paul and John". When it comes to us, "Bill Martin and Phil Coulter" rolls off the tongue much more easily than "Phil Coulter and Bill Martin" and so does the combination, "Bill and Phil" although I'm not sure that Phil would agree!

Old Jimmy Phillips liked me to meet the stars as he knew I was a salesman who could take rejection. Phil didn't like people saying, "I don't like that." I used to meet people that I wasn't supposed to meet such as George Martin, the Beatles' producer and the head of Parlophone, as Jimmy had salesmen to do that. As most of the salesmen were old drunks, it was much better to do it myself. That's how I got 'Surround Yourself with Sorrow' recorded by Cilla Black, produced by George Martin which became a number 3 hit in 1969.

Jimmy Phillips found 'Tears' and many other songs for Ken Dodd, and Ken was often in the office. The very first song of ours that sold anything was 'Dreams', which was sung beautifully by Ken. Singing wasn't just a sideline for him: he was a first-rate singer and we did other songs for him such as 'My Life'. We could have written novelty songs for him but he preferred to keep his musical career and his records separate from the comedy.

Myles Rudge and Ted Dicks wrote some good comedy songs for Bernard Cribbins. People may dismiss 'Hole In The Ground' and 'Right Said Fred' as novelties but they are among the hardest songs to write. These were the kind of records that George Martin was producing before the Beatles.

I loved 'The Old Bazaar In Cairo' that Charlie Chester wrote for Clinton Ford, and Charlie Drake had some good material, but we never quite managed it. Lionel Bart had done 'Little White Bull' and so we wrote 'What's The Matter With The Matador?' It was a good title but it never got anywhere. I knew two old-time publishers, Elton Box and Desmond 'Sonny' Cox, known as Box and Cox, and they had only published one really big song, 'I've Got A Lovely Bunch Of Coconuts', which was a smash hit in 1950. They sat at the opposite ends of the same desk. There was just room for you to squeeze in and play your song on the piano. They kept up a dialogue with each other: "What do you think of that, Mr Box?" "I'm not sure, Mr Cox." "Well, I don't think I like that, Mr Box." "I'll agree with that, Mr Cox", and they would wish you good afternoon. They were cheapskate buffoons really and were just having a laugh.

One day I went in and I got £20 for a song title and I refused to play them the melody first. "Well, what do you think, Mr Box?" "I love the title, Mr Cox." "Do you think he should get the money from us, Mr Box?" "Well, we made a lot of money from 'Coconuts', Mr Cox." I sold them a song that didn't exist for £20. It was called 'When Banana Skins Start Falling, I'll Come Sliding Back To You'."

They were a good touch for extra money and I went in with 'What's The Matter With The Matador'. "What do you think of that, Mr Box?" "I'm not too sure, Mr Cox, I don't think it will be a big song." "We quite like it, Mr Martin, but do you think you could write us something like 'I've Got A Lovely Bunch Of Coconuts'."

Jimmy took 'Matador' and that was recorded with a session singer called Deano by Bob Barrett for EMI. It wasn't a hit but I was always glad to write fun songs.

Once Phil wanted to do something like the American pianist, Floyd Cramer and we wrote a very good instrumental but we couldn't think of a title. My mother had a bunion and she went for an operation to get rid of it. When I saw her, I said, "Where's your bunion?" and she said, "It's run away." We called the instrumental, 'The Runaway Bunion'. That was a single for the Phil Coulter Orchestra and he's still playing it to this day.

My dad inspired another song. Sometimes I would ask him how a night went and he would say, "It was okay, but they wouldn't let me play my piano. I had to play the accordion."

I thought 'They Wouldn't Let Me Play My Piano' would be a great song title for Jimmy Durante. We did send the song to Durante but we didn't get a reply. That underlines my usual point: you've got to meet the artists.

We always made very good demos using singers like Sue and Sunny and J. Vincent Edwards. We often had Clem Cattini from the Tornados on drums, who played on scores of Number 1 records. We used to write songs in the style of a particular artist and then pitch it to them.We had a small hit with the Troggs' 'Hi Hi Hazel' but I thought it was good enough for the Top Five. Geno Washington did it too. The song did better in the States, but maybe the name, Hazel, is more popular there.

We did write a soul song, 'The Incredible Miss Brown' for one of our best soul singers, Herbie Goins. I thought it would be a hit but it wasn't incredible enough. I'm less impressed with 'Charlie Anderson' for the Herd. That was when we were writing six songs a day and it sounds like the sixth song! We also wrote 'Green Light' for Tony Blackburn and that got the red light.

Steve Rowland, the producer for Dave Dee, Dozy, Beaky, Mick & Tich, was fascinated by my hair because he wore a wig and my hair was thick and prematurely grey. He was also an actor and he had to wear wigs when on film. I could have sung anything and he would have taken it. 'Bang' was the opening track on their album called If Music Be The Food Of Love...Prepare For Indigestion.

We wrote 'Me And My Miniskirt' for the fashions of the day and we called the band, X Y Zee, as we were hoping it would be released in America. Actually, it was sung by record producer John Schroeder's wife who always wore a miniskirt. In the end, we were told that we couldn't call the band that in America as X Y Zee was the name of a radio station. I think we changed it to Mini and the Miniskirts.

We wrote 'I Was Lord Kitchener's Valet' and Peter Fenton recorded that. When we wrote it, Roger Greenaway and Roger Cook, who were next door in Mills Music, shouted out of the window, "That's a great idea." The next week they wrote 'I Was Kaiser Bill's Batman' and that went into the Top 10. Don't feel sorry for Peter Fenton. He was one of the guys who became rich from the marketing of the Beatles in America with the company, Seltaeb, which is Beatles spelt backwards. He was no slouch when it came to a deal. They took 90% and gave Epstein 10%.

There were two storeroom boys with overalls at Mills Music and one was Reg Dwight and the other was Eric Hall, who was Tony Hiller's cousin. Reg Dwight became Elton John, while Eric became a football agent and famous for the phrase, "Monster, monster". He has a radio show about football to this day. Reg could play the piano but he played block chords like a jazz musician. We would have big Christmas parties in Denmark Street and the only boss around would be Cyril Gee at Mills Music because every day was just the same to him. Elton wanted to play at the Christmas party in 1965 and I said, "No, no, you play block chords. You're not right." Elton keeps a diary for every day of his life and he wrote in his entry for that day, "I hate Bill Martin. I hate Bill Martin". More about Elton later.

I was discovering that there were thousands of songwriters all wanting the dream ticket and yet there are only 20 places in the Top 20 each week. Songwriting is a series of disappointments and if you are going to succeed, you have to go into it with your heart, knowing that you are writing at your best and knowing that you might fail. As the song says, you have to be able to pick yourself up, dust yourself down and start all over again.

Chapter 6 - Eurovision

I. The Early Years

My interest in the Eurovision Song Contest goes right back to 1958 when I first heard Domenico Modugno sing 'Volare', and I was surprised when it didn't win. It's certainly the best song ever that didn't win Eurovision and it must be a contender for the best song ever to be entered for the Contest. As soon as I heard it, I was determined to enter a song one year, but I didn't want to make a fool of myself. I didn't want to enter a song until I was sure I had a potential winner.

My first involvement with the contest came about in an unexpected way, in 1965, when I was still with Phil Solomon. He was starting a record label, Major Minor, and he wanted to get involved with the French star, Serge Gainsbourg, who was unknown in the UK. He said that I should meet him. Solomon said he would fly to me to a song festival to meet him, but I never realised that I would be paying for it – he deducted the expenses from my earnings.

I met Serge Gainsbourg in a bar – well, where else would you meet Serge Gainsbourg - and I told him that I wanted to write some English lyrics to foreign tunes. He was a caricature of a lounge lizard and he smoked Gitanes constantly. He was drinking Pernod, and he was exactly the same when he came to England to see Phil Solomon. I don't think he washed and he certainly didn't shave but the women were all over him. Believe it or not, Brigitte Bardot was there and she was licking and kissing him. Horrible! I was thinking, "This guy smells."

Gainsbourg spoke in broken English and he liked me for whatever reason and when he did 'Je TiAime...Moi Non Plus' with Jane Birkin (it was suppose to be sung with Brigitte Bardot but her boy friend at the time Gunter Sachs refused to let her record it) in 1969, he gave it to Phil Solomon. Like many women, Jane Birkin, who had been married to John Barry, fancied Serge Gainsbourg but she was the one girl who married him.

At the time Gainsbourg had written 'Poupée De Cire, Poupée De Son', which had won Eurovision in 1965. He didn't give a diddly about me doing an English lyric to his song. He wasn't interested in talking to me about songwriting: he was more interested in talking about women and about the meaning of life. He thought he was a bit of a philosopher, but really he was on another planet.

My lyric was called 'A Lonely Singing Doll'. I was learning my trade then and it wasn't a case of 'Les Feuilles Mortes' becoming 'Autumn Leaves'. It was a good song and I thought this was my big chance with Twinkle. She'd had some chart success with Tommy Scott, and she was quite like Sandie Shaw, smaller but with the same kind of dress and hairstyle.

I heard several of Serge Gainsbourg's songs. When Sacha Distel wrote 'The Good Life' or Claude François wrote 'My Way', they were proper songs, but I didn't feel that Serge Gainsbourg wrote like that. I suppose he was closer to Jacques Brel or Leonard Cohen and I could never get off on that style.

Although I was friendly with several French people in the music industry, my overall impression was that they weren't too concerned with what happened in England, and Serge Gainsbourg didn't take much interest in what I was doing.

The UK had done well in the Eurovision Song Contest, but had never won. We were usually second – 'Sing Little Birdie' (Teddy Johnson and Pearl Carr, 1959), 'Looking High, High, High' (Bryan Johnson, 1960), 'Are You Sure' (Allisons, 1961), 'I Love The Little Things' (Matt Monro, 1964) and 'I Belong' (Kathy Kirby, 1965) were all second, and Ronnie Carroll had done well with 'Ring-A-Ding Girl' and 'Say Wonderful Things'.

Then came the disaster of 1966. I've no complaints about Udo Jürgens' winning song for Austria, 'Merci Chérie', but the UK had its worst-ever showing with ninth. The song was 'A Man Without Love' and the singer was a Scotsman with a very good voice, Kenneth McKellar.

Kenneth McKellar sang well but his mistake was to wear national dress. It would have been ridiculous if all the performers had worn their national dress and he looked like a fish out of water. Also, he was representing the UK and not Scotland, so there were some mixed messages there. I was laughing at the time and I'm a Scot.

II. 1967 - Puppet On A String

The BBC felt that they had to do much better and to give their 1967 entry a more contemporary appeal they chose Sandie Shaw. She had had a number of big hits – 'Always Something There To Remind Me', 'Girl Don't Come', 'I'll Stop At Nothing', 'Long Live Love' and 'Message Understood' – but she had stopped selling. Her three singles before 'Puppet On A String' were 'Run' 'Think Sometimes About Me' and 'I Don't Need Anything' and I doubt if you'll know any of them.

The format for picking the British song entry in 1967 and 1968 was for the BBC to choose an Artist and all the professional songwriters were asked to submit their song. The Music Publishers panel would prune this down to 5 which would be sent to the BBC. They would then select the Artist whose record would showcase once a week on a major BBC Light Entertainment show. In 1967 it was Rolf Harris's TV Show and in 1968 it was Cilla Black's.

At the time, Dusty Springfield, Lulu and Cilla Black were doing better on the charts than Sandie Shaw but despite that, I felt that she was right for the contest. She was quirky and an attention-grabber and she looked terrific. Most of Sandie's hits had been written by Chris Andrews and this was an opportunity for other songwriters to get a piece of the action. Phil Coulter and I wanted to write for Sandie Shaw but we knew all the songwriters in Denmark Street would be thinking the same.

We decided right away that we shouldn't do anything too unusual. Sandie Shaw should have a love song, but it should also be fun.

Nothing is original in songwriting. I said to Phil, "We should start this with a long note."

"What do you mean, start it with a long note?"

"One of the greatest songs to come out of Eurovision is 'Volare' and that starts with a long note." I sang, "Vo-----lare."

"We'll be pinching it, we can't do that. We'll get sued."

"No, no, no," I maintained, "Domenico Modugno stole it from 'O-----kla-homa!' so we'll be all right."

In it went and Phil added the 'bup-bup-bup-bup' intro, which was very clever. If you are on a cruise, the band always knows the 'bup-bup-bup-bup'. In the autumn of

2010, there was an Orange ad for Gulliver's Travels with Jack Black in the cinemas: that uses just the 'pup-pup-pup-pup' and there's no missing the reference.

We wanted a circus atmosphere. We tried to get the word 'circus' into the lyric but without success. I thought of using the word 'marionette' as I could see all sorts of possibilities – a rhyme with 'we met' and things like that – but I couldn't work it in. You know, "When we met you were a marionette, but now..."

Phil said, "You can't even speak French so why are you doing this? No one ever puts foreign words into an English song".

Then the word 'puppet' came out and it was perfect. 'Puppet On A String' sounded like a winning title. It's ironic that the straight English translation of that Serge Gainsbourg song, 'Poupée De Cire, Poupée De Son' is 'Puppet Of Wax, Puppet Of Straw'.

There are lots of clever little rhymes in 'Puppet On A String'. You might not notice them but they add to the tightness of the lyric. My model was Sammy Cahn's lyric for 'Teach Me Tonight', which did teach me tonight. You didn't have to have your rhymes at the end of the lines:

"Did you say I've got a lot to learn,
Don't think I'm trying not to learn,
Since this is the perfect spot to learn,
Teach me tonight."

'Puppet' goes:

"I wonder if one day that you'll say that you care
If you say you love me madly
I'll gladly be there."

115

I took that idea from Sammy Cahn. I wasn't interested in records with great guitar solos. I wanted to write direct little ditties that would make the world sing.

We made a demo with, an excellent session musician, Alan Hawkshaw on organ and it sounded really good. I bumped into the record producer Denny Cordell in Soho Square and he said, "I think I've got a Number 1 here."

I said, "I think I've got one as well. Let's go to my office and we'll play them."

Denny came from Argentina but he was educated at Cranleigh public school and spoke impeccable English. He smoked pot all the time. He'd done 'Go Now' for the Moody Blues and I was keen to hear what he had. It was 'A Whiter Shade Of Pale' by Procol Harum. I was blown away and I said, "That's fantastic. It will be the esoteric song of the 60´s, even the Beatles couldn´t write a song like that. It will be number 1 all over the World."

He said, "Put yours on." I was a bit wary after hearing 'A Whiter Shade Of Pale' but I put 'Puppet' on and he said, "Are you going to release that?" I said, "That's going to win The Eurovision." 'Puppet On A String' won an Ivor Novello Award as the most performed song of the year and I'd like to bet that it made more money than 'A Whiter Shade Of Pale'.

The melody of 'A Whiter Shade Of Pale' was familiar and it was such a clever use of Bach. I couldn't have written those kind of words, but they worked. A song like 'Eleanor Rigby' tells a story but with 'A Whiter Shade Of Pale', you wondered what the hell it was all about.

Compared to 'A Whiter Shade Of Pale', 'Puppet' wasn't just middle of the road - it was out in the country, much like a salmon swimming upstream. It didn't bother me. I knew that there were millions of people who were anti-Beatles, anti-Merseybeat, anti-Hollies and certainly would be anti-Procol Harum. They felt apprehensive if they went into a record store. 'Puppet On a String' was for them.

As I told you, Jimmy Phillips put his name on a lot of songs, and Jimmy Kennedy, who had written 'South Of The Border' and 'My Prayer', had warned us about him. He said, "You boys have a lot of talent but beware of Jimmy. Jimmy is capable of getting his name on songs that he didn't write."

I said, "He wouldn't want his name on our songs. They are just pop songs."

"Maybe," he said, "but one day you will write something that has the potential to be really big. Jimmy will ask you to play it to him again and then he will suggest that you change a word here or a word there, something like that, and then he will want his name on it."

Jimmy Kennedy was right.

Jimmy Phillips did try that with 'Puppet On A String'. He said, "Why don't you make that note longer?"

As Jimmy Kennedy predicted, he had drawn up a contract with three names on it. Kennedy had told us, "Ask him to send you a letter saying that he would like to be part of the song. He will never do that as he knows it could be used against him."

Jimmy Phillips said to me, "In a way, I've been contributing to this song" and I could see what was coming.

I said, "I don't think so, Jimmy."

He said, "Well, Eileen's prepared a contract."

I said, "Write me a letter, Jimmy, saying that you want to be on the song and I will take it up with Jimmy Kennedy." He never did that. Kennedy was the chairman of an industry association, BASCA (the British Academy of Songwriters, Composers and Authors) and he wouldn't have wanted any scandal. Remember, he was, after all known as Honest John Turner, his pseudonym as a songwriter.

Hundreds of songs were submitted blind by the music publishers to the BBC so that the judges are not swayed by the identities of the writers. Our song, 'Puppet On A String', made it onto the short list. Four songs were chosen and because he'd written so many of her hits, Chris Andrews was given a bye. That made five songs all written by Professional Songwriters and they were:

Puppet On A String (Bill Martin and Phil Coulter) Peter Maurice Music
Tell The Boys (Peter Callander and Mitch Murray) Shapiro-Bernstein & Co
I'll Cry Myself To Sleep (Roger Webb) Eighty Eight Music
Had A Dream Last Night (Chris Andrews) Fortissimo Music
Ask Any Woman (James Stewart and Gerard Langley) Mills Music

One of the songs was written by Roger Webb, who was a superb piano accompanist for a whole range of well-known singers. Like me, he loved the Great American Songbook and he may be the only songwriter who can claim Prince Charles as co-writer. He made an album of the Prince's book, The Old Man Of Lochnagar.

In her 1991 autobiography, The World At My Feet, Sandie Shaw wrote very disparagingly about 'Puppet On A String' but she viewed it from some feminist perspective, which was ridiculous. Lighten up, Sandie.

She wrote, "I hated it from the very first oompah to the final bang on the big bass drum. Even in those days, before the phrase 'chauvinist pig' had been coined, I was instinctively repelled by its sexist drivel and cuckoo-clock tune. The writers were men, the panel of judges were men, all white faced and stiff collared. Was this how they wanted women to behave – like stupid puppets? I dismissed the song as a joke. It had no chance of being selected, it was so awful."

The five selections were performed live by Sandie on The Rolf Harris Show and Sandie wanted 'Tell The Boys' to win. When they got to 'Puppet On A String', the guitarist made a mistake and the microphone was switched off so that you didn't hear that long note but Sandie was great. I'm sure, in fact I know, that her manager, Evie Taylor had this set up – she was an old rogue - and I'm also sure that Sandie had no idea what was going to happen. Sandie couldn't hear what they were doing and said, "That's unfair to the songwriters. I've lost my timing. We'll have to start again." Evie tried to do something similar in Vienna but it was futile because 'Puppet' was a runaway winner. If you check out the clip of Sandie singing 'Puppet' on YouTube, you'll see exactly what I mean.

That must have helped us. If you're making the tea and only half-listening, you go, "What was that?" and start watching but in any event, I was sure it would win as it was so distinctive. The viewers sent off their postcards or sealed-down envelopes and 'Puppet On A String' was the runaway winner. The contest itself was going to be in the Grosser Festsaal, Wiener Hofburg, Vienna, Austria.

I was so confident now as I had felt that securing the British nomination was going to be more difficult than winning the Eurovision contest itself. It struck me as perfect for the contest and anyway, we had deliberately done that. I was so confident and then, when I went to the dress rehearsal in

Vienna and heard the other entries, I realised that we might not win. I told Jimmy Phillips that it might be over for us.

He said, "Why the cold feet? We're hot favourites."

I said, "Listen to that song for Luxembourg, 'L'Amour Est Bleu'. That's as good as ours."

'L'Amour Est Bleu', sung by Vicky, came fourth and Jimmy Phillips bought the UK and US publishing rights on my recommendation. It cost him £100 and was a great investment. As 'Love Is Blue', the English title, it was a huge hit for Paul Mauriat and his Orchestra. The single topped the American charts for five weeks. This showed me that I had a good ear for music and as Jimmy Phillips never paid me anything for my judgements, I was beginning to think that I should have my own publishing company.

The American publisher, Al Gallico, who had 'Stand By Your Man', represented Jimmy Phillips in the States and he said, "You've to got to let the kid (me) run the publishing. He'll become the best publisher of us all." Maybe he was right, but at the time I was concentrating on songwriting.

Jimmy Phillips did offer me a position in his company but at the time I wanted to build a songwriting team with Phil Coulter and then we had our own publishing companies.

In the end, 'Puppet On A String' won by a landslide in Vienna. It got 47 votes and the Irish entry, 'If I Could Choose' by Sean Dunphy was second with 22.That year in 1967, Glasgow Celtic became the first British Club to win the European Cup in soccer. The whole team were born within a thirty mile radius of Glasgow City centre. So it was like the Glasgow Boys including me had conquered Europe!

It was our first award and I found I absolutely loved getting awards. I was sitting next to David Bowie when he got his first Ivor Novello award and I congratulated him. He said, "I'd rather you didn't mention it. I'm hoping the award will soon be forgotten." It was for 'Space Oddity'. If you congratulated him on it, he wanted to punch you on the nose. Oddly enough, the David Bowie song I liked the best was 'The Laughing Gnome' where he sounds like Anthony Newley. Apart from the Eurovision Award we won the prestigious Ivor Novello Award for the most performed British song, which is quite something when you look at all the songs we beat in the year of St Pepper and Flower power, the year of 'I'm A Believer', 'Whiter Shade Of Pale', 'Release Me', 'Let's Go To San Francisco' and 'The Last Waltz'.

After the contest, we were elated when we won and we wondered where Sandie was as well as Jimmy Phillips and Louis Benjamin, who ran her label, Pye Records. They were at the private BBC party upstairs. I went up there with Phil, and the BBC executive, Bill Cotton Jr opened the door and said, "What are you two doing here?"

I said, "We've come to the party. We wrote the winning song."

He said, "This party has nothing to do with you. You've not been invited. Get out."

That was an odd reaction but Bill Cotton Jr hated songwriters because he was a failed music publisher. He had a little company that his father had given him and he had had one hit with a song for the Coronation in 1953, 'In A Golden Coach' by Dickie Valentine. He never made the grade as a music publisher and his father had got him into the BBC, where he did exceptionally well. He established many of the great TV personalities of the 70s like Michael Parkinson, Terry Wogan and the Two Ronnies but he had no time for us, or any other songwriters, that night.

I was seething but I said to Phil, "We must get into the normal party for the Eurovision delegation." We met the mayor of Vienna, who said, "Why don't you boys stay as our guests at the Rathaus (the mayoral residency)?" We stayed for a few days, they gave us a coach and horses to drive us around Vienna and we had a fabulous time.

Sandie Shaw made a great record which was helped by a fine arrangement from Kenny Woodman. The bassoon was a very good touch. 'Puppet' was a hit all over the world, except America. I thought later on that I should have got in touch with the great Columbia A&R man, Mitch Miller, as he played the bassoon and he would have warmed to recording it for the American market. Still, I've heard the song everywhere, even on bagpipes in Kenya. I'm going out for a meal tonight and it wouldn't surprise me if I heard it in the restaurant.

The last song to sell a million copies of sheet music was 'Puppet On A String'. That shows you how popular that song was. You couldn't play the other sort of pop music on the piano. That was big money for us.

As I said, 'Puppet' was a hit all over the world but not in America. Oddly enough, it was released in the States by Frank Sinatra's label, Reprise. I wonder what would have happened if they had given it to Nancy as I could imagine her recording it. The famous trumpeter, Al Hirt also did 'Puppet' as an instrumental for the States and it sounded great. There are now lots of instrumental versions of it.

I remember, years later, being at the opening night of Billy Elliot at Victoria Palace. Elton's manager Frank Presland invited me, and Elton John sat behind me with his mother. I gave Elton's mother a kiss and I gave Elton a hug. I heard Elton's mother say, "Why can't you write songs like 'Puppet On A String'? And furthermore, look at Bill's hair. He has terrific hair." That was quite a night for me as I had my wife

Jan on one side and Sophia Loren on the other. Goodness gracious me!

Sandie Shaw said that she hated the song, but she made nearly £1m from it, which is about £16 million in today's money, so if she doesn't want it, she can give the money to me. I like the song, Phil likes the song and so does the public and so does my bank manager. May Sandie Shaw live forever, but 'Puppet On A String' will last longer than any of us.

Strangely enough Sandie now performs concerts with Jools Holland and loves singing a slow version and Jools said he never realised it was such a good lyric

One last point about old honest John Turner aka Jimmy Phillips. Phil and I and Jimmy his two sons Robin and Peter all flew first class to Vienna – we had no idea the cost was coming out of our future earnings! Just as well we made a lot of money.

Chapter 7 - How To Win (Or Not Lose By Much)

I. Spin-offs

The success with 'Puppet On A String' went to our heads. We were enjoying the fruits of success but we were becoming more like celebrities than songwriters. We didn't write many more songs during 1967. I remember giving Phil several ideas for songs but he wasn't keen.

I was feeling the strain because I had two children and I felt that my marriage was over. I wrote a song about it, 'You're Disappearing Fast', for Sandie Shaw, but Phil said, "Let's enjoy our run with 'Puppet' first." That didn't make sense at all as, like all the pop stars of the period, Sandie released three or four singles a year and the follow-up to 'Puppet' was ours for the taking.

'You're Disappearing Fast' would have been perfect for Sandie – and I'm sure she would have liked it as I had written it like a Chris Andrews song. Effectively, Chris Andrews tried to write like Burt Bacharach and we were doing the same. Phil was disappearing fast and, by the time we were writing again, Phil didn't think the idea was original enough. Instead, we came up with a mundane song called 'Tonight In Tokyo'. Jimmy Phillips sent the demo round to Evie Taylor who was Sandie's manager

I remember going to see Evie who was a tough lady who lived behind the American Embassy in Grosvenor Square. I went in with another song and she came down in a short dressing gown with everything hanging out and said she wanted to manage us. I didn't want her to manage me as I can manage myself and we would end up with nothing if she did that. It was bad enough getting money out of Jimmy Phillips but, in my opinion, it would have been much worse with her.

Evie was seducing me in a major way and in order to placate her, I said that I would tell Jimmy Phillips that she was going to manage us. That was just to get out of the door. I told Jimmy that she was preparing contracts and I said, "Tell her that we're not going to do it." Jimmy said, "We're lucky. She's already agreed that Sandie will do 'Tonight In Tokyo'." We didn't get another song with Sandie as Evie then cut us dead. Still, it was better that than being tied to her, both sexually and on monetary terms.

'Tonight In Tokyo' made the top 30 during the summer of 1967 when Phil was in Ireland. I was enjoying my celebrity. I had an interesting choice in September 1967: the QE2 was being launched by the Queen in Glasgow on the same day as the Govan Fair in my home town. I was invited to the opening but I thought, "I've had enough of shipyards. I would rather crown the queen at the Govan Fair."....which I did on the day of the QE2 launch. Who'd have thought, all these years later I would be giving my music talks, having a suite and dining in the Queen's grill on the Cunard lines.

It was Jimmy Phillips who got us back together. He said, "You boys are going to write songs again." He suggested a song festival in Rio De Janeiro. I liked that but I would enter any competition. I am worse than Sammy Cahn in that respect. Sammy Cahn once said jokingly that he would have written with Adolf Hitler if there was a chance that the song would be a hit. What the hell, you do it and you have a laugh. Phil doesn't think like that and I always had to persuade him.

So we wrote 'Celebration' for Georgie Fame. It was a good song with clever words but the arrangement was terrible. I knew that the arrangement for 'Celebration' was too busy, but you could never tell Phil anything as he thinks he's a great arranger. There was no need for all those instruments: if it had been just Georgie's voice and piano with a little combo, the song would have sounded great. We had a falling out over that we hardly saw each other until the start of 1968.

I enjoyed being in Rio and I dressed up in a bowler hat, swimming shorts and a Union Jack to promote the song. The Rio song festivals were really good and I met the likes of Sammy Cahn, Henry Mancini and Quincy Jones. The song that won the following year was 'Evie' by Jimmy Webb and sung by Bill Medley, but the best song that year was a Les Reed and Barry Mason ballad called 'Love Is All', sung by Malcolm Roberts. They only came third and all 80,000 people in the stadium booed the judges. Bill Medley returned to the stage to sing the winning song and they didn't want to hear him. They knew an injustice had been done and they wanted 'Love Is All' again. It was an extraordinary moment and Malcolm Roberts, to his credit, resolved the situation by hugging Bill Medley, giving him the British flag and showing that there were no hard feelings. Malcolm got a huge standing ovation and then Bill Medley finally sang the winning song.

What the audience didn't know was that Jimmy Webb writer of 'Macarthur Park', 'Up Up and Away' had written his song 'Evie' about his feelings for Leslie Bricusse's wife, Evie with whom he'd fallen madly in love. She was an actress, Yvonne Craig, who had been in an Elvis Presley film, Kissin' Cousins.

Jimmy Phillips knew that I enjoyed song festivals and that I liked meeting people on the Continent. He had a song from the San Remo Festival called 'Quando Dico Che Ti Amo' I met its songwriter, Tony Renis, who had also written 'Quando, Quando, Quando', which Engelbert Humperdinck has been singing for 40 years. I liked his new song and wrote an English lyric, 'When I Tell You That I Love You'. Al Hirt, the American trumpeter recorded it with his orchestra and chorus and there were several other recordings. There is supposed to be one by Louis Armstrong, but I've never heard it. I'd have liked to have heard Dean Martin sing it – it would have been great for him.

"Not in small ways, but in all ways,
I love you.

Doctor Jekyll and Mr Hyde
I´ve got them both inside me"

That's Sammy Cahn-styled rhyming.

Anything could inspire me, even passing through an airport. I was always flying and I thought about all the lonely people in an airport. That led to 'Airport People' which was recorded by the Mindbenders and then Adam Faith's group, the Roulettes.

I started using the expression 'different class' instead of super or first class. When Dick James asked me for the name of a company he wanted to give Phil and I me, I said, 'Different Class Productions'. We did anything that came to mind. I don't sing well, but I would take every opportunity that arose. I made a record called 'Private Scotty Grant' about a soldier going back to rescue some troops in Vietnam. Fortunately, Phil could sing and so when he added harmonies, it sounded okay. Larry Page released it on his Page One label and we had a laugh about it. Very insensitive and appalling really given that The Vietnam War was at it's height. We thought we had something that might sell in America, but we hadn't appreciated the feeling against the war in America and it was far too flippant.

II. 1968 - Congratulations

Cliff Richard was a tremendous performer and fortunately for most of the publishers and songwriters in Tin Pan Alley, he didn't write his own songs. Three of the Shadows – Hank Marvin, Bruce Welch and Brian Bennett –were good songwriters and wrote such hits as 'Summer Holiday', 'In The Country' and 'The Day I Met Marie', but Cliff was always looking for new material. Although he wasn't a songwriter, he was a terrific judge of what was right or wrong for him and he could spot a hit. All of us in Tin Pan Alley wanted to write for Cliff. Of course, everyone in Tin Pan Alley also wanted to write for Elvis as well, but there wasn't much chance of that.

In 1968, Jimmy Phillips asked us to write a song for the Eurovision to be sung by Cliff Richard. Again, we had to go through the competition with other pro songwriters like Don Black, Andrew Lloyd Webber and Tim Rice (all of whom failed to get through that year). We wrote a song that has never seen the light of day called 'My Magic Music Box': note the alliteration, and I thought it was brilliant. We had a cast of thousands on our demo record including strings. We were about to discover that all the demos were being made with our own money. Jimmy Phillips took it off our royalties – every last penny of it.

Jimmy Phillips had a shiny red face and looked like Churchill and we played it to him. He got up from his big desk, gave us a big hug and said, "Now, boys, I am sure you have got something better in you." That meant "Get out". He didn't like it.

We had a little room with two chairs, a piano and a hand basin. We were very clean songwriters. I had no new ideas at the time. I came in the next day and I found a piece of manuscript paper on the piano. Phil had written a melody and some words:

"I think I love you,
I think I love you,
I think the world is fine,
If you will say you're mine,
I think I love you."

Although the Troggs had had a huge hit with "Wild thing, I Think I Love You", Phil's chorus didn't sound right. You can't say to someone "I think I love you". You either love someone or you don't. (Apologies to Tony Romeo who wrote another song titled 'I Think I Love You', which was a global hit for The Partridge Family). When we met up, I said, "'I think I love you' is five syllables, so why don't we call it 'Congratulations' and follow it with 'celebrations'?" Phil agreed and then we came up with the rest.

I thought that a slow down before the final chorus would attract attention and that would lead into a big finish. Otherwise, the song would be the same tempo throughout. Norrie Paramor's arrangement was very good – the 'di di di did di di di' intro – was a winning component but that slowing down made it. In fact, this was nothing new - just take Edith Piaf's song 'Je Ne Regrette Rien' as an example.

Both Jimmy Page from Led Zeppelin and John Paul Jones played on the record but they probably wouldn't want to be reminded of it. The backing vocalists were the Breakaways, three girls who had broken away from the Vernon Girls.

Cliff hadn't had a Number 1 since 'The Minute You're Gone' in 1965. Although his records were still charting, they weren't climbing as high and they were only selling to his devoted fans. The Hank Marvin song, 'The Day I Met Marie' got into the Top 10 in 1967 but it surely would have gone to Number 1 a few years earlier. The likes of The Beatles, The Kinks, The Bee Gees, The Rolling Stones and The Foundations were keeping Cliff away from the top.

Cliff was contracted by the BBC in October 1967 to sing the six songs for £1,000 on 5 March 1968 on The Cilla Black Show and then receive another £250 for singing the winning entry the following week. He would get £750 for performing in the Eurovision Song Contest.

The British entry was to be chosen from:

Congratulations (Bill Martin – Phil Coulter) Peter Maurice Music
High'n'Dry (Roger Greenaway – Roger Cook) Maribus Music
Do You Remember (Tommy Scott) Scott Solomon Music
The Sound Of The Candyman's Trumpet (Tony Hazzard) Bron Music
Little Rag Doll (Mike Leander) Leeds Music
Wonderful World (Guy Fletcher – Doug Flett) Abacus Music

How interesting that I should find myself in competition with my first songwriting partner, Tommy Scott. 'The Sound Of The Candyman's Trumpet' is an example of a good song being in the wrong place: the family viewing audience for The Cilla Black Show didn't want psychedelic lyrics.

Once again the viewing public chose our song. Cliff wasn't surprised. He knew that 'Congratulations' would win and he was astute enough to know that 'Congratulations' was a unique title. He was confident that we stood a very good chance in Eurovision which was being held in the Royal Albert Hall as the previous year's winning nation always hosted the event.

This was the first Eurovision Song Contest to be televised in colour so it was an expensive production. Bill Cotton Jr wasn't very pleased at the prospect of staging it again in 1969 as the BBC didn't have the budget.

I went to the dress rehearsal and I didn't hear anything as strong as 'Congratulations'. There was no 'L'Amour Est Bleu' to threaten us. I felt we had it in the bag. Cliff looked great, the Royal Albert Hall looked perfect, and the set was excellent. I knew the orchestra Norrie Paramor was conducting and everything was right.

I've heard it said that Cliff made as big a mistake as Kenneth McKellar by opting for that double-breasted suit with a white fluffy collar and frilly sleeves, but that's looking at it by today's standards. He looked fine at the time and on the day, I wore a similar jacket. Admittedly, I was wearing a kilt, and I'd never seen anyone who was dressed like Cliff without a kilt. You can see where Austin Powers got his look from. Cliff looked great, especially as he was so slim, but he can't dance. If you watch the clip on youtube, you will see that Cliff's dancing is out of sync.

I was convinced we were going to win and the voting was going in our favour. My mother and father were there and they were in a box next to the representatives of the Spanish television station. It was odd that the chat show host, Simon Dee was among them and he was cheering for the Spanish song. Now I wonder if he was part of some jiggery-pokery.

'Congratulations' looked like it was going to win and we were taken backstage by Bill Cotton Jr so that we could be ready to mount the stage as the winners.

There were two countries left to vote and one of them, West Germany, gave top marks to the Spanish entry, 'La La La' by Massiel. As a result, Spain clinched the victory by just one vote. Bill Cotton didn't commiserate with us. He said,

"Thank God for that" and told us to get back to our seats. It was a farce and it was a farcical song that won.

So what, if anything, happened? There have been plenty of conspiracy theories. Spain was having a tourism boom through the advent of package holidays, and General Franco may have thought that a win in Eurovision would help the industry.

Two or three weeks before the contest, the Spanish entry, a young man Joao Manuel Serrat, was replaced because he was going to sing in Catalan. Franco put in Massiel in short or Maria de los Angeles Santamaria in full. Her song was 'La La La' – there are 78 la la las in that song, I've counted them. It have to be some of the worst lyrics ever heard in Eurovision. The song was in la la la land. It was embarrassing.

Not that I am condemning a song solely for repetition. When they were writing West Side Story, Leonard Bernstein said to Stephen Sondheim, "When you do 'Maria', do not say 'I love you' as I could write a lyric like that." So what did Sondheim do? He included 38 Marias just to annoy Bernstein. The difference between 'La La La' and 'Maria' is that the melody of 'Maria' is fantastic....but more of this later

Massiel, who was not even known in Spain, suddenly had a 12 week television series in West Germany. According to the rules, no country knew how another country was voting and there were independent scrutinisers to check for irregularities before each country's results were broadcast. Did the scrutineers miss something? I don't know. God knows how General Franco and the West Germans pulled it off but there is no question in my mind that they did.

Again, we never got invited to the BBC party. That was the first time that I saw Terry Wogan at The Eurovision. He had inveigled his way on to the top table and yet they told us that we were not invited. We put together our own party in the Royal Garden Hotel with our Irish and Scottish friends.

Most people think we won Eurovision with 'Congratulations' but it was with 'Puppet On A String'. Of course we were disappointed not to win again but the fact that 'Congratulations' has sold millions of records and become a standard has been better for us. It was a turning point in Cliff Richard's career. This was his first Number 1 for some years and it knocked the Beatles' 'Lady Madonna' off the top. It revitalised his career and put him back on the map all over the Continent. It was Number 1 across Europe and further afield. Also, for the anoraks amongst you, it is the longest single word title to top the UK charts.

Cliff took his defeat well and he praised Massiel's beauty, if not her song. Cliff did Eurovision again in 1973 with 'Power To All Our Friends', written by Guy Fletcher and Doug Flett, and this time he came third.

'Congratulations' won an Ivor for being the most played song the same year that 'Hey Jude' won for being the highest seller. I am very proud of the fact that 'Congratulations' was played more than 'Hey Jude'. How cool is that? So two years running we won the 'Ivor' for the Most Performed song – not bad when you consider we were up against artists like The Beatles, The Beach Boys and The Stones.

EMI and Capitol in the States thought so little of Cliff's record,'Congratulations' that they refused to release it. EMI also did that to the Beatles first 4 records Our American music publisher, Al Gallico, got it released by Uni, a small label that was also to release hit songs by Neil Diamond and Elton John and make giant stars of them both.

I'm sorry to say this but 'Congratulations' ruined Eurovision because it led to the 'Boom Bang-A-Bang' and 'Jack In The Box' type of songs, but, unlike them, 'Congratulations' was actually a terrific tune. The others were derivatives. There have been so many rubbish songs in Eurovision. You may remember Mouth and MacNeal for the Netherlands with 'I See A Star', and I must confess that I didn't think that 'Waterloo' was that great at the time......how wrong was I and as we all know, Abba went on to be the biggest band in the world.

Before 1974, Abba had tried to represent Sweden in 1971 / 72/ 73 and had been rejected. In 1974, they were open to any offer. Their manager, Stig Anderson, offered me the all the English language territories (Canada, Australia, New Zealand etc) publishing for 'Waterloo' in exchange for the Bay City Rollers' 'Shang-A-Lang'.

What most people don't realise is that the voting for Eurovision is actually done during the dress rehearsal so all the artists come out as if it's the real thing and I was there when Abba (who looked terrific) came on stage. However, their conductor was dressed as Napoleon which I thought was a joke and I didn't buy the song, leaving the path clear for American music publisher, Ivan Mogul, to do so. He bought it for the market in the USA and from there, he got other Abba songs for America and various countries. When he sold his music publishing catalogue, he made a fortune.

.

It was a thrill to know that your songs were acceptable and that everybody knew them. When George Harrison was recording his album, All Things Must Pass, in Abbey Road in October 1970, John Lennon walked in to see what he was doing. George started singing "It's Johnny's birthday" which he'd written to the tune of 'Congratulations' a song on his new album, All Things Must Pass which was an Apple record, pressed by EMI and which went on to be number 1 all over the world.

I said to Jimmy Phillips, whose company was also partly owned by EMI, "We can stop the presses at EMI as George Harrison has stolen our song." There was a precedent. When the Beatles had done 'All You Need Is Love', the musicians had let themselves go at the end and gone into 'In The Mood'. The publisher of 'In The Mood' threatened to sue and the publisher was given one old penny a record. I said we should stop the presses unless we were given four pence a record. We got our credit and the album sold 12 million. I've even got a gold disc on the wall at our home in London, which George presented to me personally. When George was dying, his lawyer Nick Valner, asked him whether he should take 'It's Johnny's Birthday' off 'All Things Must Pass'. George said "No, leave it on as I like Bill." That was in 2001 and sadly Nick died in 2014, aged only 60.

When George was with the Travelin' Wilburys, they wrote a song called 'Congratulations'. I don't know who chose that title but I do wonder if George Harrison had selected that title as a little dig at me.

I was with Jimmy Phillips one day in 1968 at Claridge's Hotel in London when we met Irving Berlin who was in his 80's at the time. He was a diminutive fellow, but very dapper. He had written the seasonal songs, 'White Christmas' and 'Easter Parade'. Another great composer, Jerome Kern once said, when asked, "Irving Berlin has no place in American music – he is American music."

Irving Berlin had heard 'Congratulations' and, as Jimmy and I walked away, he said, "I don't know how I didn't think of that one, Bill." I walked on, skipping down the road, delighted, and Jimmy said, "He means that, you know. If he'd thought of that title, he would have written it."

I always give the Salvation Army a donation when I see them as I got 'Puppet' and 'Congratulations' from the brass bands I heard in Govan. Although I was a drummer in a pipe band, the brass band meant more to me. Think of the sounds in those songs, they are trumpet, or brass band songs. It was in my subconscious.

There was a church in Denmark Street and when songwriter Jimmy Kennedy (who wrote great songs like 'My Prayer' and 'South of the Border) died in 1984, Denis Thatcher gave the eulogy. Some years later I was invited to Number 10 Downing Street by Mrs Thatcher and I shook her hand. I told her about this service and she said, "What were you doing there?", and I said, "I knew Jimmy Kennedy and I wrote 'Congratulations' for the Eurovision Song Contest." and she said, "That must have been a thrill", and I replied, and this shows you what a creep I am, "No bigger thrill than when our victorious troops from the Falklands were sailing down the Solent and the brass band was playing 'Congratulations'." She said, "Would you like your picture taken with me?" So we had our picture taken together.

It is a delight to hear 'Congratulations' when I don't expect it. In the early 70s, I was at Hampden Park in Glasgow for a Scottish Cup Final. Rangers were beaten 4-0 by Celtic and I was feeling sick by the end of the game. That's how it is when you lose to Celtic. I was feeling awful when suddenly the loudspeakers blared out 'Congratulations'. It was revenge as they were being forced to listen to a song written by a Rangers' supporter !

When my mother was 95, I phoned her up to tell her that it was the Queen Mother's 100th birthday and she saw the brass band playing 'Happy Birthday To You' and then 'Congratulations' on the television. I could see the Queen mouthing the words "Congratulations" and the Queen

Mother was pretending to conduct the band. That was a big thrill for me.

I never thought that Cliff would sing it at Wimbledon in the rain to a tennis-starved, rain-soaked audience, let alone at the Queen's Diamond Jubilee Concert in 2012. Cliff wrote me a lovely letter in which he said he was proud to be associated with a song that has become almost as big as 'Happy Birthday To You'.

'Congratulations' was also played by the band outside Buckingham Palace when Prince George was born. It was also played for me when I collected my MBE in June 2014 for services to music and charity in Scotland.

So, as you can see Eurovision played a huge part in my life. When you look at the size of the event nowadays, it's hard to believe that it started life in 1956 with just 7 countries taking part and that didn't include the UK.

It played its part in history though. In 1974 the signal for the start of the Portuguese Revolution was when the nation's Eurovision entry began on TV.

Some great songs have come out of Eurovision – 'All Kinds Of Everything', 'Volare', 'Save Your Kisses For Me, 'What's Another Year', 'Love Is Blue' and 'Waterloo', not to mention mine (modesty aside) but the biggest interval act in the history of showbiz was Riverdance which was first performed during the 7 minute interval of the 1994 Eurovision in Dublin. I knew it would be huge as soon I saw it on Eurovision. It was six minutes of sheer joy. I was even on the phone trying to buy the music publishing rights before they'd finished performing, but I was too late.

It made multi millionaires of dancers Jean Butler and Michael Flatley, who is a terrific fellow, and score writer Bill Whelan but the producers behind the subsequent stage show, which toured globally, were the ones who made the real fortune. In turn, Flatley made his fortune when he split from the original production and set up his own, Lord Of The Dance....and it all started with Eurovision. Unfortunately, it's a totally different kettle of fish these days. Finland won it in 2006 with a band called Lordi who were dressed as Vikings. It was a load of rubbish and you can see why people run down the Eurovision and say that no big star would dare enter.

An interesting anecdote to end this chapter. Katie Boyle was a beautiful elegant ex-model and BBC presenter with a perfect public school accent who frequently hosted Eurovision including 1968 at The Royal Albert Hall when Cliff sung 'Congratulations'. Katie was married to a very successful theatre impresario, Sir Peter Saunders, who owned the worldwide rights to the Agatha Christie play, 'The Mousetrap.' On the play's opening night, he was approached by two Hollywood executives who wanted to buy the movie rights and Sir Peter agreed but insisted on a caveat that said the movie could only be made once it has finished its run in the West End. As I write this, The Mousetrap is in its 65th year and the Hollywood executives have both passed away.

Chapter 8 - Branching Out

I. All Kinds Of Everything

In 1969, Phil didn't want to be involved in Eurovision again, but I thought we should go for three in a row and write a song for Lulu. I knew there was a danger in being called Mr Eurovision instead of Mr Martin, but that would be worth it.

We did write 'Peppermints And Polka Dots' for Lulu and it was getting through the selection process okay. Then Bill Cotton Jr rang up Jimmy Phillips and said, "That's a Bill and Phil song" and Jimmy responded with "You're not supposed to know that." Bill Cotton Jr said, "We can't have them representing the UK again as it looks like a fix", so we weren't even included. I thought that was unfair because we weren't dropped because the song was poor. I'd have liked to have done it for three consecutive years.

Elton John and Bernie Taupin wrote a song for Lulu in the Song for Europe heat that year but it didn't get far. There is a picture of me in the NME calling it the worst song and saying it would come last. I'm sure I was again criticised by Elton in his diary. The song did come last, but I knew Elton had a great talent. Their Eurovision song was a formula song based around the title, 'I Can't Go On Living Without You'. From that day on, Elton and Bernie never wrote in the same room again and their first hit, 'Your Song', was very clever and a classic.

Phil and I had been signed to Jimmy Phillips for three years and we honoured our contracts. We had done well for him.

As we came towards the end of the contract, I asked Jimmy to create a new company for us on a 50-50 basis and we would stay with him if he included 'Puppet On A String', 'Congratulations' and all our other songs in that company. He said, "I couldn't do that."

I said, "But you will then have us for life. We will have a joint operation and I will run the company."

Old Jimmy Phillips didn't see that my youth and my music brains could have helped him. I would have had songs that I loved and he would have had modern stuff. It would have been a great marriage.

We branched out on our own. We formed Mews Music and we hit Number 1 very quickly with two songs, 'All Kinds Of Everything' and 'Back Home'. By some quirk of fate, we were also to have 'Saturday Night' for the Bay City Rollers, a number one hit in the USA and Canada, in Mews Music.

Phil had been given 'All Kinds Of Everything' by two Irish guys, Jackie Smith and Derry Lindsay. They weren't really songwriters, but their song had potential. We went over to Ireland and knocked it into shape. Phil arranged and produced it for Dana, but we couldn't put our names on it as we weren't allowed to write for Ireland.

I thought that Dana would walk the contest. She was a little girl sitting on a stool, and the line "snowdrops and daffodils" is very Rodgers and Hammerstein. The song could have come from The Sound Of Music.

The British entry was Mary Hopkin's 'Knock Knock - Who's There', written by two good and experienced writers, John Carter and Geoff Stephens, but it was a waste of her great voice. She had a fragile, folky voice and she would have been better suited to 'All Kinds Of Everything'! 'Knock Knock - Who's There' was the wrong song for her and she was a salmon swimming upstream. Mickie Most, the international hit record producer, had produced "Knock Knock -Who's There" and he was confident about it. He thought it was unbelievable that we could win with 'All Kinds Of Everything'.

A couple of people have tried to write themselves out of the Eurovision story. One is Sandie Shaw of course and the other is Julio Iglesias. He has claimed that he has had nothing to do with it but he was representing Spain in 1970 and he came fourth. Instead of going out with the Irish crowd, I went out drinking with him. He was a very handsome guy with a black scarf and a black cloak. He was even more attractive to the ladies than Serge Gainsbourg - and he was cleaner too!

I think we were doing the Eurovision Song Contest in the best years and now it has gone downhill pretty rapidly. You could even say that the decline started in 1969, the year after 'Congratulations' as Lulu came first equal with 'Boom Bang-A-Bang', which was a load of bollocks in my opinion.

Unfortunately, it's a totally different kettle of fish these days. Finland won it in 2006 with a band called Lordi who were dressed as Vikings. It was a load of rubbish and I couldn't sing you the tune now as I can't remember it at all, so you can see why people run down the Eurovision and say that no big star would dare enter. That's true to an extent but I think Terry Wogan has to take some of the blame as he constantly knocked the contest and took the mickey out of it.

It does reach farcical levels at times, for instance, how do Israel qualify, let alone Australia? In whatever guise, and whether you agree with me or not that its best days are long gone, it is here to stay as it's now one of the biggest gay parties in the world and the TV audience is in the region of 100 million but Eurovision stopped being a song contest way back in the 70s. It has just become a visual extravaganza and they are more interested in costumes and dancing than in the songs these days. The point scoring in recent years has reached levels bordering on the farcical with blatant political and geographical voting.

As for songs, I have not heard one that I consider world class song for years in Eurovision. The British entries haven't had much originality. 'Ooh Aah...Just A Little Bit' by Gina G in 1996 was quite good. It was catchy and it made it in America. A really great ballad would have a hard time now because of the audience participation and the visual presentation, but I would like to see Susan Boyle with a great song as she could win Eurovision. A new song I have written with Carol Widenbar, a songwriter, 'Clearly Invisible', would be a possibility. She would start "Clearly invisible, nobody notices me" with that wonderful voice and she would have a chance

In 2009, Andrew Lloyd Webber used an American lyricist, Diane Warren, for his Eurovision song, 'It's My Time' which was sung by Jade Ewen. I've nothing against Diane Warren, who's a good songwriter, but that was a disgrace as he should have used a British writer. I think it's wrong that people didn't contradict him. It is a classic example of people not wanting to speak up because he is Andrew Lloyd Webber.

Most songwriters are afraid to enter Eurovision because they might fail. In 2010, hit songwriter Pete Waterman entered it because he was either brainless or too cocky. He was old-fashioned in his approach and he didn't have the ability to do it on his own. The song he wrote, or rather co-wrote, 'That Sounds Good To Me' sounded like a joke to me and it came last, yet Pete is one of the best pop songwriters I know and a great promotions man.

I knew that Blue wouldn't win the 2011 Eurovision with the song 'I Can' and I think they will regret that they did it. It was a retrograde step for them and having seven people to write a song reminds me of the Cole Porter story. Cole was with his musical publisher in Sardi's restaurant in New York when he heard a tune playing. He said to the publisher "This is a lovely tune, who wrote it ?" The publisher replied "Rodgers and Hammerstein". Cole replied "It took two of them to write that ?" This was perhaps a little unfair as the song was 'Some Enchanted Evening' and is considered by some to be the single biggest popular hit to come out of any Rogers and Hammerstein show, but you get my point. Imagine what Cole would have thought of it taking seven of them to write 'I Can'. That's an absolute disgrace to the profession of songwriting.

The songs in the contest are nothing today, all of them instantly forgettable. Where is the 'Volare' , (the English lyric of which was written by Mitchell Parish who also wrote the classic, 'Stardust ') the 'Ciao Ciao Bambino', the 'Love Is Blue', the 'Walk Away', the 'Puppet On A String', the 'Congratulations', the 'All Kinds Of Everything' of today? I'm reminded of what I said to Bill Cotton Jr all those years ago, "It's called the Eurovision Song Contest and for that, you need songs and professional songwriters".

Whilst I think that Sir Terry Wogan had one of the best radio voices of them all I am so glad he was not around in the Eurovision from 1967 till 1970 when we had our three great songs "Puppet on a String" "Congratulations" and "All Kinds of Everything". Terry began to make it his show and was usually condescending to the songs and artists for cheap laughs. It slowly became a joke and now Graham Norton has taken over it´s like a breath of fresh air. Terry retired from the show and his Radio breakfast programme. He was excellent as a radio broadcaster. I was pleased when, on his demise, the BBC gave his career great coverage on both radio and TV and renamed Broadcasting House as Wogan House. A National Treasure that is greatly missed.

It is not just the Eurovision Song Contest where standards are slipping as I see the malaise everywhere. The Ivor Novello Awards are meant to be about the quality of songwriting. You are voted for by your peers and the Songwriter Of The Year is the one to get. The ceremony is not televised because that would spoil it, but it is trying to become trendy now and they often pick the younger guys. They should look back on its history and go for songwriters with real quality. Long after the record company executives have been sacked and the music publishers have changed ownership, the great songs will still be around like stars twinkling in the sky. They'll never die. Cole Porter and Noël Coward will be remembered long after contemporary Ivor winners such as Plan B and Ben Drew.

II. Several Drunken Nights

Wouldn't it have been fun to have had the Dubliners in the Eurovision Song Contest? It would have been a daring choice but it is quite possible that the audience would have warmed to them as they had so much personality. I always thought that the Dubliners were a terrific group. It's a shame it was a black and white period as they would have looked phenomenal in colour with all their beards and funny clothes. We could never have got sponsorship from Gillette.

I first came across them when they were with Phil Solomon. They were brilliant musicians and had enormous presence. Luke Kelly, in particular, was a wonderful singer. Money didn't play much part in their lives at all – it was booze and the craic for them. I probably got on better with the Dubliners than Phil because I could drink with them. I'd sit with these boys and drink Guinness and discuss songs with them.

They were great favourites on the pirate radio stations and so they had a big hit with 'Seven Drunken Nights. I didn't mind the pirate stations even though they paid no royalties on the songs they played. I thought they were terrific and they really changed popular music in the UK. They made it all happen in the 60s.

We wrote 'The Ballad Of Ronnie's Mare' about lead singer Ronnie Drew and he sang it. He would speak the songs rather than sing them. He thought he was singing but everybody else knew he was talking. Ronnie had a wonderful corncrake of a voice and he and Luke Kelly shared the lead vocals on another song we have our name on, 'Free The People'. That song sympathised with the IRA prisoners, but, unlike Phil, I was very uneasy about making political statements in songs. Although my name is on that, it is really Phil's song.

We wrote a film theme for The Molly Maguires, which they recorded. The film starred Sean Connery and Richard Harris and we foolishly gave it to Richard to pass over to the director, Martin Ritt. It's very easy to forget when you're on the piss and falling about! Martin Ritt never heard the song and in retrospect, we should have chosen a more conventional route.

Phil came in one day and said he had written 'A Town I Love So Well' about Derry and he didn't want my name on it. He felt that it was his testimony to his home town and a song that he would be remembered for because of all the troubles in Londonderry between the British Army and the IRA. I was very impressed with it. It did come out first as Martin and Coulter but I don't mind just his name being on the song. It is the only song that he wrote entirely on his own during our time together.

One of our best songs is 'Scorn Not His Simplicity', which was written when Phil's first son was born. The baby was named Paul after Pope Paul and we had a massive celebration around Highgate when he was born as only the Irish can do. The following morning Phil told me that the baby had a hole in his heart and a large head. The diagnosis was Down's Syndrome. I met him in a pub in Highgate and he was crying and I said, "There's no point in crying, Phil. Why don't we write a song about it? We may be able to do some good."

As a result we wrote 'Scorn Not His Simplicity' and I'd like to quote the full lyric:

"See the child with the golden hair
And eyes that show the emptiness inside:
Do we know, can we understand just how he feels
Or have we really tried?
See him now as he stands alone
And watches children play a children's game
A simple child, he looks almost like the others
But they know he's not the same.

"Scorn not his simplicity
But rather try to love him all the more.
Scorn not his simplicity
Oh no, oh no, oh no.

"See him stare, not recognising that kind face
That only yesterday he loved
The loving face of a mother
Who can't understand what she's been guilty of.
How she cried tears of happiness
The day the doctor told her, 'It's a boy'
Now she cries tears of helplessness
And thinks of all the things he can't enjoy.

"Scorn not his simplicity

146

But rather try to love him all the more.
Scorn not his simplicity
Oh no, oh no, oh no."

"Only he knows how to face the future hopefully,
Surrounded by despair.
He won't ask for your pity or your sympathy
But surely you should care.

"Scorn not his simplicity
But rather try to love him all the more.
Scorn not his simplicity
Oh no, oh no, oh no."

It was obvious that the Dubliners should record it. Luke Kelly sang it so beautifully, one of the best records you could possibly hear. There have been many other versions including the Three Irish Tenors, the New Seekers and Sinead O'Connor but I still think the Dubliners are best. Phil and I are known for our 'feel good' songs so I'm glad that we wrote this. When I've been talking on cruise ships, I've had people tell me about their own problems with handicapped children, so I know the song has done a lot of good.

III. Single again

I never felt guilty about anything in the Sixties. I never took drugs but I drank on a Friday night with my mates. I wasn't too much of a Jack the Lad, but I was certainly not the home-at-the-weekend, doting husband. I was always looking for the main chance. There was always a way that meeting somebody would get you into something and you'd end up with a commission.

More and more I found myself out every night doing the rounds of the Bag O'Nails, the Scotch of St James and other London clubs. I had two little kids and I was trying to be a success. Everyone in the industry knew about Bill Martin and Phil Coulter, Bill and Phil.

One day I made up my mind: I was going to divorce Mag, which was a terrible thing to do. I left Chelsea and I bought Mag and the kids a house in Sunbury-on-Thames.

Mag had trusted me all her life, she had done nothing wrong, and I was the person making the money. She got a shock when she got a letter from my solicitors saying that I was divorcing her and the girls who were aged 5 and 3 at the time, told me that they'd never heard their mother cry so much. I didn't need telling. I knew I was behaving abominably and I walked into the street and the tears were pouring down.

I would regularly walk around the streets. I liked to pick up street sounds, snippets of conversation and whistle tunes in my head. It was all part of my creative process. This time I was walking around when I left Mag and I must have been inspired as I wrote:

"You watch the water falling down
Falling down outside your head,
You do your best to turn the tide
But can't forget everything he said
The pressure's getting far too great
The word 'Together' came too late
What do you do when your love breaks up?
Do you fall apart like a butter cup?
Forget about tomorrow,
Surround Yourself with Sorrow."

I get that sensitivity from all the music my father put in me. Songs like 'We All Make Mistakes' and 'Who's Sorry Now'. Although I may come across that way, I am actually not all brash, pushy and jolly, jolly, jolly. I've got 'Surround

148

Yourself With Sorrow', 'Scorn Not His Simplicity' and 'My Boy' in me because I've a lot of sensitivity.

I had written 'Surround Yourself With Sorrow' in ten minutes. It had come to me through a broken heart and I went to Phil and I said, "Don't change anything." He arranged it and even if I listen to it now, it sounds remarkable.

I took the song to George Martin who said, "It's the best song you two have written" and he produced it for Cilla Black. Cilla loved it too. It was a great record and Roger Greenaway and Roger Cook thought it was the best song we'd written. To me, 'Surround Yourself With Sorrow' sounds like a Bacharach and David song and I'm very proud of it. I thought it was going to replace Peter Sarstedt's 'Where Do You Go To, My Lovely' at the top. Then Marvin Gaye charged up the charts with 'I Heard It Through The Grapevine' and that was that. If you look at the UK chart for the week of 29th March 1969, you'll see those three songs at the top. At least we were kept off the top slot by one of the greatest soul songs of all time.

Cilla was a terrific talent and she always listened to the songwriters. She wasn't someone who said, "I can be a songwriter." When her husband, Bobby Willis, died, I wrote her a letter that said, "Don't surround yourself with sorrow, Surround yourself with family and friends".

Mag and I got divorced in 1970 and it was a very sad period. She was very bitter for a while and my parents were horrified. My mother, in particular, thought it was scandalous. I had to win her round.

I let Mag take the children to Belgium as she was, by now, with a Belgian chap who ran a restaurant. There was a danger that they might go to a local school and not speak English. I didn't want to meet my kids when they were 21 and not be able to talk to them so I sent them to the British school in Brussels. They both speak several languages now.

I sold our home in Sunbury on Thames and I gave Mag the money to buy a house, but the Belgian was a con-man and said to Mag, "We won't buy a house. The interest that the money's making will pay for the mortgage," and then he gambled the money away. So again she was let down.

She's married to a nice chap now and she seems very happy. In fact, we're all happy.

When people say to me, "It's all right for you with your Rolls-Royce and your mansion and your money," I say "You don't know what I've sacrificed to make the grade. You've no idea what I've been through. You've no right to talk to me like that." It was the hardest thing in my life to leave two little girls, but I was right to do it and my love for them has never changed.

In 1969, Phil and I were asked to do an advert for Silexine Paint. I wasn't keen on doing adverts as it took us away from pop writing, but it was always good money. They wanted a Batman and Robin sort of thing, so I went for the interview and it was at the Rupert Chetwynd Advertising Agency in Fleet Street. The girl with hot pants and long legs who met me was Janet Olley, known as Jan. I had met her a couple of years before when she had worked briefly as a secretary at Keith Prowse Music. She was drop dead gorgeous with amazing blue eyes.

I was trying to be cocky and she took an instant dislike to me. She told her boss that I was the worst of the three candidates as I didn't have the right attitude. Then they played our piece of music and we got the commission. She had to admit that this terrible Scotsman had the best piece of music and she phoned me up and said, "If it had been up to me, you wouldn't have got it." I said, "Maybe I can change your mind about me over a drink" and that's how we started going out.

Jan said, "If you have written all these hits, why do you need to write adverts?" and I said, "Because I have just got divorced and I need the money." I told her about the divorce and about leaving the children. That was shock, horror really and I knew I wasn't coming over in a good light. Somehow, I charmed her over.

My mother didn't like the fact that I was divorced and at first she wasn't friendly towards Jan. She may have felt that Jan had broken up a happy marriage which wasn't the case. I was on the randan anyway then. If anything, Jan settled me down. She has been terrific in every way. Everybody loves her. My mother adored her in the end.

Jan's father, Bruce, had been a Major in the war and had dropped the title when he came out. Real war heroes do that. Her mother came from Preston and was a very attractive and pleasant lady. Her father had worked as the advertising manager of The Daily Sketch, The Evening News and The Daily Mail. Finally he was invited to be the Advertising Director of the Mail on Sunday and was part of the transformation that turned it into tabloid form and he joined the board of Associated Newspapers. Through him, I got to know everyone in Fleet Street. It is possible that the England World Cup Squad wouldn't have recorded 'Back Home' without him, but more about that later.

It may have been connected with my troubles, I don't know, but I was having some health problems around this time, including a deviated septum, the legacy of an old football injury. I met Tom Jones who was always having trouble with his voice and I was close to losing my voice forever which may well have made a lot of people happy! He said to go and see Dr Sweevack who worked in Notting Hill and it turned out to be a nursing home run by nuns. I thought I would be in for a week but I was in for six. I had been 16 stone but I was losing weight rapidly and I came out four stone lighter. I was fit and healthy but lighter and I thought that I would stay like this. I didn't go over 12 stone again for years. The operation and treatment on my deviated septum took its time but it was successful.

In 1971, Jan and I had just become engaged and we went to Dublin and there is a big castle where the Eurovision Song Contest was being held. Jan had a long lime green dress on and looked lovely. I was in black tie and Phil Coulter was there too. Eamonn Andrews, who, at the time, had a programme on TV called This Is Your Life, was commentating and he was following me. We were in this Government building and I said to Phil, "This is it. They're going to do us on This Is Your Life." We went into another room and someone asked me to sit on the throne. I thought, "This is it. It's This Is Your Life." Eamonn Andrews came in and he made straight for Jan. It wasn't This Is Your Life at all – he just fancied Jan like mad it was her he was following!

IV. Life Is No Fairytale

Dermot Harris, the brother of the actor Richard Harris, wanted to manage J. Vincent Edwards, who had been in the West End production of Hair and was a good singer. He needed songs for him. Phil and I had written 'Thanks' which we thought would be perfect for Tom Jones but by this time Tom was flying around the world and hard to pin down. We recorded it instead with J. Vincent Edwards and it got nowhere. We thought that was that but then it was issued in the Netherlands and got to Number 1. It was so successful that he bought two pubs in Holland and married a Dutch girl.

We were desperate for Tom Jones to do 'Thanks' as he was a giant star and breaking big in America. He did it once in his act and the song was also heard by a country singer called Bill Anderson, whose version was a big hit on the country charts. I still live in hope that Tom Jones will record it. There's another song that we wrote and recorded with J. Vincent Edwards. 'Rely On Me', that would be perfect for Robbie Williams. He'd need to remodel it a bit but not much.

Another songwriting team was told in 1969 that their career was almost finished before it started. They were allowed to go into the studio for one last chance by the MD Brian Brolly who a few years later would become Andrew Lloyd Webber's Chief Executive.

Their single had a cast of thousands but again it flopped, except in Holland and Belgium. For 12 weeks we were Number 1 with 'Thanks' and then they were at Number 2 with 'Superstar' from Jesus Christ Superstar. Then they were massive in America and Australia. The singer was Murray Head and the songwriting team was Andrew Lloyd Webber and Tim Rice. If you listen to the Jesus Christ Superstar album, you will find that they were rushed into finishing it: it is just piano, drums and guitar as they only had a small budget.This then became the corner stone of the great careers that Andrew and Tim quite rightly enjoy.

J. Vincent Edwards had a great voice and we made an album, Thanks, with him. It included Jimmy Webb's song, 'Didn't We', which was first recorded by Richard Harris. It had been his follow-up to 'MacArthur Park'. Richard came back from filming somewhere and he said, '"That album by J. Vincent Edwards is fantastic. I didn't know you two could make records like that." To be honest, up until 'MacArthur Park', we didn't know Richard Harris could sing like that.

Richard Harris lived in Kensington in a house that looked like a castle – Jimmy Page of Led Zeppelin lives in it now – and it is next door to the late Michael Winner's mansion, which now belongs to Robbie Williams. It is a huge house with turrets but he didn't have much more than a fridge, a bed and a throne in the sitting room. The pictures on the sleeve of the Richard Harris/My Boy album were taken there.

Richard was a mercurial character and he was getting divorced. Elizabeth was leaving him as she had had enough. Once he went out to buy the evening paper and he didn't come back for two months. He was outrageous and like the Dubliners, he liked the craic.

I knew that the French singer, Claude François must have another song in him after writing 'Comme D'Habitude', which became 'My Way'. You can't write one great song and not have another one ready. Claude François lived in a windmill which had been converted from a working mill into a home with underground bedrooms where the grain used to be kept.He was a very handsome fellow with a house full of beautiful girls. He wasn't much of a singer and he had a ridiculous ego. He fell out with me because I wouldn't help to make him a star in England.

We took another of his songs 'Parce Que Je T'Aime, Mon Enfant', which became 'My Boy'. The demo was just Phil playing and me singing. We gave it to Richard Harris who thought it was phenomenal. Richard was getting divorced and this song was about someone considering divorce. We took 'My Boy' and Richard Harris to the Radio Luxembourg Grand Prix Music Contest in 1971 and we won. That's when we said we should do an album. Alan Keen, head of Radio Luxembourg stopped Richard misbehaving on a plane on the way to London, when Richard tried to persuade the pilot to divert to Dublin. Harris certainly was a one off.

We then wrote some other songs around it like 'Proposal' and 'This Is Our Child'. He could identify with the songs and he loved what we were doing. Richard wrote a sleeve note to say that the whole album had been created around his divorce but that's not true. That's his ego talking. The songs could have been for anyone, but maybe he thought he could sing it better if he felt that way. Richard never knew that I was going through a divorce at the time.

Richard had a good timbre to his voice and he had just bought the touring rights to the musical, Camelot. In one sense, he regarded this album as another exercise on his way to becoming a singer.

Richard knew that he was unreliable but when he did Camelot, he knew that he owned the rights and he wasn't going to mess it up. If you were a promoter who had hired him to give a concert, he might stay in the pub. He knew that if he didn't turn up for a performance in Camelot, he might lose the whole thing. The theatre chain might kill the show dead and so he became very disciplined. He toured for nine years with Camelot and he became a multi-millionaire because of it. He made money from acting of course, but he made his fortune from Camelot.

As for Claude François, I had seen his bathroom downstairs in that windmill and he had a bookshelf in there. He must have read books in the bath. The light went out one night and he stood up in the bath to change the bulb and electrocuted himself. That's how he died, like something out of the spoof rock 'n' roll film, This Is Spinal Tap.

It was even worse for his manager, Johnny Stark, who also looked after Johnny Hallyday, Sylvie Vartan and Mireille Mathieu. He had a mane of white hair and was a gangster. Johnny Stark was a tough man with an extravagant life style and his house was modelled on John Wayne's in Albuquerque.

The first time I went to see him, I visited his tiny office with a huge desk and no room for anything else. The door closed and he pulled out a gun and said, "I've heard you're a tough guy," and I said, "Not as tough as that, Johnny." The next thing he said to me was, "Do you like chocolate cake?" I said, "I love chocolate cake," "Okay, that's good enough for me let's go to the patisserie." I never went to his office again but that's how I got songs recorded with Sylvie Vartan and Mirelle Mathieu. Sylvie Vartan recorded the French version of our pop group, Kenny's hit, 'Julie Anne'.

Johnny Stark got me record deals with Eddie Barclay who ran Barclay Records. One of the reasons that 'Puppet' and 'Congratulations' were so big is because I got to know the people on the Continent. I knew that you could get new versions recorded in different languages, and I met French and German lyricists.

Believe me, Sandie Shaw had nothing to do with obtaining the "Puppet" continental lyrics except singing them phonetically.

Johnny Stark introduced me to some of the foreign lyricists but he knew a whole pile of other, very dodgy people as well. He was involved with the Marseille Mafia and I have my doubts about his death from a heart attack in 1989. The industry story is that he was found hanged in a park in Paris.

'My Boy' wasn't a UK hit but it did well in America and that is probably how Elvis Presley came to hear it. In 1973, Phil said to me, "I've heard that Elvis is singing 'My Boy' in his act." I asked my secretary, Denise Semmence, to take a letter.

I started, "Dear Elvis", and she said, "Elvis who?" I said, "Elvis Presley."

156

She said, "Have you been drinking again ? You can't write to Elvis" and I said, "Just take the letter." I wrote to Elvis´ because I knew that he always kept a million dollars in his current account so that he actually felt, and knew, he was a millionaire. I actually wrote to his bank, his doctor, his manager, his lawyer and Elvis himself.

I wrote Elvis several letters, hoping for a response and hoping that he was going to record 'My Boy'. I was so into golf at the time that I didn't even consider going over to Las Vegas to watch him sing it in concert.

Elvis did record 'My Boy' in December 1973 and it became a Top 5 record in the UK and number 1 on the   Billboard Adult Contemporary chart in the US. The ending is very powerful with Elvis really giving it his all. I've met the recording engineer who told me that Elvis listened to the playback over 30 times. His father Vernon said, "Hot dog, Elvis, I'm getting tired and hungry, we've got to go home." I'm sure that Elvis loved that song because it conveyed what he felt about his wife Priscilla leaving him and taking his daughter, Lisa-Marie.

Phil and I rented a house that Phil used in Beverly Hills as he wanted to write scores for American films. In August 1977 he was taking his family back to Ireland for a month and so Jan and I went over to the house. My American lawyer had arranged for me to meet Elvis in Las Vegas but we decided to stay in LA for a week and get a sun tan – we weren´t to know that Elvis would die that week. That was one sun tan I wish I'd passed up. Elvis died on August 16 and that night we were at the opening of Star Wars. I was having breakfast in the Polo Lounge when they announced over the loudspeaker that he had died. It rained all day and that continued for the next two days so it was like the skies were crying for Elvis. In the Beverly Hills Hotel they never announce when a star dies but they did that day.

I knew Mark McCormack who had built up a company called International Management Group (IMG). He brought television and show business into golf and made stars of Arnold Palmer, Jack Nicklaus and Gary Player, and he had also transformed the Wimbledon tennis tournament. We met on a plane.

I used to fly first class to New York and Mark McCormack would be in the Pan-Am first class bubble. You would get lunch and McCormack knew who was on the plane and flying first class. He would choose where to sit and he came and had lunch with me. He had a yellow pad, and he would be talking to you and writing down notes. It was very disconcerting. I said, "Why are you doing that?" He said that he had so much in his brain that he had to write things down when it concerned business deals for Jack and Arnie.

He said, "I like the song 'My Boy' that you did for Elvis Presley" so he had found out all about me. He said, "This is one of the few businesses that I am not in and I would like to get into it. I'd like to buy you out."

I said, "I'm not for sale."

He said, "It's something you should consider."

I didn't bite but he did get involved with the songwriter Barry Mason, a good pal of mine, for a musical project, American Heroes, becoming his agent in the process, taking 20% of his earnings at the height of Barry's success. It didn't work out but he formed a little company, Marksmen Music, and did attain some success. He wanted me to run the company with him, but I felt I would be swallowed up. He backed Def Leppard, who became a huge success, and then he did Aida at Earl's Court.

He said to me once, "I have fixed for you to play golf with me, Arnold Palmer and Ben Crenshaw down in Royal Sandwich." I was Songwriter of the Year in 1975 and ready to celebrate so I met up with some great friends in Kent on the way down but I stayed the night in a pub called the Ivy House, singing, drinking and carousing, and I didn't turn up for the golf match which was outrageous. Quite understandably, Mark never spoke to me again.

Ian Wooldridge, the great newspaper writer, told me that Mark had died of vanity! He had a face lift and died on the operating table. That aside, he was a brilliant businessman.

V. Film & TV Music

It's not worth having a full chapter on our involvement with films. Phil and I wanted to write film songs, but you have to devote yourself to that. You have to be knocking on the doors of agents and it would be best to move to America. Phil did that but he can't take rejection so nothing happened for him in Hollywood. Perhaps it was a lost opportunity but we just did bits and pieces here and there.

We got started in 1966. The film producer, Peter Rogers kept coming into Jimmy Phillips' office. His brother, Eric Rogers, did the incidental music for his Carry On films. I was hanging about the office and Jimmy introduced me to Peter. He said that he would like a title song in a Carry On film, and I said, "We'd love to write one." "OK," he said, "Do the next one." I went to see him and he had a huge desk at Pinewood Studios, full of little Wedgwood corgis. The next one was being made with the Carry On team but was called Don't Lose Your Head. It was about the French Revolutions. Do you fancy writing a song called 'Don't Lose Your Head'? It wasn't an easy assignment but we did it. We also sang the song on the soundtrack so we were a pair of cheapskates.

The film has since been rebranded as Carry On Don't Lose Your Head but our song still gets played when the film is shown.

The following year, we wrote the soundtrack music for a 40 minute film, Money-Go-Round, which was performed by an excellent Liverpool group, the Koobas. They were managed by Tony Stratton Smith, who later signed Monty Python. It was a film about the Stock Exchange and it worked out rather well.

One of our best songs was for Take A Girl Like You, a 1970 film starring Hayley Mills and Oliver Reed and based on a book by Kingsley Amis. It was performed by the Foundations who did a good job but unfortunately they had already peaked as a pop group and it failed to chart.

I knew the TV comedian, Dick Emery, and his agent, Tony Lewis, and he and I were known as Martin and Lewis (after Dean and Jerry). Tony Lewis was a very funny man and he would take me out with Dick Emery and we had great laughs: we were funnier than Dick.

Dick used to say, "Ooh, you are awful" and I said, "You should have that as your catch-phrase, and you should have a song like Bob Hope's 'Thanks For The Memory'." So, Phil and I wrote "You Are Awful (But I Like You)" which turned out to be a good signature tune for him and it's an indication that I was heading towards musicals. The B-side was good fun too, the very camp 'Dance Dance', and is the sort of thing that would suit someone like Lily Savage or Graham Norton.

At the time I lived in a huge house, called Kenwood, in St. George's Hill and Dick lived there in a much smaller one. When he saw me pull up in a brand new Rolls Royce, he went to Tony Lewis and said "Tony, I've got to stop being a comedian. I want to be a songwriter", but he never was. He may have dressed up in sketches as a woman but Dick had a real eye for the ladies and was married 5 times. He suffered from dreadful stage fright but was a super fella who became a good friend.

In 1971, we wrote a song for a spaghetti western, A Man Called Sledge, which starred James Garner and Dennis Weaver. In 1976, we did a comedy with Leslie Phillips and Terry-Thomas called Spanish Fly. I saw quite a bit of Terry-Thomas and thought he was perpetually drunk. I didn't realise that he had Parkinson's disease.

Some directors like to get their music off the shelf and companies like Keith Prowse Music would release albums of original background music that could be used in specified situations. We wrote tunes with 60s connotations like 'Discotheque', 'Big Moody' and 'Big Bass Boogie'. We took a song, 'In My Calendar', which had been recorded by Helen Shapiro without any success, and we gave it a new career as background music. It's a lovely piece of music and it still makes us money. We were very lucky as five pieces of our music are used in the Spider-Man cartoon series. Keith Mansfield and Johnny Pearson also made albums like this and Johnny was particularly lucky as he ended up with the theme music for News At Ten. I still receive CD's from Spider-Man fanatics trying to persuade me to change the songs to more contemporrary titles.

As you will have gathered from this book, there are many songs of ours that have scarcely been heard or never been issued. The biggest disappointment was a musical that we could never get off the ground. It is all about Robbie Burns and I realise why it wasn't acceptable at the time. We gave it to a young Cameron Mackintosh in 1969. He didn't like the title, Rabbie. He thought that people would think it was called Rabbi and about a Jewish priest.

161

One song, 'A Poet Should Be There', was about a poet being there to record the moments in history. In a way, it was like 'Flash, Bang, Wallop!' from Half A Sixpence which was about recording things in photographs.

"With his paper and his quill,
He could make time stand still.
Recording what he's seen,
For those who've never been.
He could register each fact,
Each strong dramatic act,
For those who were never there
So everyone could care
A poet should be there."

It would be good to revisit Rabbie sometimes to see if I could get it on the stage or television.

We also wrote for the movie 'The Water Babies' but more of that later.

Chapter 9 - Back Home

Did you know that there was an official World Cup single for the England team in 1966? The team had a mascot called World Cup Willie and a song of the same name was written by Lonnie Donegan with the TV comedy scriptwriter, Sid Green, and recorded by Lonnie for the Decca label. It wasn't really a song for the terraces and nobody paid it any attention. It didn't even make the charts.

When England won the World Cup in 1966, I was watching it with my brother in Scotland and England were winning 2-1 and then Germany scored in the last minute, and most Scottish people thought that was great. We supported Germany, but that was more in fun, I suppose. When Bobby Charlton came back from the final, he asked his Manchester United colleague and Scot, Denis Law, "What did you think of the game?" He said, "I was playing golf, I never watched it."

With the scores level at the end of 90 minutes in the 1966 final at Wembley, the game went into extra time. Geoff Hurst then scored a goal and there has been much debate as to whether it should have been allowed. There was some brilliant commentary when the BBC commentator Kenneth Wolstenholme said, "Some people are on the pitch. They think it's all over..." Hurst scored again and he added, "It is now." England had won 4-2.

England was going to Mexico in 1970 to defend the title and it made sense to have a good football song, something more appropriate than 'World Cup Willie'. My friend, Tony Lewis, who was Shirley Bassey's agent, was also friendly with Bill Cotton Jr at the BBC. He suggested to Bill that we wrote a song for England that could be sung by the team and it could introduce the broadcasts from Mexico. Although we had had our run-ins with Bill Cotton Jr, he could see the sense of it.

We needed a strong idea for the song, and I remembered the story of Jimmy Phillips and "Lili Marlene". Before the war, he had been in a pub when he heard some German soldiers singing this song. He knew it was a great song, so he found out who the publisher was, bought the rights and then wrote an English lyric, so both sides sang it during the war. You know the old joke about the Second World War being started by Vera Lynn's agent – well, this was the same situation.

I had the idea of writing the song like a war song and I came up with the line, "Back home, they'll be thinking about us when we are far away." You can see what I mean when I say 'Back Home' as it has been used when our boys have been returning from Iraq and Afghanistan.

We wrote "Back Home" but we recorded our demo under difficult circumstances. Phil had broken his arm the night before and was in plaster from his wrist to his shoulder. I held his hand as he played the notes and I sang, and the demo was sent round to the BBC. Bill Cotton summoned his producer to listen to it with him, held up the demo and said, "This is the song for Mexico". They listened to it together. "Christ! That sounds like a man playing with a broken arm," said Cotton and threw it out.

I thought I had better bite the bullet and go and see the team's manager, Alf Ramsey. I knew it might be difficult but I had an ace up my sleeve.

Being a director at Associated Newspapers, Jan's father, Bruce Olley, had told me stories about Alf Ramsey's brother, Albert, who was known to be a bit of a drinker and a gambler. Terry Venables had told me about him as well and I knew that he was a source of unease for Alf. Terry by the way, is the only footballer to play for England at all international levels (schoolboy, youth, amateur, under 23 and for the full international team), something that no-one else will ever achieve as amateur caps are no longer awarded.

Alf had taught himself to speak properly but he was from Dagenham, same as Sandie Shaw and Terry as it happens. I went to see Albert in Dagenham and it was like meeting a drunken Alf Ramsey as there were so physically similar.

Ken Stanley was the agent for the England World Cup Squad and he got me in to see Alf at Hendon Hall. I told Alf about the song and Alf didn't like the fact that I was Scottish, never mind the song. He said, "How dare you come here with this suggestion. My boys are athletes, not entertainers."

I said, "That's not what your brother said last night when I was having a drink with him in the pub."

Alf panicked because I had brought up his brother and this was his Achilles heel. He said, "Please don't mention him. Would you mind going upstairs and talking this through with the boys? It's up to them."

I went upstairs to talk to these legends and they were shuffling their feet and looking around while I was talking about the song. I don't know what possessed me but I thought I would take the opportunity of giving them my views on football in order to grab their attention. I said, "The trouble with you, Alan Ball, is that you've got a lot of energy but you are running around like a headless chicken. You have to preserve your energy. You, Bobby Moore, have got a little bit slower and you, Bobby Charlton, can't carry the forward line forever. You will have to move deeper."

Now I had their full attention as I was discussing football and being outspoken.

Then I said, "What do I know? All I know is about making records and writing songs. We will have a lot of fun making 'Back Home' and I can guarantee it will be Number 1 and you will be on Top Of The Pops and get a gold record. In years to come, you will be able to say, 'That was me on Top Of The Pops.'" They liked the idea of meeting Pan's People and they told Alf they would like to do it.

I knew Louis Benjamin at Pye Records would be interested because he had had Sandie Shaw's 'Puppet On A String' and, sure enough that's where we recorded 'Back Home'. Phil was the conductor and I had put down some vocals to show them how a bad singer could do them. Jeff Astle and Geoff Hurst were decent singers, but Alan Ball was the best. He may have spoken with a wee squeaky voice but he was a really good singer. Some players like Bobby and Jackie Charlton weren't interested in recording the song, but half a dozen could sing and so we had a decent nucleus....and, funnily enough, they all wanted to sing it once we invited them on to Top Of The Pops.

We were going to put in the middle that piece of commentary, "They think it's all over, it is now." We dropped the idea because we thought we'd be tempting fate.

"Back Home" was released as a single and it rocketed up the chart. We were selling 100,000 records a day before the World Cup had even started. It went to Number 1 and it was still selling during the World Cup.

We got all the boys, except Paul Reaney who had broken his leg, in black tie on Top Of The Pops. I wasn't in the line-up. Then they went by coach to the Hilton Hotel and Alf surprised me by asking me to join them for dinner by taking Paul's place. It was marvellous. I felt like part of the team.

The B-side of 'Back Home' was another of our songs, 'Cinnamon Stick', but we hadn't put much effort into it. However, I was in a taxi a few months ago and we were discussing the World Cup and I told the driver that I had written 'Back Home'. He said, "God, I love the B-side, 'Cinnamon Stick'." I couldn't believe that, and then I was in a bar and somebody said exactly the same thing and that it was the first single he'd bought. I could hardly remember the song.

We made an LP, The World Beaters Sing The World Beaters, and I designed the sleeve as a souvenir in the shape of a football. There was a table in it for you to write down the scores. Again Phil and I sang some guide vocals but they were more confident by then. Bobby Moore did a great version of 'Ob-La-Di, Ob-La-Da' that is so Cockney. I admit that nobody today would want to hear the England World Cup Squad of 1970 sing 'Sugar Sugar' and that is why you see so many of them in charity shops or on ebay, but it was a Number 1 album at the time.

There was another single but it wasn't an official one. 'Mexico' was written by Tony Macaulay and John Macleod for Long John Baldry. It made the Top 20 but I didn't think much of it. It couldn't touch 'Back Home'. Our song was too good and I was disappointed that we didn't win an Ivor Novello Award for it. Having said that, I had honoured my word - a Number 1 hit, Top Of The Pops and a gold record.

The England squad arrived in Mexico on 4 May and the tournament began on 31st May with England's first game on 2nd June. They had to acclimatise to the altitude and to the heat. I know Bobby Charlton lost a stone in one match alone. They were in the Parc de Princes Hotel in Mexico City, over 7,000 feet above sea level.

Unbeknown to everybody, there had been a fracas the night before the game with Germany and none of the players have ever spoken about this.

Kenneth Wolstenholme had a great deal with a travel agent. If he filled the plane with stars, meaning that more fans would be attracted, he would get free trips to Mexico. He got Geoff Hurst's wife, Judy, Bobby Moore's wife, Tina, Peter Bonetti's wife, Sue, and Martin Peters' wife, Kathleen on the plane.

Once they were there, some reporter told Bonetti that his wife was allegedly having it off with a Mexican. They were married with kids and so the night before the big match with Germany, Bonetti went to the hotel to speak to her as he doubted the rumours. There was a big argument and he stayed up until 6am talking things over with Sue. She said that she would be at the match and he drove back to join the team for breakfast.

Alf Ramsey said, "Where is Gordon Banks?" He couldn't stay off the toilet and so he couldn't play, thus, at the 11th hour, a decision was taken to put Bonetti in goal.

When they came out to play, the players' wives were watching by the entrance but Peter Bonetti's wife was not there. She never thought that he would be playing after being up all night and she didn't go. What does Bonetti think when his wife isn't there? He thinks his wife is back at the hotel with the Mexican.

The game started and Franz Beckenbauer and Bobby Charlton couldn't get past against each other: they were like chess players. The England players in their famous red shirts were winning 2-0 with 20 minutes to go when Bobby Charlton was called off to be saved for the semi final. He had lost a stone in the heat and Alf didn't want him to lose any more weight!

Beckenbauer seized the moment and the first goal went under Bonetti's arms. Then there was a second goal and a third and England was losing 3-2. There is a shot of Alan Ball in the tunnel after the game and he looked like he was going to kill Bonetti. Alan told me that he knew something was wrong with Bonetti and that he may have heard the rumours. As I wasn't there, I can't vouch for all this, but Alan Ball, Bobby Moore and Kenneth Wolstenholme all told me this same story.

If Bobby Charlton hadn't come off, England probably would have made it to the final and maybe won the World Cup again and 'Back Home' would have sold 50m singles. Instead, England lost and I couldn't give them away as ashtrays. The single went right out of the charts.

December 1970 I decided to take Jan to Scotland and introduce her to the rigours of skiing in Scotland. We flew up and stayed in Aviemore. It so happened that there was a TV crew on the slopes and they were filming the opening segment for the New Year's Eve special. They had got an olympic ski champion to be filmed coming off the ski lift and to ski off down the mountain. However it was extremely icy and on the first take the olympic medalist fell and broke his leg.

I decided if it could happen to someone as competent as that we two amateurs would have no chance so we gave the skiing a miss and we headed back to the hotel.

I decided to teach Jan the art of snooker so found the games room and I suggested a glass of something might make it easier and was just about to go to the bar when Jan asked the young man in the snooker room if he would like a drink too.   I went off to get the drinks and Jan asked him if he was on holiday with his parents. He said 'yes, he was with his mum and dad' and then asked Jan 'is that your father you are with'. Jan didn't tell me this conversation until much later!

A few days later we were back in Glasgow and Jan and I were invited to the 'Old Firm' derby game at Rangers' home ground of Ibrox. I made an error of judgement and decided to drive there in my green Rolls Royce.   Celtic, of course, play in green so I had to park my car a bit away from the ground as it would almost certainly have been vandalised had I parked any closer.

We got to the ground and went upstairs to the director's box. Five minutes later my brother Ian arrived and asked the doorman if I had arrived. He said 'yes he has just gone up the stairs with his daughter'.   Twice in a matter of days was a little hard to take!

Although Jan was wearing a full length fur trimmed leather 'Dr Zivago' styled coat and a fur hat it was cold even in the box.   Halftime arrived and Ian and I followed the other men into the bar...Men only and Jan was shown to the ladies lounge.   There she politely asked for a large vodka and tonic and was told by a sweet Scottish lady 'och no dearie, we don't serve alcohol in here but I can offer you a cup of tea and a wee piece of cake'.

Suitably refreshed I returned to my seat next to Jan who relayed her story through the whisky fumes emanating from the gentlemen seated around us.

The match was heading for a 0-0 draw when Jimmy Johnstone scored to give Celtic the lead in the 89th minute. The Rangers fans started to leave then with just seconds left on the clock Colin Stein snatched a dramatic equaliser for Rangers.

Two goals in the last minute. What a finish!   Sadly though the match is not remembered for this. Unbeknownst to us, as the game finished and the supporters began to leave, some stumbled on the steps of the now infamous staircase 13 at the Rangers end of the ground. A human tidal wave caused a surge and steel barriers crushed under the impact leaving people trampled underfoot.

For those of you who have not realised this was the day of the Ibrox disaster when 66 people lost their lives including 4 boys who lived in the same street.   It remains the worst football disaster in Scottish history.

We all remained in the director's box out of respect whilst the medical teams and emergency services tended to the injured people on the pitch.

In 1974 we wrote the World Cup song for Scotland when we were flying high in the charts with the Bay City Rollers. The Scottish squad was going to Germany and it was easy to write,

"Yabba dabba do,
We support the boys in blue."

'Easy, Easy' made the Top 20. When we did the album, we brought in Lulu, Marmalade, Gallagher and Lyle and other Scottish acts. They did their songs and we put the boys in with them. It was a laugh. We had them singing 'Back Home' too. That was my commercial instinct but they protested about doing it. They sang it but they hated it but again the LP was a hit.

Scotland did very well although we didn't qualify from the group stages. We drew with Brazil and Zaire and we never lost a match. Rod Stewart said that he was hiring a jet plane to Hamburg for £180 each and he was taking his brother, Bob. I thought I would take my brother, Ian, and Junior Campbell, guitarist and lead singer of the band Marmalade, was taking his brother, Phil. That was six of us. We got on the plane which had two propellers, and when they closed the door, it was shaped like a coffin. Rod said that there was a big blonde waitress to serve us, but I didn't give a diddley. I was thinking of the Buddy Holly and the Big Bopper plane crash. I'd be like the singer Ritchie Valens: nobody would know I'd died if Rod Stewart and Junior Campbell had gone. The headlines would be "Rock stars Rod Stewart and Junior Campbell die in plane crash along with the songwriter Bob Martin" as I would be mixed up with the dog tablets man.

I said to Rod, "I'm not going back on that plane, that's not a jet, so you owe me £90." We joke to this day as to who owes whom the £90.00.

After the game, the football team smuggled me back to their hotel and Rod and Billy Connolly were there, as was Willie Ormond, the manager. We were all drinking and laughing. Willie said," Can we organise a cabaret and Billy says, 'Not me, I'm not getting up.' Rod Stewart says, 'Not for me.' I got up and told a few jokes. I said, 'We have got one of Scotland's greatest stars here' and I could see Billy and Rod thinking, 'Oh no', but I said, 'Give a big welcome to Scotland's Lonnie Donegan.' Lonnie got up and played, and knocked everyone out. He'd get up anywhere – typical Glaswegian.

By 1997 Glasgow Rangers had won the league nine times in a row and Celtic had never done any better than that. I wrote "Nine Times In A Row - When Will You Give Us The Ten?" with Mike Stock and Matt Aitken. They are great producers and songwriters and they really know how to use the recording desk. My football songs peaked at 'Back Home' but it was nice to do the Rangers' song and the lead vocalist, their striker Ally McCoist, had a decent voice.

The song was dead in the water as they never made the tenth title. That was a shame as I thought the songs they were singing on the terraces, 'The Sash' and 'No Surrender' were both provocative and out of date. Football, after all, is now about family entertainment.

Frank Skinner and David Baddiel used 'Back Home' as the theme tune for their programme, Fantasy Football, and they never gave me any credit. I wrote to them and they put up the credit but they must have thought, "We should write our own football song", and sure enough they wrote and recorded 'Three Lions' with the Lightning Seeds.

I've heard 'Three Lions' being sung on the terraces, but I still think 'Back Home' was the better song. We introduced that clapping to the terraces, When Frank Skinner was on Desert Island Discs, he picked 'Back Home' as one of his eight favourite discs. There have been lots of football songs, but there have been none like 'Back Home'. Funnily enough, John Lennon told me how much the song meant to him, that it made him think of being back home in Liverpool.

In 1993 Bobby Moore's funeral was held at Westminster Abbey. At 51, he was too young to die and he died of an illness that most of us had not heard about – bowel cancer. All the 1966 team was there in the Abbey and Jimmy Tarbuck and Bobby Charlton spoke. Bobby Moore got the send-off that he richly deserved. I went to the Abbey with three of my best friends, Peter Bradley, Wally Ball and Alan Crossman.

Oddly enough, there were two funeral parties. One was headed up by Tina Moore, who was his ex-wife and the other by Stephanie, who was his new wife. One of the factions went to Langan's and the other to Motcombs. I was at Motcombs, which was owned and run by an Irishman, Philip Lawless who knows anyone and everyone in London.

In 2007, a statue of Bobby Moore by Philip Jackson was unveiled at the new Wembley Stadium. It is a superb likeness and well worth seeing. The inscription by the sports writer, Jeff Powell, is perfect. It reads, "Immaculate footballer. Imperial defender. Immortal hero of 1966. First Englishman to raise the World Cup aloft. Favourite son of London's East End. Finest legend of West Ham United. National Treasure. Master of Wembley. Lord of the game. Captain extraordinary. Gentleman of all time."

Kenneth Wolstenholme was Jan's godfather and he died when he was 81 in 2002. He had commentated on 23 FA Cup Finals and 16 European Cup Finals. He had been a member of the RAC for 47 years and he was their golf captain in 1977.

I knew him very well as we were both past captains of the golf club. The family asked me to give the eulogy at his funeral and so I phoned the vicar. He said, "How long are you going to speak? I suggest two minutes." I said, "I can hardly say his name in two minutes." He said that he would be saying something. I said, "Have you been in the church a long time?" He said that he'd been a barrister, so I knew he loved the sound of his own voice.

I went to see the vicar and, since the music publishing days and knowing songwriter Jimmy Kennedy, I've able to read upside down. It's a very useful attribute. I could see his speech and at the very end, he said, "They think it's all over. It is now." What a crass way to finish.

This is how I started the eulogy: "There were three Kenneth Wolstenholmes: Kenneth Wolstenholme the war hero, Kenneth Wolstenholme the commentator, and Kenneth Wolstenholme the family man. He came from Bolton and he joined the RAF and flew Lancasters and he flew over 100 sorties, and he was awarded the DFC twice. He was a very modest man and he never accepted a knighthood. Then he was a commentator and he spoke the best sports line ever heard on TV in 1966 when Geoff Hurst scored his hat trick goal and some people were on the pitch with 'They think it's all over. It is now.' He was a family man and he had a daughter who died of leukaemia when she was young. I explained all this and then I turned round and looked at the coffin and I said, 'Kenneth Wolstenholme, when you left Bolton as a little boy, you could not have anticipated what would happen to you. You became a war hero, a commentator and a legend. You never expected to become a legend...you are now." Everybody applauded including members of the 1966 World Cup Squad.

Chapter 10 - Rollermania

I. Bay City Rollers

I always wanted to make a success of someone or some band from Scotland. I nearly made it with the Beatstalkers and the Boston Dexters (who at the time were the best I'd seen from Scotland) and then in 1970, I had the Dream Police. Guitarist Hamish Stuart was an outstanding musician who later spent many years in Paul McCartney's band. They recorded a song of ours, 'I've Got No Choice' and it had a very good chance of making it. They were a white soul band but they were unhappy with us and our songs and with the UK. They wanted to do their own music and I should have picked up on the potential of their instrumentals. They went to America and became the Average White Band and 'Pick Up The Pieces' was an international hit and a number one Stateside, earning them a Grammy. So I missed them and it taught me that I should listen to what other people want to do. I was thinking 'Pop, Pop, Pop' all the time.

I then had success with two Scottish acts and I couldn't have predicted either one – the Bay City Rollers and Billy Connolly.

In 1971 the Bay City Rollers had a Top 10 hit with 'Keep On Dancing', an American song from the early 60s. They hadn't been able to follow that up with another hit but two years on, they still had a big following in Scotland. They didn't have Les McKeown in the band yet and their lead vocalist was Gordon Clarke, known as Nobby.

The Rollers recorded for Dick Leahy's Bell Records. Whereas Mickie Most at RAK had golden ears, Dick Leahy had silver ears and both could spot a hit. Dick didn't want to give up on the Rollers. He was desperate to find something good for them and he asked Phil and I to help.

I was pleased to be asked but I had one reservation. I couldn't stand their manager, Tam Paton who had been around for years in Scotland. He had been a potato salesman and he was as common as muck. He had no style, no flair, nothing at all. I didn't like him, but I thought he was dopey, not evil, and that I could manipulate him to get to the Bay City Rollers to do what we wanted. I would butter him up to get what we required. I was never able to quite put my finger on what was so objectionable about Paton but my instincts were correct – he was later given a 3 year prison sentence for gross indecency with teenage boys.

Phil and I wrote a song, 'Saturday Night', for the Rollers, but Phil, due to illness, was unable to turn up at the studio and so I recorded it with them. The record has a chant, similar to an American University football match "S-A-T-U-R-D-A-Y night" and they got excited as we recorded it and increased the tempo. I told Dick Leahy that Phil had been ill and that's why the production wasn't great, although the drums were very good. I'd allowed them to go fast and had not redone it. Dick said, "Well, I like that fast bit." It was released as a single and it flopped selling about 180 records (thanks again, Mum!), but Dick wanted us to try again. Meanwhile, Nobby Clarke had left and their new lead singer was Les McKeown, who was only 18. He became the cheeky one of the group. I liked him a lot and we are friendly to this day.

I had written a song called 'Remember' and Phil took some 'sha la las' from something he'd written the week before so we had a new song, 'Remember (Sha-la-la)'. In the same way, George Martin took a Paul Mccartney song, 'We Can

Work It Out' and Lennon's 'Life is Very Short' and combined them to produce the former. Remember (Sha-la-la) became a hit in February 1974 and climbed to Number 6. That really was the start of the Rollers.

They needed an image and preferably something to emphasise their Scottishness. Tam Paton showed me a letter from a fan, who had an idea for doing something different with tartan and clothes. It reminded me of the old Lerner & Loewe musical 'Brigadoon' where everyone wore tartan, even trousers, in this mythical Scottish village.

I had a secretary, Sheila Lazarus, who was extremely protective of me. She wouldn't allow anybody in to see me. I said, "We need a receptionist, we are so busy", and she said, "No, I can do that." This always happened – I can do the accounting, I can do this, I can do that. When I told her the idea for tartan gear, she said, "I can get these clothes made." I said, "How can you do that?" She said, "My mother makes clothes. I will buy all the material and we can do it." You may remember that the trousers were short – well, Sheila hadn't bought enough material. We also had to buy these ringed stockings and the big boots. I wouldn't have worn them myself but it looked great. We gave the prototype for the clothes to Tam who had them made up in Scotland.

'Shang-a-lang', another song of ours, took me back to the sound of the shipyards when the cranes were lifting the heavy plates of steel, the riveters were bashing and hammering and the cutting machines were slashing and drilling. I used to hear 'bang, crash, clang' all day. There already was a song, 'Clang, clang, clang went the trolley', but 'Shang-a-lang' came to me. Actually, I had been using the phrase for some time. If somebody said something that didn't interest me, I would say, 'Oh, shang-a-lang'. People would think I was swearing but of course I wasn't.

So we wrote 'Shang-a-lang' and it became one of the Rollers' biggest hits, making number two in May 1974. It was kept off the top spot by the Rubettes' 'Sugar Baby Love', which was written and produced by Wayne Bickerton and Tony Waddington, and I was somewhat disappointed about that as I thought 'Sugar Baby Love' was extremely similar and had the same feel to the Diamonds' 'Little Darlin'', a number three hit in 1957.

I also felt that 'Shang-A-Lang' had the country behind it. The Rollers should have been Number 1 and you'll meet people in Scotland who think it should be our national anthem! It was the biggest of all the Rollers' songs in Scotland. If the Bay City Rollers had gone on Eurovision with 'Shang-a-lang', they'd have walked it. Judy Murray, mother of tennis star, Andy, chose it as her favourite song on Desert Island Discs. Thanks Judy !

We consolidated our success with two more Top 10 singles, 'Summerlove Sensation' and 'All Of Me Loves All Of You'. We also made their first album, Rollin', which was Number 1 and on the charts for over a year. I like that album as it is like the Beatles' first album with covers of Brill Building songs like 'Please Stay' and 'Be My Baby'. Jeff Barry, the American songwriter who had written 'Be My Baby' wondered why they had done the song and I told him that I was a big fan of his songwriting and that's why it was on the album. We had used session men like drummer Clem Cattini for the backing tracks and the Rollers just did the vocals.

The packaging for that first album, Rollin', from 1974 is very interesting. Photogenically they were fabulous, but the photographs must have been taken just before we got the right image. They look like an American band. I don't know why but the drummer Derek Longmuir is given pride of place on the cover and although we were trying to pass his brother Alan off as early twenties, he looks several years older. Alan and Derek were good musicians and they were the cornerstone of the band. They held the Rollers together musically on bass and drums. Eric Faulkner was okay as a guitarist and Stuart Wood, known as 'Woody', was an afterthought. If that sounds harsh, he was chosen for his good looks which appealed to the younger fans, especially when they went to America.

We were promoting an image of a clean-living, innocent group and yet we slipped up as, on the LP sleeve, they list their favourite drinks as "dark rum and peppermint" and "Cointreau with lime and lemonade". Notice too on the record sleeve how inexperienced Les McKeown was: he has written his autograph as he would a legal document, "Leslie R McKeown". There's no question in my mind that Les was the true personality of the group.

Phil and I as the songwriters, producers and publishers were being both greedy and silly. We were greedy because we hadn't let them write their own B-sides. That's not to say we did anything wrong but that would have kept the boys happy, especially Eric Faulkner who saw himself as a writer. On the sleeve of Rollin', he says his ambition is to write a Number 1 song, but having ambition is not enough. I did listen to their songs, and, without being harsh, if they had been any good, I would have done a publishing deal with them but they weren't and I didn't get involved. They formed a publishing company with Freddie Bienstock at Carlin but he wouldn't have helped them at all. In my opinion he was a collector of songs as opposed to being a creative music publisher. I also doubt that the contract was a generous one.

Maybe Phil and I were at fault here. Perhaps we should have encouraged Eric and taught him something about the craft of songwriting. Eric and Woody did write a big hit in America eventually although without wishing to appear uncharitable, anyone could have written a hit as they were

180

so big by then that the fans would have accepted anything. Their song was called 'Money Honey' and there's an example of their naïvety as there was already a well-known song called 'Money Honey', associated with Elvis Presley. It was the group's momentum that made it a hit and the Rollers failed in the end because their own songs weren't creative enough.

We were foolish because I made the mistake of telling the media that they didn't play on their own records. I thought it was funny but really I was destroying the group. I should have had more sense – look at the troubles there had been with the Monkees and Love Affair. There was some backlash from this – BBC DJ Johnnie Walker wouldn't play the Rollers anymore on Radio 1 as he thought the fans were being conned. Even now, he still doesn't play the Rollers on his 70s show on Radio 2 but that's his problem as they were one of the biggest selling groups of the 1970s.

Obviously, it was quicker for us to record the tracks with session musicians, but we had hurt their feelings. We should have built up their egos and not destroyed them. We hadn't been considerate enough and we were just being cost conscious for the record company. That's how we were. We could make a single in a morning and do an album in three days back then.

Clive Davis is one of the most successful record executives ever in America. He had worked with Bob Dylan, Barbra Streisand and Paul Simon at Columbia, and now he was setting up his own operation, Arista. He had the rights to Bell Records, which owned the Rollers recording contract for the US, but he wasn't releasing any of the their singles.

I rang Clive Davis about this, told him who I was and he started berating me. "Who are you? You've got the Rollers but they are nothing compared to the Monkees. I've not heard one song that appeals to me so don't tell me how to run my business." I cited the fact that I'd written hits for Sandie, Cliff and Cilla but he was unimpressed saying that they had all had hits before my songs and that I'd discovered nobody. I replied, "Well, can I fly in and see you?" He said, "I don't know where it will get you because I don't plan to release anything here."

I went to see Clive Davis. He was a lawyer who dressed like a London City Gent and, accordingly, he liked the fact that I dressed smartly. He was bald on top while I had a full head of white hair and this intrigued him. I am sure that half the time he was looking at my hair trying to spot the join. He had a yellow lawyer's pad next to him and he would be constantly writing. His brain worked so fast that he had already made up his mind what to say next, so he was jotting down things to do. As I said, the only other person I've met who did that was Mark McCormack.

Anyway, my visit worked. Clive changed his mind about the Rollers and he said he would release our product on Arista. He was having great success with Barry Manilow's 'Mandy', which was another British song, co - written by two of my friends, Scott English and Richard Kerr. That had originally been recorded as 'Brandy' and was about a dog but Clive Davis thought the tempo should be slowed down and the title was changed to 'Mandy'. Then it became an American Number 1.

Clive Davis spoke to Tam Paton and he had been told that, after five hits and a Number 1 album, the Rollers wanted us out as record producers and songwriters. They wanted to record their own songs. That was a bit of a blow, but we said, "Okay" and we negotiated for Arista to buy our record producing rights on the previous releases by The Rollers. We sold them for a substantial amount, but we kept our songwriting royalties and our music publishing rights.

Meanwhile, the Rollers had cut a very successful new single, 'Bye Bye Baby', produced by Phil Wainman, who worked with Sweet and it had become their first UK Number 1. It was a good record but by then, Rollermania had taken off to a phenomenal extent. We had built them up to an extraordinary level and if they had recorded the phone book, it would have been Number 1. That said, 'Bye Bye Baby' was an excellent tune from the prodigious Bob Gaudio/Bob Crewe writing team and a hit for The Four Seasons and a focal point of the global smash stage show, Jersey Boys.

The public loved the Bay City Rollers because it was all innocence and fun. They had a TV series, Shang-a-lang, named after our song, and when they appeared on a Radio 1 Fun Day at Mallory Park in Leicestershire, young girls were swimming across a lake to get to the island where they were performing and had to be rescued.

In the history of the music business, there has only ever been Beatlemania and Rollermania. Think about it - the 'mania' moniker has never been attached to anyone else and that includes One Direction, Take That etc. In those days, the additional merchandising was negligible so just think what the Rollers would be worth in today's terms. Once again just YouTube or Google it if you want confirmation. Marketing people have told me that they would now be a £1bn + merchandising industry.

Clive Davis wanted to create a similar excitement in America but he wasn't sure about 'Bye Bye Baby' as it had been a hit a few years earlier for the Four Seasons. He wanted something new or, as it turned out, something old. He wanted to release the Bill Martin/Phil Coulter song 'Saturday Night' in the States. I couldn't believe it but I didn't object. We went into the studio and took off Nobby's lead vocal and replaced it with Les's voice.

I think Clive liked 'Saturday Night' because it was a cheerleader song, the way those girls with pom-poms spell O-H-I-O or whatever at American Football matches. The song was ideal because Howard Cosell, a big U.S. TV star, hosted a programme called Saturday Night Live on ABC. Cosell was a big sports promoter and he thought that the Rollers with all their plaid (that's the American term for tartan) would come across well, so he used our song as his theme and gave The Rollers their first show in the States and the rest is hysteria.

'Saturday Night' became Number 1 in America, Japan and Australia and sold 12m copies internationally. Dick Leahy should have reissued it in the UK but bizarrely, he never did and it has never been released to this day . 'Saturday Night' still makes us a lot of money as it is used in films and TV movies. In Japan in 2010, it was used to advertise a beer called Asahi and when I go there, they bow down to me because of that song. Indeed, in August 2012 Japanese TV did an hour long programme with me, based solely on 'Saturday Night', showing just what a global phenomenon the Rollers had become.

There is an hilarious video from a TV show on YouTube. The beautiful film actress/singer Ann-Margret, who starred in Viva Las Vegas with Elvis, is singing 'Saturday Night' with the Rollers to an audience of pensioners. I love the pensioner who is knitting and not noticing what is going on in the video.

Phil Wainman is a talented producer but he wasn't a great songwriter in the eyes of the songwriting fraternity. The Rollers needed good pop songs and we could have had two more great years with them – pop bands are unlikely to last longer than that. Eric Faulkner got his way and the Rollers recorded his songs but they stopped having the big hits. It worked for a while when they still had momentum but ultimately fizzled out due to poor quality of songs.

But the Rollers' big problem was their manager, Tam Paton. Everything was wrong about this man and I don't know how he got away with it for so long. He was a crook, a pervert and a drug dealer - Operation Yewtree would have had a field day with him. He was a bad man and he was using the band to get to little boys, and he should have gone to prison. He's dead now and the world is well rid of him. For the record, I said all of this on TV and Radio long before he died. He was an objectionable man. Tam Paton didn't buy the Rollers houses: he leased everything so they had nothing. They were reputed to have sold 138 million albums but they didn't see much money.

They were simple, trusting lads and though people think it is better now with lawyers and accountants, young musicians are still being exploited. They should have been multi-millionaires and now they complain about not getting their money from the manager.

I don't know where the money went. Tam Paton may have got a lot of it but he never looked wealthy. He lived on a farm towards the end of his life and he looked exactly like Marlon Brando in Apocalypse Now. The money went somewhere and Phil Coulter and I were lucky as we got paid direct as writers, producers and publishers. I would like to stress that we only received what was rightly ours and we never took any of the money due to the Rollers. In fact, I never ever wanted to be a manager because I didn't want musicians ringing up and saying, "Why are you still in bed?" or "Why didn't you come and see us last night?" I could have managed so many people but I preferred to lead my own life. I feel very sorry for the Bay City Rollers because they were twenty-somethings who should all have been millionaires. Just the merchandising alone was worth millions: Jan and I met someone on a cruise, Brian de Zille, now a friend, who had made some of his fortune from Bay City Rollers sweaters.

I don't think Tam Paton was clever enough to steal all that money, but he might have been. If it had been me chasing my royalties, I would have looked at the lawyers, the accountants and the promoters from those days. The Rollers' money should have gone through an accountant and a lawyer and then to the manager and the promoter and then to the boys. The chain allegedly had too many weak links in it and the band suffered.

II. Kenny

I knew that there was one song by the Bay City Rollers that had been overlooked – 'The Bump', which was the B-side of 'All Of Me Loves All Of You'. It had been made as a quick B-side. We had used professional musicians for the backing track and because the Rollers were getting fed up, they had done some lacklustre vocals. They hadn't wanted to be associated with it. We took the backing track and put our vocals on it instead. It sounded good but I couldn't see how we could go on Top Of The Pops to promote it. We looked too old and I had white hair. We'd look ridiculous doing the Bump. We had to find a band that would do it for us.

We advertised for a band and I remember two boys turning up and one of them was a bit lippy. It was the Chegwin twins, Keith and Jeff, and we weren't keen.

An agent, Peter Walsh, who had the pop group Marmalade, and was one of Phil Coulter's friends, told us that he had a group called Chuff. We said, "When can we see them?" and he said, "Well, one of them works in a banana warehouse in Enfield." We went to see them in the banana warehouse and they looked good. They had had some experience as they had been supporting Hawkwind and the Edgar Broughton Band. I wanted to change them from Prog Rock to Glam Rock and they didn't seem to mind.

Around that time, we were making records with everyone. Paul Gabriel, who worked in the office, had a good voice and so we gave him a song, 'Sweetheart', which was released as D'Arcy. Nothing happened to it, but it was a good record.

In 1973, we had written a hit, 'Heart Of Stone', for an Irish vocalist, Tony Kenny, which was released under the name of Kenny. It was a Top 20 record here and really big in Ireland. Another of our songs for him, 'Give It To Me Now', was recycled with the Bay City Rollers. Tony didn't want to work as just 'Kenny' anymore so we thought we would continue with that as a group name.

I put the big K on them, which looked like an advert for Kellogg's; in fact it would have been good if Kellogg's had sponsored them. They appeared on Top Of The Pops and 'The Bump' was a huge single on Mickie Most's record label, RAK. It would have been even bigger if the Rollers had sung it properly in the first place. We followed it with another Top 10 single, 'Fancy Pants' and again, that could have been a Number 1 for the Rollers. There wasn't a great deal of effort in writing these songs. The title of their third hit, 'Baby, I Love You, OK!', came from some graffiti I spotted somewhere.

We wrote a song for Kenny called 'Forget The Janes, The Jeans And The Might Have Beens' and it has also been recorded by Tony Christie as well as being turned into a country song by Bryan Chalker in the UK and Bill Anderson in America.

It sounds cynical but we were giving the teenagers what they wanted. They wanted good-looking young guys and as they couldn't play properly, it was better to have them singing to backing tracks on Top Of The Pops. It wasn't cheating as they were entertaining the audience and that's what counts. They did come to the studio and stuck their voice on some things, but they never played anything. I can't remember what they did in concert as we had nothing to do with that.

Okay, I look at the sleeve of their album, The Sound Of Super K, and I can't name them, but the public didn't remember them either as lead singer Rick Driscoll was in the identify parade on TV show Never Mind The Buzzcocks and the teams couldn't pick him out. We hardly saw them to be honest. I wouldn't know any of them if I met them today."

That album, incidentally, is where Phil started his nonsense. Look at the credit: "Produced by Phil Coulter - in association with Bill Martin for Martin-Coulter Enterprises." I said, "Why are you doing that? Our whole thing is Martin-Coulter." He said, "Well, I am the producer."

The members of Kenny were getting £40 a week from their manager and we didn't pay them anything as it wasn't our place to do so. Like the Rollers though, they wanted to write their own material. They had two songwriters in the band, Rick Driscoll and Yan Stile, and they wrote 'Happiness Melissa', which was the B-side of our song, 'Nice To Have You Home'. We had four Top 10 hits with them – 'The Bump', 'Fancy Pants', 'Baby, I Love You, OK!' and 'Julie Anne'.

After those hits, Peter Walsh took Kenny to Polydor Records and that's when things became nasty. We were taken to court and we foolishly said that we had created the falsetto and the other gimmicks that they had used. We said that nothing was down to them, which was true. I suppose Kenny had a strange job. Success was being handed them on a plate but they were being asked to impersonate a non-existent group and maintain the subterfuge.

We thought we had done well and were going to win, but in the papers, it said, "Boys from the banana warehouse live on peasants' wages and don't even play on their hit records." The judge said that we were treating them like slaves and we got a very bad press. It was very unfair as it had been their manager Peter Walsh who was responsible for paying them not us. He gave them the Oliver Twist wages, not us.

My conscience is totally clear. We were hired to make the records and they were released on RAK. The management got their royalties and we as producers got ours. We wrote the songs, we made the records and we published the music. They went on the road and somebody would give them a wage, and that somebody would be Peter Walsh, not us.

We were only involved in the court case because Kenny wanted to leave us as producers and songwriters in the way that the Rollers had left us. We got paid for losing our production deal with the Rollers, but we didn't with Kenny. We had started the thing – it was our idea, but it came out all wrong in the press.

Kenny were free of us. They recorded an album of new material Ricochet and had a single, 'Hot Lips', which sounded like one of our songs, but without the chart success. They toured with some success in Germany but then Yan Stile was injured in a car crash. His arm was paralyzed and the group was finished.

'The Bump' was a fun thing, a great dance record. I have met Quentin Tarantino and we were talking about the use of songs in films. He had used 'Stuck In The Middle With You' for the torture scene in Pulp Fiction and I said that 'The Bump' could be good for when he had a murder scene. He thought the title referred to gangsters so I have high hopes about that !

III. Slik

After the Kenny case, Polydor wanted to be friendly with us as they knew that we could make hit records. I said to John Fruin, their head man in London, "Okay, if you want to be friends, you can pay our legal costs for the Kenny court case and give me that little band that I gave you called Salvation." They had recorded one of our songs, 'The Boogiest Band In Town'. Polydor paid our legal fees, a few quid on top and gave us Salvation.

I didn't like the name Salvation but I liked the band and changed it to Slik. We did think of Lord Slick, Oil Slick etc but that was silly, and we gave them that baseball image. That was American and we were hoping that they were going to be as big as the Rollers. We had a Number 1 on Bell with 'Forever And Ever' and that one could have been the Rollers' biggest ever Number 1. Once again, management let them down.

All the boys were very talented and could play on their own records. Oddly enough, Midge Ure, although the member to find the most fame later with Ultravox and Band Aid, wasn't the best talent in the band. That was Jim McGinlay, But Midge was a hard worker and I knew that he'd make it. He had more push than the others. Kenny Hyslop was a very talented drummer too. That band could have been huge, but punk came in. Just as the Rolling Stones were the negative image of the Beatles, the Sex Pistols were the reverse of the Rollers. Teenybopper songs and Glam Rock was over.

'Forever And Ever' is songwriting at its easiest. Just look at the Lord's Prayer. We took it from there − "Forever and ever, Amen." It was dead easy to write. It even starts with the words, "Ashes to ashes", dead easy but dead clever.

Everybody wanted to buy Slik. I liked Bell Records and I liked Clive Davis. Clive phoned me and said, "I must hear your new band." I said that I would see his guy, Tony Roberts, who was the son of the Fifties songwriter Paddy Roberts, who wrote 'Softly Softly,' a number 1 hit in 1955 for the Irish singer Ruby Murray. Incidentally, that was one of 5 hits that Ruby had in the top ten at the same time.

We agreed to sign the band to Bell in the UK and elsewhere, but I didn't give him the rights to North America, or to Germany, Austria and Switzerland, which are known as the GAS countries. Clive Davis went ballistic. They wanted to release the record in December 1975 but I said only if the contract is signed the way I want it. We missed the deadline but it didn't bother me. It was a very good record and we didn't need Christmas to push it. We could get the momentum going in January.

I would go to the factory and see the workers who manufacture the records. I would inspire everybody and get them on side, behind the record. We had Gary Farrow plugging it and he was one of the best in the business. I knew that once we had 'Forever And Ever' out, it would shoot to Number 1.

It was a great success and at the music conference, MIDEM in Cannes, France, I was going to sell the rights to the GAS countries, and Clive Davis told his people to buy them for whatever they cost. They had to pay us a fortune as they couldn't have records being pressed by another company in Germany, say, which could then sell them all over Europe.

I could have sold the American rights to Russ Regan, the guy who signed Elton John and Neil Diamond and made them stars. He really wanted the group but I thought I had better stick with Clive Davis. Clive then killed the record and killed the group. You know why? He had invested so much money in the Bay City Rollers that he couldn't afford another band taking over. By signing with Clive, I had signed Slik's death warrant.

It was a great shame as Slik was actually a better band than the Rollers. We hadn't realised how politics came into things and from then on, we couldn't be bothered dealing with pop bands. We had had three bad experiences with the Bay City Rollers, Kenny and Slik.

Slik's manager was Billy Connolly's manager, Frank Lynch, and he made a bad mistake. When they made Number 1, he never put them on the road. He could have made a fortune. He thought that he would keep them back and then launch them later, but the public can't wait. They want to see them now. There was one other single, 'Requiem', which we did and that was a great track. They did another one themselves but they wanted to pack up when punk came in. Nobody stood a chance then. We wrote 'The Kid's A Punk' and that was the end of Slik and as it happens, Martin and Coulter as well.

I gave Frank Lynch a young Glaswegian named BA Robertson, who had come to me as a writer. He was the most big-headed songwriter I have ever met but he did write 'Wired for Sound' for Cliff Richard and 'Bang Bang' for himself. He has written one truly great lyric, 'The Living Years', for Mike and the Mechanics.

Johnny Fruin was one of the best record men. He could have been the head of EMI but he went to Polydor and then left to work with Wayne Bickerton at State. That was his downfall as some people are better inside a big corporation. There is a line in 'Bang Bang', "Her life was in ruin, She loved Johnny Fruin" B.A. Robertson had put that in to ensure his record would get airplay and the whole company would get behind it.

In June 1979, I was asked to make a speech at a Variety Club dinner to celebrate Radio One. I'm a good after dinner speaker now but instead of trying to do it my normal, natural way, I did it my brother's way.

Ian is a great after dinner speaker. He has a very good retentive memory and he does jokes – he is like Ken Dodd, joke after joke. He picks on people in the audience and tells jokes whereas I tell stories.

I took one of his scripts and adapted it. Paul Williams was the BBC radio producer of The Jimmy Young Show and I said that it was like trying to impress the Ayatollah when you wanted him to play a record. Instead of laughing, they took it seriously. Geoffrey Everitt, Head of Radio Luxembourg, who was hosting the event, said, "Thank you, Bill, for your well read speech" and I knew I'd blown it. I apologised by letter and Jimmy Saville, of all people, sent a handwritten note back, saying, "Forget it." He had a good attitude about things like that: you gave it a go, sometimes you get it wrong, but you've still done it.

I wanted to make amends for my gaff. I got all the songwriters to put up £1,000 for a page in the Variety Club brochure and I raised £118,000 for charity and they gave me a silver heart. I then gave a speech that was a big success. I was natural that night. I had B.A. Robertson then and I said, "To quote one of my songwriters, the Variety Club has 'knocked it off', the title of a B.A. song at the time.

Frank Lynch was really buzzing because he managed Billy Connolly, but then he stopped managing Billy and Slik and his company, the Unicorn Empire, collapsed. It was comprised of bars, restaurants, the Apollo Theatre and Billy's management. Frank offered it all to me for £130,000 but I turned him down as I was not interested in bars or, as I've said before, management.   All of a sudden, he absconded. Nobody knew where he went and rumour has it that he took a suitcase full of money with him but who knows. That is the danger a performer faces and that is why I don't have anybody looking after me. If I can't do it myself, then there's no point. I'm the best judge of my own time. I spend my own money and I look after myself. I have to be the master of my own destiny. I simply don't trust most of the people in the music business.

I am hired by Carnival (Cunard), P&O and other cruise liner companies to travel round the world on their ships, giving my talks on such topics as The Golden Age of Musicals, The Rat Pack, Eurovision, The History Of Rock 'n Roll and Classic Standards. In 2011, I was asked to give talks on the maiden voyage round Great Britain on the new Queen Elizabeth and the captain informed me that we would be stopping in Liverpool, the birthplace of Cunard, where there would be a service in the cathedral. He added that Lesley Garrett would sing and several people including Jimmy Savile, who was I was told was also on board, would give a reading.

I bumped into Savile in the cigar room but he was emaciated and could barely stand. He was obviously dying and puffing on his last cigars and I didn't know what to do so thought I'd just say my goodbyes.

Savile remembered my speech at The Savoy and said "You wrote some great number ones Bill, the guys and gals will remember them."

"Jimmy," I said, "The guys and gals will remember you."

"Don't worry about me Bill, he replied, "The world will remember me."

I said my final goodbye and immediately went to the captain and told him that he couldn't let Jimmy speak as he'll never make it up the cathedral steps, let alone the pulpit and, if he does did, that he'd fall on his way down. When the ship arrived at Liverpool, Jimmy was immediately driven home in a car. A few weeks later he was dead and not long after, the press stories started.

I would obviously have treated him completely differently had I known about the skeletons in his cupboard and the appalling things we've since learned. In my opinion he should be stripped of his knighthood and the medal returned.

Chapter 11 - The Big Yin

Billy Connolly was born in Glasgow in 1942 and we have already talked about him working on the docks. He completed his apprenticeship as a welder but he left the job to work in folk clubs with Gerry Rafferty as the Humblebums. They made several albums of original material for the folk label, Transatlantic. Their best known songs were 'Shoeshine Boy' and 'Her Father Didn't Like Me Anyway', but they weren't hit records. Billy was a good banjo player and they were doing all right but neither had quite found their calling.

The Humblebums did a lot of gigs and Billy found that his introductions were getting longer and funnier and clearly he had the makings of a great comedian. The group split up in 1970 and Gerry continued as a musician and, as I mentioned earlier, found fame with Stealer's Wheel and then his famous solo smash, 'Baker Street'. Billy could play the banjo really well and he was a good guitarist. I don't think that he ever wanted to be a musician, yet he had the patience for it —but this ability to be a raconteur was too great.

Although Billy was still singing, he wanted to be a stand-up comic. He was one of the several comedians emerging from the folk clubs in the early 70s who also included Jasper Carrott, Mike Harding, Max Boyce, Bernard Wrigley and Bob Williamson. In my opinion though, Billy was by far the funniest and most creative of them. He was never a teller of jokes. He is a storyteller who is funny. He had tremendous drive and he drank a lot back then, but everybody drank a lot in Scotland. It was a way of life and it's partly due to the fact that we like company. We enjoy being in pubs for companionship.

He is very observant and so he can describe a hotel room to you and he will find something funny in that room. He is the best raconteur I have ever come across, and I would call him a genius. Every show is different. His brain is so fertile and funny that he can go off on tangents, but he always returns to the subject.

Billy Connolly was the first comedian to use swearing for comic effect. He doesn't need to swear and he didn't swear on the records we made. The language came from the shipyards. My parents didn't swear but when I went out, everybody was swearing, in the shipyards, at the football matches and in the pubs. I swore naturally and I had to teach myself not to. It was laziness to use the f-word for adjectives. Billy could see the comic potential of all that.

Scottish comedians like Jimmy Logan and Chic Murray had loyal followings and they didn't get bottles thrown at them. They knew how to get the crowds rolling with laughter. We were also weaned on this at the Five Past Eight Show at the Alhambra Theatre. In 1974, I helped Billy Connolly to realise a dream. I secured his first big recording deal with Polydor Records and he wanted to play the Alhambra. I flew up some BBC producers, a record executive and told Billy not to swear as Glaswegians, the likes of Billy and myself just swear naturally, and furthermore I told Billy that my mother was in the audience.

I could remember Jimmy Logan singing a parody of Adam Faith's hit, 'What Do You Want' at the Alhambra: "What do you want if you don't want briquettes?" Billy remembered Jimmy doing that too the first time he played the Alhambra in the 60s. As he went on stage that night in 1974 I again reminded him not to swear, adding that my mother was in the audience. He said, "Aye, ok" but I don't think he planned to take any notice. He bounded on stage dressed as a Teddy boy with a long coat, crepe shoes, a guitar and proceeded to sing to the tune of Buddy Holly and the Crickets' 'Oh Boy!':

"All my life I've been kissin'
Your left tit 'cause your right one's missing."

The place erupted with laughter.

Billy was also highly intelligent, enabling him to talk cleanly on many subjects when he wished.

As with the Humblebums, Billy Connolly was recording with Nat Joseph for Transatlantic and he made a novelty song called 'The Welly Boot Song' which was on Billy´s new album. The song actually belonged to me as the music publisher. You're not allowed to release a new song as a record until a publisher, in this case, me, gives you the rights and so I told Nat Joseph that I could stop the record. I said to Nat, "I own the publishing rights and I can stop the record coming out, but I will let you release the L.P. if Billy is then released from his contract for future records." Nat was taken aback but I know how to negotiate about Music Publishing.

As it happens, Billy, Phil and I did extremely well out of this. I managed to get Billy Connolly out of his contract with Nat Joseph. In its place, I got a contract for Billy to record for Polydor. Billy was paid £350,000 (equivalent to about £3.7 million in 2015) and I asked Phil Coulter to be the producer for our company, Martin-Coulter Productions, whilst I was Billy's 50/50 partner in Sleepy Dumpling Music, a music publishing company. Billy had done really well out of this thanks to me. He had got a huge advance, a giant record company, a producer, a publisher (and some very good promotion) who were determined to get him to the highest level.

Billy Connolly was very witty and very funny and he knew how to make people laugh. I thought at the time he was too Scottish to make it all over the world.

He was doing very well and then he became a sensation when he did Parkinson in 1975. In fact, it made both of them. The audience loved the fact that Michael Parkinson was laughing so much. It was a great programme to be on as he was the best TV interviewer of them all. He listened and he asked good questions.

In 1975, we got Billy to Number 1 in the UK and Australian Charts with a comic version of Tammy Wynette's country song, 'D-I-V-O-R-C-E' and then we recorded the Village People's 'In The Navy' as 'In The Brownies'. He was very, very good at doing parodies of things but he always wants to move on. It would be interesting to release the outtakes from the recording sessions one day as there are dirty versions which didn't come out. By this time, Phil and I were doing very well. We had Number 1 records as writers, producers and publishers all over the world. In fact, at this time, Martin Coulter Music was the third most successful music publishing company in the UK.

People don't realise how hard Billy Connolly worked to make the grade. He was on the road a lot and he was very disciplined. He was always there and he was always funny. We went to the Europa Hotel in Belfast, which had been bombed a number of times, and the sycophantic manager said to Billy "How did you hear about our hotel?" And Billy said, "News At Ten."

In 1978, Billy played the Troubadour in Los Angeles and despite the reports, he didn't die a death, they just didn't take any notice of him. Everybody was talking away and when Billy came on with those yellow wellies, nobody even laughed at them. After two minutes, he said, "Oh, fuck the lot of you" and walked off. I thought then that he wouldn't make it in America but he made it in a big way through a television show called Billy.

Billy's wife, Iris, now dead, was a typical Glasgow girl, all mouth and chatter. She drank quite heavily and the last time I saw her was at a party in Billy's house in Scotland. Before that Jan and I gone with Larry Page (record producer of The Troggs and manager of The Kinks) and his wife, Lee, to see Frank Sinatra in Vegas. The party at Billy's developed into mayhem.

Some time earlier, Jan and I and Larry and Lee had come across a company in LA called A Guy With A Pie. They came at you when you least expected it and hit you in the face with a custard pie. I found a company in the UK that would make cakes that you could stick people's faces in and I ordered some. Billy loved it. There was a big chocolate cake and Billy stuck my face in it. Frank Lynch, Billy's manager, had married a Victoria Beckham lookalike, and Billy stuck her face in it too, although that didn't go down too well.

I first saw him with Pamela Stephenson at Victoria Palace and I asked Phil Coulter who she was. She was very beautiful, tiny and slim. Billy never discussed women, so I hadn't seen or heard of her before. She had been married to Nicholas Ball from Hazell, a detective series co-written by my friend, Terry Venables. To me, Billy looked like Rasputin with a beautiful china doll. It reminded me too of the Scottish comedian, Chic Murray and his wife Maidie, but Pamela was far more attractive than Maidie.

Then there was Billy's fortieth birthday. He lived in Fulham and although the name of the street escapes me, his building had once been a fish factory. Billy wouldn't live in a normal place. The party was fancy dress and, as I was in my golf club stage at that time, I went in a double-breasted suit as a golf secretary. Pamela Stephenson was nine months pregnant and she opened the door as Humpty Dumpty. Billy was in some fancy outfit and George Harrison just wore a white shirt and I spent a lot of time with him. The cake arrived and out of it came the Pope. ....what I mean is that it was an actor who looked like The Pope and he was very funny.

We had been making Billy's records and when Phil Coulter became the King Sod (more about SODS later), we were all invited to Les Ambassadeurs. Phil couldn't make it because of a kidney stone. Phil's first wife, Angela, was there and Billy Connolly was a guest on the table. I became the King Sod for the speech and took Phil's speech with the Lady King Sod, Angela, who had to say something as well. She was nervous and shaking, and Billy was sitting next to her, holding her speech notes. Angela was a very soft-spoken girl from Belfast and Barry Mason, the co-writer of 'Delilah', kept calling out, "Speak up, love." He was encouraging her but it sounded like heckling. At the end of the evening in the Red Room at Les Ambassadors, we are all leaving and Billy Connolly jumped on Barry Mason and started pulling his hair. He thought that Barry had been rude but he hadn't been. They are both about the same size and Barry was fighting back. When Billy was finally pulled away from Barry, he had a big clump of his hair. To this day, Barry Mason says that Billy Connolly gave him his bald patch.

When I was captain of the golf club in 1980, I told Billy that I would like him to be there in a black tie, but he didn't have to give a speech. I was going to get Alex Hay, the golf commentator and the captain of the Royal & Ancient, Ronnie Alexander, who owned Alexander's buses, to do that.

There were 200 men at the RAC Country Club and I put Billy on a table with all my best friends. I told Billy not to let me down and wear a Black Tie and Dinner suit.He turned up in a proper dinner suit with black tie, but he also wore pink socks and slippers. He said, "You never told me about the shoes." I had a great Scottish friend, Andy Gordon, God rest his soul, who was on this particular table with some of my friends, Billy Connolly and my brother. There was raucous laughter and I knew it must have been caused by Connolly. Andy was laughing so much that he fell over backwards and there was a commotion and they carried him into the foyer. Andy was covered in blotches and couldn't breathe and they called the club doctor, who happened to be walking his dog nearby. He said, "Is there a dog in that room?" I said, "There's no dog here, there are 200 gentlemen, it's the Golf Stag Dinner." He said, "Well, this man is allergic to dogs." Just then Billy came out to see if Andy was okay and when he lent over him, Andy couldn't breathe. Andy wasn't allergic to dogs: he was allergic to Billy Connolly's hair and beard!

That night Billy really got plastered as it was during his heavy drinking period, pre-Pamela. There was an old-fashioned lift with two gates and Billy Connolly was lying across them in the lift. Nobody knew what to do with him. We got him up and got him to bed. Months later he met Pamela Stephenson and she sorted him out. His whole life changed when he married her. He stopped drinking, became an actor and was very sensible about his career. I don't think that he ever wanted to be pigeonholed and that's worked great for him. Look at how good he was in Mrs Brown, where he was nominated for a BAFTA. Then there are his brilliant travel shows. I jokingly call him the Alan Whicker of comedians.

Billy never boozed before he went on stage as he didn't need Dutch courage but he was happy to imbibe afterwards. He can handle himself in any situation. There was a pub in Tonbridge with a sign outside saying, "Welcome to the musical lunatics asylum". My father, who was visiting us from Scotland, played the piano there one night and I asked Billy to come up from Hastings, where he had been performing. He came in the limo from Hastings with Michael Parkinson. My father was a great fun guy and in fine form that night but he got so excited that Billy Connolly turned up, that he fell off the piano stool.

When I produced the musical, Jukebox, the after show party was at the Pheasantry in King's Road. At the time, Billy was being managed by Harvey Goldsmith. I didn't think that Harvey was right for Billy as he was more involved with rock stars. That night something happened as Elton John`s Manager took over Billy`s management, and they brought in a guy called Steve Brown, which was another turning-point for Billy. He is Billy's manager to this day. Harvey Goldsmith, who doesn't admit defeat, said to me, "I didn't want to manage him anyway because he's not funny anymore." Some mistake!

In April 2001, I went to Scotland for three funerals and a wedding. The first funeral was for my brother's best friend, George Robson, and it was a normal little funeral. The second was for the Scottish comedian, performer, producer and impresario Jimmy Logan in Glasgow Cathedral. Then there was one for Jim Baxter, the great Glasgow Rangers footballer. The Rt. Hon. Gordon Brown, Denis Law and Sir Alex Ferguson were there.

There were a lot of people at Jimmy Logan's funeral and you had to say you were from the Kelly family which was the password that got you near the front. I saw Billy on the other side in the pews at the front of the Cathedral and I was next to the Scottish comedian Johnny Beattie. Billy went to the pulpit and looked round and said, "I've played some places but this is something else. I never knew Jimmy Logan." What a start, eh ?

He continued, "I met him first at the Alhambra and it was Jimmy's show and theatre. There was a female Scottish singer about to go on. We had tied a toy snake on the microphone so when the microphone came up from the floor, she would see the snake. Jimmy gave me a bollocking for that." The next time I saw him was at the BBC canteen in Glasgow and he was eating a ham sandwich. Jimmy said, "This is a good sandwich", and Billy said, "Well, you've been hamming it up all your life so you should know."

The coffin was draped with the Scottish flag, The Saltire. Billy said, "It was Jimmy's wish to have a coffin with a Scottish flag draped over it as that way, we would never know if Jimmy had bought a cheap coffin."

In 2008, his wife, Pamela, who is a psychologist, wrote a book about him, "Billy", which became a best seller. I appreciate that you need notoriety or sex in a book to become a big seller, but I don't think she should have revealed that his father had interfered with him. It is terrible for his children to have a memory that their grandfather might have been a paedophile. Only Billy knows if it happened and I and a lot of other people think he shouldn't have brought this up.

Billy was on Parkinson to promote the book and I could see he was uneasy when Parky mentioned his father. Actor Ricky Tomlinson came on next and he said, "I don't know about Billy but my old man was the greatest. Even when I went to prison, he stood by me." You could see Billy's head falling and he knew he had made a mistake, and Ricky Tomlinson had seized the moment. Billy is the greatest Scottish comedian of them all and he shouldn't have tarnished himself for the sake of Pamela selling some books.

Having said that, I know that Billy is very close to his sister and, as she hasn't fallen out with him over this, it could well be true. Even so, it was best left unsaid for the sake of the children and grandchildren.

I don't see Billy very often these days but we are always friendly. When he got his toes tattooed, he sent a photograph of his feet to me on a Christmas card. He's a wonderful guy and a great comedian. He told me once what he wanted on his gravestone – "Is that it?" Billy has the most retentive and most attentive memory of anyone I've met. Thus, the fact that he is now suffering from Parkinson's Disease makes it all the more poignant. Knowing Billy, he'll make light of it and I wish him all the best. His recent Knighthood is well deserved.

Chapter 12 - Kenwood

In 1970, when I was getting divorced from Mag (my sweetheart since I was 14) I bought a place in St George's Square Mews in Pimlico. It was a bachelor pad and I was to buy five more properties in that square as an investment. When Jan and I married, we moved to Fulham but we wanted children and thought we would rather live in Weybridge. The place we found in St. George's Hill was rather special.

There was a mansion set in nearly three 'highly desirable acres', as the estate agents say, in Weybridge that was originally called The Brown House. It was bought by Ken Wood, who made his fortune from Kenwood Mixers and he renamed it, Kenwood. There was a master suite with a dressing room and study, four en suite bedrooms, three more bedrooms, five reception rooms, a games room, a sauna and a swimming pool.

Brian Epstein wanted the Beatles to live somewhere secluded. They should live outside London but within commuting distance. Paul McCartney wouldn't leave the city and he bought a property in St John's Wood, very near EMI's recording studio in Abbey Road. Epstein spoke to some friends who were lawyers and accountants and some of them lived in St George's Hill and they said that it was secluded and secure.

Thus, John Lennon bought Kenwood in 1964 and lived in it until 1970, first with his wife, Cynthia, and then with Yoko Ono. In 1968, Cynthia had returned from holiday to find Yoko in residence. In 1970, John and Yoko moved to Tittenhurst Park.

After John Lennon moved into the area, the Gordon Mills Management brigade joined him – with his protégées, Tom Jones, Engelbert Humperdinck and Gilbert O'Sullivan, all of whom had properties in the area along with the comedians Eric Sykes, Dick Emery and Tommy Trinder who all lived there too.

John didn't use a lot of Kenwood. He spent most of his time in his music room in the attic and that's where many of the Beatles' songs were written. It still had the same blue window when we moved in. The Beatles had their annual Christmas parties at Kenwood and the sleeve for Rubber Soul was taken in the grounds. Besides the other Beatles, the visitors to the house included Bob Dylan, Peter Cook and Michael Nesmith from the Monkees. There was a large, psychedelic eye mosaic in the swimming pool which has since become famous in its own right.

I didn't buy the house from John Lennon. Billy Atkins, a local, somewhat dodgy character, had bought it from him but the house was in limbo for a long time because he went bust and refused to let anybody in. I kept seeing the picture of this house in the papers and I wanted to buy it. Billy Atkins went bankrupt so I went to see the liquidator in 1976 and he said, "You can't see around it as Mr. Atkins won't get out of the house."

Coming from Govan, nobody scares me. As I went to the door, at Kenwood it was opened by two big guys with baseball bats and Alsatians, which were snarling at me. Billy Atkins himself was a small chap and I told him that I wanted to buy the property.

He said, "I'm not selling it to you. I'm getting a special deal in cash from somebody else."

I said, "I will match that special deal in cash but I have to see around the house first."

He let me look around and I knew right away that I had to buy it. Billy Atkins wanted cash on the side, but I said, "I can't give you cash for nothing. I have to buy the property from the liquidator. If I am to give you some cash on the side, then I would have to buy the kitchen furniture or whatever."

As a result, he left me everything that was in the house, which was just as well. He had been planning to smash the place up, which was would have been terrible as there were, for example, some beautiful leaded windows. I'm sure that the carpets were as they had been in John Lennon's day. I know John had several cats and there was still a smell of cats' wee.

I did find something unusual and I can't believe that Billy Atkins would have bought it. It was a little model of a girl throwing a snowball and at first, I thought nothing about it. It must have been bought by John or Cynthia and it turned out to be worth £10,000. That was more than I'd given the fellow for all the goods. I'm not the stereotypical Scotsman but I do get some things right.

Only a fool tells all but it's now documented that John bought Kenwood for £20,000 in 1964 and spent about £40,000 on it, hoping that some mad millionaire would buy it, or maybe another pop star. I don't know what Billy Atkins paid but I bought it for £56,000 and it was a magic house, a great investment.

The only drawback was our house sign that said 'Kenwood' was buried in the ground outside the gates. As soon as we put one up, fans would take it. We gave up in the end. We took the sign, "The public are requested not to walk on the grass", with us from Kenwood and we see it every day

Bill Martin with his Soldier Toy 1939

Clyde Shipyards

*Mag and I standing on
Victoria Falls*

*Bill Martin visiting Taransay Street
where he was born*

*Bill Martin
and Phil
Coulter
1976*

Andy Williams, Claudine
Longet 1969

Georgie Fame Rio
de Janeiro Song
Festival 1969

Sammy Cahn in Los Angeles 1968

Sammy Cahn

Wednesday
April
3

My Good Chum Bill,

It was awfully nice to hear from you and to open the
letter which exploded into the kind of publicity clips
that only a Sammy Cahn could get! Come to think of it
your problem is that you are The English Sammy Cahn!
(I'm glad you are over there TWO of us any place would
be too much!!!)

I am back in Los Angeles just to take the Nose-Dive at the
Oscar Race. I think that it will be either Look of Love (Because everyone thinks I win EVERY year! And Burt Bachrach
has never won!The same could happen for Bricusse who has
never won!) Oh well we shall see! About me winning - don't
worry about the key chain, IT'S LIKE THE GIRL SAID, "IT
CAN HOLD A WEE ONE!!!"

It looks now like I may be back in Rio for the next festival
along with Paul Anka (a good chum) and if you are going to be
there it will be fun to meet up again!

Nothing much else except that I am working hardeer than ever
and wait until you get a load of some of the title songs they
have hit me with, ready? " A FLEA IN HER EAR!" and "THE
ODD COUPLE!" and "STAR!" Fool with that for a while. The
way my luck is going they may have me do the title song for
that Chinese Movie Star "LOTTA NOOKY!" Maybe you better
write it!

My warmest to you and make sure you say Hello to all my chums
and special one to Cyril Simons!!!

Sammy.

Cliff Richard, Cilla Black 1968

Bill Martin and Lionel Bart 1975

Lionel Bart 1965

Yoko Ono 1982

Sandie Shaw Eurovision Win 1967

England World Cup 1970 - on Top Of The Pops singing "Back Home"

Bernie Ecclestone 2004

Sir Alex Ferguson at Royal Ascot 1995

Denis Law,
Rod Stewart
1974

In my office
at Alembic
House
1980

Rod Stewart and Dennis Law at the launch of the 1974 Scottish World
Cup Song

Sevriano
Ballesteros after
playing with Bill
at the RAC Golf
and Country Club
in 1980 when
Seve was the
Open Champion

KENWOOD,
St. George's Hill, Weybridge, Surrey

John Lennon at Kenwood with his son Julian 1967

Bill Martin at Kenwood with his son Angus 1980

John Lennon and Bill Martin's house Kenwood in 1967 and 1980

Scottish World Cup Squad - Denis Law and Willie Morgan leading the players

Bobby Moore, Geoff Hurst and Alan Ball reaching number one with "Back Home" 1970

Sir Tim Rice is tall!

Sir Matt Busby, Rod Stewart 1974

Terry Venables 2002

Jose Mourinho 2004

Luis Figo 2004

Sir Geoff Hurst and Kenneth Wolstenholme

*Billy Connolly at RAC
Golf Dinner 1980*

*Bill Martin by Lord Litchfield - my
Royal Automobile Club photo as
Golf Captain in 1980*

LORD LICHFIELD 1982

*Lord
Litchfield
and I at
lunch at
the House
of Lords*

*Bob Hope STV Golf
Day 1981*

Arnold Palmer 1981

Jack Nicklaus and
Gordon MacRae 1981

Bill Martin with the Ryder Cup
Trophy

Jimmy Tarbuck - The UK's answer
to Bob Hope 2016

Gary Barlow 2009

The great lyricist Hal David 2010

Errol Brown 2004

Katherine Jenkins 2010

Mike Batt Mitch Murray, Paul McCartney, Wayne Bickerton 1995

Michael Parkinson 2010

Sir Bob Geldof at Elton John's Party 1998

Hugh Hefner 1979

Lord Olivier 1993

Sir Sean and Micheline Connery and 1998 Jan Martin

Sir Terry Wogan

Terry O'Neill International Photographer 2005

*Marty Wilde, Bruce Welch, Me (King SOD),
Justin Hayward and Sir Tim Rice 1995*

*Sir Elton John 2002
Man of the Year*

*Chuck Berry
the Cole Porter
of rock n roll!
1990*

*Holland Dozier & Holland Motown
Hit Songwriters 2004 Ivor winners*

All the SODS in the Houses of Parliament 1991

Paul and Linda McCartney with Bill Martin
1987

Paul and Linda McCartney at the Capital
Awards 1987

Meeting the Queen for the first time in 1985 at the Royal Variety Performance of my musical "Jukebox"

Margaret Thatcher, Jan Martin, Sir Bernard Weatherill (Speaker of the House) at 10 Downing Street 1991

1991
THE RT HON MARGARET THATCHER & SIR BERNARD WEATHERILL
PRIME MINISTER   SPEAKER OF THE COMMONS

Meeting the Queen at Windsor 2016

My daughter Alison and her husband John on their wedding day.

My daughter Melanie and her husband Rupert on their wedding day.

Angus Macpherson and Alison McClure with Jan and Bill Martin at Buckingham Palace 2014

My daughter Meran and her husband Wilf Moore on their wedding day

My granddaughter Jessica Vander Motte

Team Townsend.....Barnaby, Melanie, Poppy, Rupert and Huxley

Jan Martin on her Wedding Day with Ushers Stuart Olley, Phil Coulter, David Bateman, Ian Macpherson and Best Man Michael Mander 1972.

After we left our wedding reception we joined Barry and Sylvan Mason's wedding with fellow friends Ernie Wise, Stuart Reed, Barry and Sylvan, Les Reed and Tony Macauley all stamping on Mitch Murray.

through the window of our home in Portugal, although we have no grass out there.

Later in the year in 1976, I spoke to Bernard Brown, who had worked at Apple and then for me and was going to New York to see John about a court case. I said, "Please ask John what songs he wrote at Kenwood." John sent me a lovely, affectionate letter. He loved Kenwood as he called it "an old friend". He told me some of the songs he had written there including the ones for Sgt. Pepper.

He was so modest in that letter as he could have listed so many songs. I have always said that 'Help!' was my favourite Lennon and McCartney song because I believe John was actually crying for help. I always enjoy hearing 'The Ballad Of John And Yoko' which is John's take on Chuck Berry with some very funny lyrics. He didn't take himself too seriously.

Lennon and McCartney were a great team and they were at their best together. I love 'Help!' and 'Hey Jude'. I loved the Beach Boys and Brian Wilson was an amazing songwriter but 'Back In The USSR' is, in my view, on a par with any Beach Boys song. When it comes to their solo albums, I think McCartney was better. I love 'Maybe I'm Amazed' and his 'Live And Let Die' should have won an Oscar. I would rate him higher than Elton John and George Michael in that regard. He has the melodic flair of Mozart and I think he's great.

When I spoke to George Harrison, I told him that Dark Horse was a great name for his record company as he was the dark horse of the Beatles. Lennon and McCartney got all the acclaim but at least 8 songs should be Lennon-McCartney-Harrison because of his guitar contribution. George said in his laconic way, "But I didn't write them."

209

If I were on Desert Island Discs, I would not choose one of their songs but a song that they didn't write. It would be 'Twist and Shout,' 'Money' or 'Please Mr Postman,' because they sounded so raw and so fantastic on that and I would have loved to see them doing it in the Cavern. They were sensational recordings

Much as I love Lennon and McCartney, I do think Burt Bacharach and Hal David are brilliant songwriters with songs like 'I Say A Little Prayer', 'Alfie', 'Walk On By' etc. Hal David was a lyricist every bit as good as the great songwriters of the Thirties. He once told me that his favourite song from the "Bacharach/David' catalogue was Alfie.

My memories of Kenwood are first class. Jan wasn't too keen as the area was rather hilly but I liked it and I was at the golf club a lot. It was a long and winding road to get to it and I believe that Weybridge also inspired Paul McCartney to write both 'The Long And Winding Road' and 'Fool On The Hill'.

We loved entertaining and we had great dinner and lunch parties at Kenwood, but there were problems. There were big gates with a little door at the side and we couldn't keep the fans out. They turned up all the time, especially the Japanese. They would wander in without an invitation and want to photograph the pool. One fan even stole the little door of the official gate of the house. That was a nightmare.

People used to say, "I gather you live in John Lennon's house" and I would say, "No, I live in my own house."

Gordon Mills lived in St. George's Hill. He had seven acres and a zoo and I had three acres with the old Lennon house. He had a power complex and he owned a gorilla, an eagle and a tiger. We went to his house one day with a few songwriters and their wives and he was ever so proud of his gorilla. Barry Mason and his second wife, Sylvan, Jan and I, Roger and Brenda Greenaway, Les and June Reed. We saw the gorilla (Ollie was his name - after Oliver Reed) as we drove in. There was a gatehouse and there he was. He would wander over like a human being and he went to Sylvan and held her dress. Gordon shouted, "Leave her dress alone." The gorilla stepped back and his strength was such that he pulled her dress right off. She was there in a pair of knickers, high heels and what was left of the dress. It was like a scene from King Kong. Gordon jumped into the cage and started whacking the gorilla to get the dress off him. Most of us decided that discretion was the better part of valour and went back into Gordon's house. In future, whenever Sylvan came back to the house, the gorilla, because he still had the dress, would sense that she was at the roundabout nearby and would be bouncing off the cage. She is now a top music business photographer, Sylvan that is, not the gorilla !

Gordon saw me as a big publisher and Bill and Phil as talented songwriters. He had MAM publishing which included 'My Way'. He said, "Why don't you write for my company?" I said, "Well, you need to buy Martin-Coulter Music Publishing first and then I'll run MAM and that would be a perfect fit."

It never happened but one day he said, "Would you believe what that bloody Gilbert O'Sullivan has done? He was a nanny to my kids and I gave him a house in the garden and 'Clair' was written for my daughter and she laughs on it, and now he wants to leave me. He says he is not getting this and not getting that and I own his songs. Greedy little bastard."

A few days later, Gilbert called me up and said he wanted to leave Gordon Mills. He said, "I am going to sue him for my publishing." He also asked me if I would represent him but I declined as he had a great lawyer called Charles Negus-

Fancy, whose sister, incidentally, owned the rights to the soft porn movie, Emmanuelle.

I said, "You can leave anybody but you don't understand the power of these people. You'll get your songs back but your career will be over."

He said, "I still want to sue him."

Gilbert having Charles Negus-Fancey as his lawyer, it was relatively easy to get the songs back because his contract was terrible and disgraceful. The upshot was that he never got another decent recording contract and he has only recorded with small labels since then. He made the wrong decision and he would never be a big star again. He should have stayed where he was and negotiated. I could have done that for him and he would have done well. He could have got a good deal and Gordon would have kept Gilbert's copyrights for a limited time.

When John and Yoko were making Double Fantasy in 1980, I tried to buy the new Lennon songs from the album as May Pang, Lennon's former girl friend, told me that they didn't have a publishing deal. Back in 1969, I remember the publisher, Laurence Myers telling me that he was making a bid for Stevie Wonder's next album and it would be an advance of £50,000. He claimed that within a month he would have his money back

This was the first John Lennon album for several years and I thought it might be worth considerably more. I didn't know for sure, but I felt that the songs were going to be great and if there was one huge hit, I would soon recoup the money. I bid £250,000 and oddly enough, the deal went to David Geffen for precisely that amount, and he got both the record and the publishing. He was one of the founders of DreamWorks along with Steven Spielberg and Jerry Katzenberg. John and Yoko liked him a lot and he was the first person that Yoko called when John was shot. He also had a great reputation as a music man.

Bernard Brown and George Harrison said they spoke to John regarding my request for a letter and John sent it to me which made me very proud. John also phoned me from New York and said he wanted to come over and see Kenwood lived in properly by a family - but as the world know, he never made it! After his murder on December 8th, Lennon entered the legends pantheon with Elvis and James Dean and he would have loved that.

I had framed my letter from John and I put it on the bookcase in the study. In 1980 I was captain of my golf club and I was coming back from the club in the inevitable Rolls-Royce with a driver and I'd had a lot to drink. I got into bed. Duke Ellington's band could have been in our bed, it was so large, and suddenly I heard this noise and I said to Jan, "That's the kids." All the kids had microphones in their bedrooms and she said they were okay. I looked at the clock, it was 4.10am, and went back to sleep.

Jan got up the following morning and told me that John Lennon had been assassinated in New York. What I had heard during the night was a tape recorder playing backwards and nothing looked wrong in the house except that the framed letter from John Lennon had fallen on the floor. John Lennon was killed at the exact time that I looked at the clock. No other framed photos or letters had moved. I'm not saying that this is a psychic happening, that's up to you to judge, but I am just telling you what happened.

His death had a profound effect on me as I realised, perhaps for the first time, that anybody could kill anyone else if they really wanted to.

You can't say accurately or assess how the world has been deprived. Double Fantasy was a great album and John may have written more great songs in the intervening 34 years. On the other hand, he was one of those radical types who could have gone off the rails completely.

Although I bought Kenwood for a very low price, I moved out on a very different level. I made a good profit but I will always regret selling it. I didn't need to sell it but I wanted to be back in London. I recently saw Kenwood offered for sale for £15.8m.

Dear Bill,

      A line to thank you for lending Bernard to me...thanks Bill!

I hear your living in an old freind of mine..keep an eye on the pool!

George (H) sends his best..he was in N.y. both he and Bernard

said you were interested to know which songs were written there.There

were so many....here;s a few,

I Am The Walrus

A Day In The Life

Across The Universe

Rain

We Can Work It Out..(middle 8)

Help

and on and on and on...

John Lennon

p.s. I won the case.(maybe B.B doesn't know?)

215

Chapter 13 - Alembic House

The Star Tavern in Belgravia was my local pub, tucked away in a cobbled mews and run by an Irishman, Pat Kennedy. It was well named as it was the discreet watering hole for some of Britain's brightest stars. On a typical day, you might find several of Britain's best actors in there and certainly some dodgy characters, even gangsters. The Star apparently is where the Great Train Robbery of 1963 was planned.

There was the Welshman Stanley Baker, who had starred in the war film The Guns Of Navarone. He was often cast as a tough villain, but in reality, he was an astute businessman, sometimes producing his own films including Zulu, the film that launched Michael Caine's international career.

Richard Harris, who had come to fame with his portrayal of a rugby professional in This Sporting Life, would be there, often with his brother, Dermot. Aside from his stage work, he made great films like Camelot but mostly he made films for money. He had an immense talent but he did waste it.

Richard Harris wasn't that tall, probably 5ft 11, a bit taller than me, but he was broad, so he had an overpowering presence. He would come right up close to you when he was talking. It was never "Hello, how are you?" from a distance. He was always hugging you.

Richard was majestic, absolutely majestic. I've never seen anybody drink a bottle of vodka so quickly and he could move from that to Jameson Irish Whiskey, and he would still be lucid and talkative. He would be laughing and exciting and demonstrative. I would be smashed but he would still be larger than life. He was sensational company but he was a voracious drinker. I can't recall him eating at all. He wasn't argumentative but he was a great debater. You had to put your point back to him. He could be a Catholic talking about the Pope and saying the Pope was totally wrong. He loved to talk and he wanted you to come back at him. He never was a man who liked fighting and punching and I knew I would never get a punch from him, no matter what I said.

There was also the Canadian DJ Mike Lennox who made his mark with the breakfast show on the pirate ship, Radio London. He would sometimes bring along the BBC radio producers, Don George and Bernie Andrews. We'd call Don 'Two Lunches' as he would accept invitations from promotions men who were trying to get their records played on the BBC. He would think nothing of eating a lunch at noon and another one at 2pm. I'm not implying that there is any payola or bribery here – just that he ate a lot of lunches!

The veteran actor Trevor Howard who had made Brief Encounter during the war also drank in the Star.

Stanley Baker and Richard Harris were both generous, gregarious and lots of fun. Sadly Trevor Howard treated me with disdain referring to me as that "noisy little Scottish prat." because he hated the Scots. Of course, he never refused a drink from me – and he would always want a large Scotch – but he never once bought one for me. These were all-day session drinkers, almost from dawn to dusk and beyond, and I was often carried along. My capacity for standing up has often surprised me. Still, there was always great craic, as the Irish say, egged on by the Star Tavern's manager Pat Kennedy, who would join us for a drink, throw up in the loo and return to the bar for another!

Thugs loved to be around Richard Harris – Johnny Bindon, a good-looking gangster who allegedly had an affair with

217

Princess Margaret, loved him. Bindon was one of the most violent men in London, a terrible fellow. He came in one night covered in blood and he said that he had just hacked a guy's leg off with a Samurai sword! I believed him as he was a bad, bad guy.

Johnny Bindon had a huge 'John Thomas', that's to say he was well endowed. Richard Harris used to say, "Come on Johnny boy, get it out." He could balance nine half-pint jugs on it by the handles. You may not believe that but I have seen him do it in the pub. The landlord said, "Come on, we've had enough of this, boys." Richard said, "For Christ's sake, Pat, we've all got one of them." The landlord said, "Not like that!" Johnny Bindon became an actor, invariably playing thugs, but he should have been starring in porn movies. The cause of his death at just 50 is unclear, with both liver cancer and AIDS having been cited.

One afternoon in August 1967, I was standing at the bar listening to another Scot who was chatting away. Property in London was booming and everybody wanted to be a part of it. "Do you want to buy a building?" he asked Stanley Baker and me. Instead of saying no, we said, "Where?"

Apparently, in 1965, Felix Feinstein, a Mayfair property magnate, had built Alembic House, a tower block at 93 Albert Embankment in south-east London as a present for his son. He wanted him to have the best penthouse and best view in London. It had been designed by the architects, Oscar Carry, but it wasn't their finest hour and viewed from outside, it was a blot on the landscape. Inside, it was something else and it offered the finest waterfront views of London that you could imagine. You could see the Houses of Parliament, St Paul's, the Shell Building, the River Thames and the City of London.

In order to protect the existing Thames skyline, the Labour Government had been putting a block on new developments, but Felix had found a loophole in regulations. He maintained that it was a warehouse, despite it being a 14-storey, glass-fronted tower on the Thames.

Then he told Lambeth Council that as they already had M15 and the CID in their area, they might like the CIA as well. The first nine floors of Alembic House were earmarked for the CIA, but Felix never said that this was not the famed Central Intelligence Agency but the Chemical Industries Association. By the time the council found out, nothing could be done about it.

The council agreed with the proviso that the 10th, 11th and 12th floors should be private apartments, and the top two floors should be one single, luxurious penthouse. This was to encourage wealthy people to live in the area. Felix implied he could get Frank Sinatra for the penthouse, although, of course, there was nothing in the contract about this.

After the building was completed, Felix's son was on the last flight that used to go from Glasgow to London when it crashed and he was killed. He was only 21. As a result, Felix believed that there was a bok (a Jewish word for bad luck) connected with the building and he wanted to sell it. There were 365,000 square feet and he wanted just £365,000.

This is what was being put forward to Stanley Baker and myself.

Stanley and I were intrigued so we decided to take a look and the 3 of us jumped into a taxi. It certainly had magnificent views and we were very impressed. We went back to the Star and told Richard Harris that he should join us to buy it. "Yeah, why not?" he said, nonchalantly. Stanley also brought in two of his friends, Michael Deeley and Barry

Spikings, who had had considerable success in the film business. As a result of this, I was cut out of the deal and was rather annoyed.

The film composer John Barry was a friend of Stanley's and he had written the music for his film Zulu. He took the lease on the 10th floor (the lease that Jeffrey Archer later took over including John's telephone number ending 007), Stanley the 11th and Richard Harris the 12th. Felix didn't get Frank Sinatra for the penthouse but it went to Bernie Ecclestone. The place quickly became a thriving hub of actors, actresses, musicians, producers and directors...and probably some ladies of the night. I was often there as Stanley said that I could use his office at any time. There were some fabulous parties and everybody enjoyed the views, which were featured in many TV shows. The board room scene in which the crooks meet in The Italian Job was filmed in Stanley's apartment on the 11th floor.

Everybody who moved into the building had bad luck. John Barry wrote the scores for the James Bond movies and he had a huge tax bill. He left the country so quickly that he even left his suits in the wardrobe. Years later he paid the tax he owed back to the Government and was allowed to come back to the UK earning an OBE on the way. John probably became finest film composer the UK has known and was given a great tribute after his death at the Royal Albert hall hosted by the incomparable compere, Oscar winning songwriter Don Black.

For a time, Henry Mancini's music publisher, Larry Shane, lived there. He and Mancini split up and their company, Compass Music, was finished. More bad luck.

Stanley Baker kept falling ill and his two associates struggled with their finances and their film company, Oakhurst Productions, was skint, even after the success of The Italian Job. Richard Harris didn't have financial troubles but his brother, Dermot, died in the building in 1986. Bernie Ecclestone, who, despite his court tribulations is wonderfully mystic and great fun, was in his penthouse when the UK property market crashed in 1974.

Even the CIA – the Chemical Industries Association – moved to new premises. Various smaller companies took their place. The Bank Of Boston failed there and so too did Jim Slater, the stock market legend who became famous as a 'minus millionaire'. When he left the building, he became successful again.

In 1972 Stanley and his associates set up Oakhurst Properties to buy the whole of Alembic House, which they did with an enormous loan from Barclays Bank. When the market crashed in 1974, they were in deep trouble. In his own book, Michael Deeley admits that they did not see the crash coming.

As a result, in 1975, Michael Deeley and Barry Spikings took me to lunch, behind Stanley's back, at the White Elephant Club. It was a restaurant where film deals are made and I remember seeing Richard Burton and Elizabeth Taylor there many times.

They offered me the lease on Stanley's apartment, the 11th floor, for £35,000. They also persuaded me to buy the office safe for £1,000, but that was a con as the safe was unmovable. I ended up with a lease that would run until 1998 for just £3,000 a year and it was to be worth many millions in the long term.

It turned out that Stanley Baker, Michael Deeley and Barry Spikings were directors and shareholders in the same company. Stanley was away and so they had a board meeting and voted on selling the lease to me. I don't blame Stanley for being furious but it wasn't my fault.

Weeks later Stanley Baker came round with a massive minder and I thought I was going to be beaten up. I explained about the meeting in the White Elephant and said that it wasn't me he should be beating up. He calmed down and said he wanted to take a few things from the flat and I said that he could. Sadly, Stanley Baker, whom I liked a great deal, died of lung cancer in June 1976. Deeley and Spikings went off to America with my £35,000, which in my opinion helped them to get the finance for their classic movie, The Deer Hunter and an Oscar for them as producers.

At the time, there was no point in having an office in Tin Pan Alley. That had gone. All the publishers had been there on cheap rates – that's why they were there; they were all cheapskates. As I said at the start of the book, Harry Hyams had got planning permission nearby and built Centrepoint. He thought it was going to be a huge success and so he then bought up the leases in Tin Pan Alley. In so doing, he destroyed Tin Pan Alley. I'm sure he wanted to build a second Centrepoint but he didn't manage to fill the first one and he didn't get planning permission.

I moved into Alembic House with Phil Coulter for Martin-Coulter Productions on 30 January 1976. At the time, we were Number 1 around the world. The Bay City Rollers had 'Saturday Night' at the top of the American charts, and we had Number 1 songs with Slik's 'Forever and Ever' and Billy Connolly's 'D.I.V.O.R.C.E' but we were jinxed too. Phil and I had the discipline to write songs together, but now we would only meet once a week for a few hours. We never wrote any hit songs there and I had a writing block until 1985. When I look back on working with the Rollers, Cliff, Sandie, Billy Connolly etc, I am proud that Phil and I achieved Number 1s all over the world.

I had to get out of the building and indeed, I faced five years of acrimonious court actions with Phil as we dismantled one of the most successful songwriting, music publishing and production partnerships in British pop history. It was like a painful divorce and it was ruining my life, my career and my marriage. I even got breathalysed and lost my licence for a year. Now I never drink and drive.

As luck would have it, an Australian property company approached me and asked me if I could secure the penthouse for them. Bernie Ecclestone's penthouse was filled with beautiful ivory and Netsuki porcelain Chinese art, but he was getting divorced (more bad luck) and he wanted to be out of the building. I offered him £2m for the penthouse and we shook hands on the deal, but the Australians let me down and I had to apologise profusely to Bernie for the mess. The sale wasn't going ahead. Fortunately, a guy called Ron Shaw heard about the penthouse and said he wanted to buy it, so that was good news. Bernie hated to be let down, he believes in his word being his bond and it is, but it didn't take me long to get his friendship back as he got his money.

While I was negotiating with the Australians, Jeffrey Archer moved into the 10th floor on a short-term lease. A talented former Tory MP, he was also bumptious and arrogant but was enjoying huge success as a novelist. I knew the length of all the leases and when his time was up, we had to sort out the sale. Bernie Ecclestone wanted to move on and Ron Shaw didn't want the penthouse after all and did a deal with Jeffrey Archer to buy the penthouse. Bernie knew exactly what was going on with Shaw and Archer. Archer bought the Penthouse for 2.2 million pounds.

Through my golf club connections, I approached Legal and General who now owned the whole building. I told them that if they put up the money, I could sort out the leases and then they could sell the property. I had to deal with Jeffrey

Archer who was a sitting tenant as his lease was up. He wasn't paying the rent for his 10th floor flat and he was refusing to move. He owed them something like £41,000.

So, in 1993, the country's biggest selling author, and an ex-MP to boot, was ostensibly squatting as his lease was up and he wanted the freehold! Legal and General wanted him out but didn't want to sue him because of his so called power. With the agreement of Legal and General, I told Jeffrey that he could have the penthouse and Legal and General would overlook the money he owed them if he gave me the keys. This was an astonishingly good deal. He said okay and I asked him what I would get for doing this deal. He offered a 20% arrangement fee. I wanted it in writing and he turned to his secretary and said, "My god, the barrow boy asks me for a piece of paper. My word is my bond." And did I get any money for arranging his move and clearing everything up? No, of course not, but I have the paperwork to prove his obligation to me re the owed rent and unpaid commission. Maybe he'll read this book and honour his commitment. Yeah, and a pig may fly past his penthouse window.

One of the richest families in Hong Kong bought the building and again I was asked to sort out the leases. Eventually, the building was empty, except for Jeffrey Archer grandly installed in his penthouse suite. The plan was to convert the other 12 floors into 36 flats and I was offered one of the refurbished flats in lieu of a fee. However, in view of the disastrous history and bad luck associated with the building, I politely declined and took the fee.

The refurbishment started in 1995 and a tragedy occurred immediately when two workmen were dismantling a mast and their work platform turned over and they fell to their deaths from the ninth floor. Some Chinese investors bought the building but they felt it lacked feng shui and wanted to sell it. It was developed by Regalian Properties PLC, who had invested in London Docklands and had built the M16 building just a few doors away from Alembic house.

Alembic House was converted into flats but only a week after moving in, the head of Bell's Whisky died in an air crash. It was all too spooky for me. I don't know if there really is a curse on the building but opposite the building, on Millbank, Pimlico is the quayside where convicts were put on transport ships and sent to Australia. There is now a Henry Moore sculpture and plaque to tell you that this was the boarding point for the convicts. This is the source of the acronym 'POM's as when they arrived in Australia, they were known as the Prisoners of Millbank.

One of those convicts had committed fraud. His pregnant wife was standing with her mother on the shingle on the other side, exactly where Alembic House would eventually be. They could see him in manacles and leg irons being pushed onto the ship. His wife wailed and screamed and was in so much distress that she miscarried. She died on the spot along with her baby. Her mother, a gypsy, was said to have put a curse on the very spot where she died, and maybe there is something in that.

These days the building has been redeveloped with a new façade. It is now called Peninsula Heights. Perhaps the building has got over its bad luck but I won't be moving in again. Oh, and Jeffrey Archer is still in that penthouse. Think of the bad luck he has had with prison, the public humiliation over his mistress and the loss of his reputation. The penthouse looks fabulous but knowing the building's history it could almost be referred to as a glass coffin. As my mother used to say, "You can lose your house, you can lose your virginity, you can lose your job but don't lose your reputation because you can never buy it back."

Chris Smith a labour cabinet minister said at a Labour Party conference "The Labour Party are a Party of convictions – the only convictions the Tories have are Jeffrey Archer and Conrad Black. Jeffrey would have got his peerage because of his phenomenal work for charity and auctioneering.

Chapter 14 - Breaking Up Is Hard To Do

I. Goodbye Phil

There was a trade press advert in 1974 that listed our successes and it looked very impressive, and the next year we were awarded The Ivor Novello for Songwriters of the Year. We were having global success and it went to Phil Coulter's head. Then suddenly, it was zilch. We had stopped. What happened? What went wrong?

Phil was hardly involved in the day to day work and I had built up a very impressive publishing catalogue. We had East Memphis Music, which included 'Knock On Wood'. '(Sittin' On) The Dock Of The Bay' and 'In The Midnight Hour' as I had travelled round the world buying songs. I had Booker T. & the MG's 'Time Is Tight' which was used for the BBC's test cricket broadcasts. In today's money and based on the viewing figures, we would be paid over £100 each time it is used.

I discovered Eric Bogle, who was from Peebles and based in Edinburgh. I had my catalogued administered by Sony at one stage and they were wary about some of his song titles, not realising that they were ironic. He had some unusual titles that, on the face of it, looked objectionable.

Eric Bogle was an exception to my rule: normally, I have no interest in folk songwriters as their songs all sound the same and they write dirges. That's a wild overstatement of course, but I've never been able to fathom what John Martyn, for example was all about. Eric Bogle was different as he had some really thoughtful songs. His big one, 'And

The Band Played Waltzing Matilda', was a brilliant song about Anzac Day in Australia.

When punk came in at the start of 1976, nobody seemed to want decent songs anymore. Groups thought they could write anything and get away with it, and rubbish was being released everywhere. The record companies didn't know what to accept anymore. Some people say, "Of course there were good songs. What about Elvis Costello?" but I'm afraid he's never impressed me. I also thought it was disgraceful that he took Elvis Presley's first name and Lou Costello's second. I can't warm to him although I do like 'Oliver's Army'. His father, Ross McManus, who sang with Joe Loss and his Orchestra, was a far better singer.

I preferred Sting to Elvis Costello, and his 'Fields Of Gold' is a very pretty song. 'Every Breath You Take' is a spooky song, all about a stalker, but I would like to have heard Elvis Presley sing that. I met Sting at the Ivor Novello Awards one year when we were both guests of the MD of EMI Peter Reichardt and I called him by his real name, Gordon. He said, "Call me Sting". How pretentious is that, especially when his father is a milkman called Ernie. Makes you wonder if Benny Hill knew him.

In my opinion, the best song that Sting ever sang wasn't one of his. It was a very good version of Vivian Ellis' 'Spread A Little Happiness'. I knew Vivian Ellis and went to his 80th birthday party. All the music industry songwriting giants were there and he crept up on me and said, "The best song written since the early 60s is 'Puppet On A String'." Not quite true - he must have fancied me.

Mitch Murray who wrote 'How do you Do It' and 'Bonnie and Clyde' among many others was a great songwriter and he is such a brilliant and witty after dinner speaker that you wondered why he isn't still writing, but he won't. He says that the arrival of punk in 1976 killed it for the 60s songwriters. That's true but it's also a very negative outlook. There are always people who will record your songs if you go looking.

It is even easier to make a recording now. Kids have great equipment at home and they can post a song on the web within minutes. I don't care for The X Factor or Pop Idol as the winners, with the odd exception, like Will Young and Susan Boyle, are mostly pub singers or club acts who won't last.

The mid-70s was also that time of real excess with the top rock bands. I knew Alan Callan who worked for Peter Grant, the manager of Led Zeppelin. They were the first big rock band to collect money at the arenas. They made sure that they got every dollar in cash and they would pack into briefcases from the turnstiles and give it to Pinkerton. The van would be driven away from the arenas before they played so they always knew that they had the money.

Alan Callan was responsible for paying the bills. There was a hotel in California, Montmartre, which is where the Eagles' Hotel California is set. Rock stars and film stars stayed there and Led Zeppelin had famously had their motorbikes inside the building. They had complete excess in everything they did - excess all areas!

The sycophantic clerk who was preparing the bill said, "Lovely to have the Zeps here. 300 bottles of Dom Pérignon, yes, 50 cases of Budweiser, yes, 16 television sets thrown out of the window, yes." He added, "I have always wanted to do that."

Peter Grant said, "Have a television on us."

He said, "Thanks very much. Can I do it now?"

Peter Grant said, "Okay", so he went upstairs and Led Zeppelin watched him throw a television set out of the window. He came down and changed the bill to 17 television sets thrown out of the window.

While Phil Coulter was away in America with Angie and his children, I was given this new song, 'Isn't She Lovely' by Stevie Wonder, and told that I could record it. I had already produced an album with Buddy Greco and I had one of Phil's arrangers with me, John Drummond, who was a good guitarist and songwriter and had been in the Boston Dexters: sadly he's blind now. I wanted to do that song and Gilbert O'Sullivan's 'Matrimony' with Buddy Greco. 'Matrimony' had a reference to frozen peas in the lyric, and I was talked out of presenting it to him. It was a mistake as he would have done it very well.

By now, we had a big music publishing catalogue and Coulter had half of it so he had nothing to complain about. I was never jealous of anyone else's talent and could spot a good song. I was a large publisher and should have been gigantic but I lost my way when we split.

Geraldine Branagan his mistress at the time split us up.

Phil had been seeing Geraldine for five years and I didn't know about it. His wife didn't know about it either. How devious and deep the guy was. His father had been a chief detective and you have to be clever and keep your own counsel in that job, so I suppose he had picked up something from him.

At first, I didn't know that Geraldine was his girlfriend and I certainly didn't know I was paying for her flat in Dolphin Square through our joint company. He made some dreadful records with her. He got Geraldine to represent Luxembourg in the 1975 Eurovision Song Contest and we wrote 'You (Toi)' for her. It was the year that Teach-In won for the Netherlands and she came fifth. In the end I said to him, "Phil, we have spent £100,000 on this Farrah Fawcett-Majors lookalike with a big bust and she can't sing. Let's get rid of her."

Phil said, "You're talking about the woman I love."

I nearly died!

That is when I found out that she was his mistress. I was shocked: I could understand myself having an affair but not him. He had a wife and three children.. His father was a chief detective, his brother was a priest and his sister did a lot of good work. The link between us was broken but it took another seven years before we finally drifted apart.

As there was a flat within our office, Phil, with my permission, moved into Alembic House with Geraldine and it was an acrimonious seven years. They had a baby in their first three months there and I couldn't bring people to the office to do business because they would hear the baby. You can't run a business like that. The door would open and a nappyless kid would walk in. It was disastrous. I built a wall between us and the grand piano was on my side near the door. I had such a laugh about this as I used to say Phil's hands would come through the letterbox to play it.

We had started a new company and I wanted to call it Razor Records and the singles would be numbered Cut 1 and Cut 2 etc and so on. We'd have an old Gillette razor blade as the logo. Phil thought it sounded too punk and thought of a label called Coma. I didn't realise it at the time but he was putting his name first - COulterMArtin. He had always wanted his name in front of mine. Phonogram paid us a fortune in advance, but the records went into a coma and never recovered.

I knew that our partnership was over and I had to get rid of the staff and sell the business.

Phil took me to court so he could remain staying in the flat with his new family and he had music lawyers and I had other lawyers; foolishly not my music ones. His lawyers were told that I owned the lease and I was selling that lease to Legal and General. That was nothing to do with him as I was doing a deal with Legal and General for the whole building. I was getting the whole building clear so they could turn it into flats, except for the penthouse suite to which Jeffrey Archer had the freehold.

One day in the midst of all our troubles, Phil said, 'I could have you killed.' I said, 'What are you talking about? The IRA?' He said, 'It costs less than you think.' I don't know if he was bluffing or not, but that shows you how bad it was between us. I thought, "What are we descending to? Now I'll have to look over my shoulder."

But mostly, it was like a French farce. At one stage, I was inside the office/apartment and Phil was taking our gold records from the walls and, as quickly as he did, my wife Jan was taking them back again. Phil said "Can we change the date of our leaving to December 28?" Geraldine was pregnant with twins but I said no. It was a tough decision given her condition but basically, I evicted them from the building.

Geraldine has had now six children with Phil, making him a sire of 10 in total ! When people tell me that Phil has got yet another honorary doctorate, I always say that he should have one from Dr Barnado's.

The court case was very disruptive. I was wandering around without much purpose and drinking too much. I sold Kenwood when I didn't need to sell it. I sold it because I didn't want the association with Phil Coulter as he'd been there. I was leaving my office because he'd been there. I blamed him for the failure of my musical Jukebox and we'll come to that later. I wasn't thinking properly and I was destroying myself. I wanted him kicked out of my office, kicked out of my life, kicked out of everything. I didn't need to sell the Martin-Coulter companies to avoid the association with him as I could have given it to EMI to administer for a small percentage until I got my head right.

It was the worst period of my life, and I've had some bad ones. We were a great team and we could have been one of the West End as great songwriters with musicals. I had the push and drive and we had the talent for working things out.

When Phil and I split up, Billy Connolly took Phil's side and I was sorry about that. I think he had poisoned Billy against me. I'd taken the publishing and Coulter was running me down. That made me sad as I like both of them.

I didn't see Billy for 11 years and then I went to see him in 1989. His manager, Steve Brown, gave me tickets and I took Jan and my daughters. Billy gave the worst show I had ever seen him do. It was like he was talking to me. You know, I'm a multi-millionaire now and I have got this beautiful wife and he was telling me how big he was since we had split up. That said, we saw him backstage and he was okay.

On the Friday night, Jan and I had tickets with some of my best friends, Alan Crossman, Wally Ball and Peter Bradley, and we were put in the back row. I said that I wasn't going backstage again. Billy came out flying and he was sensational that night. Phil Coulter was in the third row, and Billy introduced him as a musician, a songwriter, a producer and a man with so many talents and here's a joke that Phil told me. Maybe I'm paranoid, but I was sure he was having a go at me again.

I had Jan with me, and I always give people the opportunity to make amends. The show finished and I was waiting outside and I saw Phil Coulter coming up and I said, "Phil" and Geraldine gave a little gasp. Phil said, "Bill, Jan, how are you? The four of us must get together." He was going backstage to see Billy and I said, "I was there earlier in the week and I'm not going tonight." Phil said we must all get together again but he didn't mean it. I didn't see him again until we got our Gold Badge awards from the British Academy of Songwriters, Composers and Authors in 2009.

Phil Coulter has achieved his ambition of being an Irish star in his own right. He now plays 'Danny Boy' at the piano with a violin string section and that's what he always wanted to do. Van Morrison and I call him Paddy Clayderman and he doesn't like that. But nothing is original in being a piano player. Liberace, Clayderman, Russ Conway, Bobby Crush etc

In 1988, Jan and I were back in Ireland and we were with an English couple in a taxi and I was in the front of the taxi and the other three were in the back seat.

I said to the cab driver, "So you have a big film business here?"

He said, "Oh, we're as good as Hollywood. We made millions last year."

I picked up Tom cruise the other day oh and Speilberg.

"And you've got that rock group, U2."

"Yes, they're bigger than the Beatles. Last year they made £358m."

I said, "Have you ever heard of that guy that plays the piano, Phil Coulter."

"Oh, the lovely Phil. He plays the piano beautifully."

"And will I see him?"

"You might, you might, you might. He does a lot of concerts and TV."

"And he wrote songs too."

"He did, he did, he did. Lots of songs for the Bay City Rollers and he won the Eurovision Song Contest. He has had number ones all over the world."

"Aye," I said, "But didn't he have a partner?"

"Yes, he did he did it was some foreigner but I think he's dead."

Phil and I will never be that close again as we have both moved on and if you met him, you would never believe that he had done anything wrong. He had four children from his first marriage (one died) who knew my four children and they were all pals, and I am sorry that they lost contact. I have never met his other six children. What saddens me is that I had created a magic name, Martin and Coulter, a brand like Crosse and Blackwell. It. was exhilarating and it was sad to see it sinking into oblivion.

I considered Phil Coulter to be a sad man, not a bad man. I had no time for him but I am pleased to say that, having met him at his wife, Angie's funeral in July 2014, along with the children from his first marriage and my kids, we have reconciled somewhat. It was a pity that we met again under those circumstances as I had been very close to Angie when

Phil and I were partners, but at least some good came out of it. Who's to say we will not write together again.

II. Sky's The Limit

When we split up, Phil kept the production side which was chiefly Billy Connolly and the Irish band, Planxty. I have to credit Phil with finding Planxty a brilliant Irish folk. That was a group of very talented musicians - Liam O'Flynn, Donal Lunny, Andy Irvine and Christy Moore.

On the other hand, I had Sky from day one. In 1979, Peter Lyster-Todd, who was a photographer's agent, came to see me. He looked after Norman Parkinson and Lord Snowden. He was putting a group together with John Williams, Herbie Flowers, Tristan Fry, Kevin Peek and Francis Monkman, and they were going to be called Sky.

It was a fantastic combination of talents and it worked perfectly. They were a great group. Herbie Flowers played the tuba for many years in an RAF band and he played bass on Lou Reed's 'Walk On The Wild Side'. He had been a member of Blue Mink, who sang 'Melting Pot' and he was a great bass player, being heard on hundreds of records. He had written 'Grandad' for Clive Dunn from Dad's Army, the Christmas Number 1 in 1970. In spite of all our hits, I never had managed a Christmas Number one. I liked Herbie and wanted to be involved with him as a publisher.

John Williams, who came from Australia, wasn't really for me as he was in the classical field, but he was a brilliant guitarist, arguably the best in the world. Kevin Peek was also a guitarist from Australia and like John Williams, he had studied music academically. He had worked on a lot of hit records and had toured for several years with Cliff Richard but sadly died recently in Australia.

Tristan Fry had been a drummer with the London Philharmonic Orchestra and he had worked on pop and classical records as well as with some avant-garde composers.

The organist Francis Monkman had had hit records with a prog rock band, Curved Air. He had had some weird ideas but I knew he could write film scores. Phil Coulter thought of himself as someone who could do that, but this guy really could. Francis was married to a Japanese girl, Gingko, and at the time, he was already writing a film score that he had promised to someone else. That was The Long Good Friday, a phenomenal gangster film set on the Thames with Bob Hoskins and Helen Mirren. That was also Pierce Brosnan's first movie in the important role of 'First Irishman'!

They were all really nice guys and I could see that this was a group made in heaven. I put the money behind Sky and I owned half the management with a piece of the record sales and I took an admin fee. Our Martin-Coulter company owned half the publishing with their own company, SKY Writing. We had a share in anything they wrote for Sky including 'Toccata', which was very popular and became a hit. Anything they wrote outside Sky, they could keep for themselves. They sold millions of records but they broke up through bad management, but it was inevitable as all five of them had individual careers.

Peter Lyster-Todd was a nice guy with the gift of the gab. In my opinion, he was not nasty at all but he treated management as a game and so was incompetent and lax. When finally, he found himself under pressure, he had a heart attack. He recovered and he learnt from his experiences. He is now a huge promoter in Australia with Paul Dainty. He is married to a beautiful girl, Isobel Griffiths, who is the main fixer for some big film scores. A Fixer is someone who get's musicians work. She is highly respected and she was awarded a Gold Badge by the British

Academy of Songwriters, Composers and Authors (BASCA) in 2007.

III. Speaking to celebrities

Commercial radio was big business by the early 70s and I knew I had to get my songs on their playlists. There were two bright guys running Radio Clyde, Andy Park and Richard Park, not brothers and not related, and Richard ended up running Capital Radio in London. They gave me the opportunity to make some programmes and I was interviewing songwriters such as Henry Mancini, Johnny Mercer and Sammy Cahn and footballing celebrities too like Denis Law and Matt Busby. Making programmes for Radio Clyde was a great experience and also a great way of being friendly with a Scottish radio station so that they would play my songs. Both Parks were very kind to me by playing our songs a lot.

In 1976, I went to a dinner at the Savoy where Princess Margaret and Danny Kaye were on the top table. Danny Kaye said, "In this terrible world we live in, we should have less of that (mimes punching) and more of this (holding hands), and none of that (finger pointing) and a lot of this (hugging). When we can all get that, we will be better people." He sat down to great applause. He and Princess Margaret wanted to smoke so they went outside for a fag together. The photographer Doug McKenzie told me to walk out with them for a photograph with Kaye as he knew the camera liked me and I was songwriter of the year. I touched Danny Kaye's sleeve and he said, "Get your hands off me, kid." I said, "Less of this and more of that." I repeated his own poem –I got the photograph!

Way back in the 1960s, Sammy Cahn told me that I was tailor-made for New York. He said, "You have that aggression and New York is very aggressive. You walk down the street and a tourist will say, 'Can you tell me where the Statue of Liberty is?' And the guy will say, 'What do you think I am? The tourist board?' He'll walk on because nobody gives a shit about you."

He gave me this advice, "When you go to New York, get in the taxi tell them the address and that's it. Tell them to shut up."

I had a black coat with a black velvet collar, my gloves and a briefcase. I got in a taxi when I arrived in New York just for one night and said, "Plaza Hotel please."

The taxi-driver said, "Are you in business?"

I said, "None of your business."

"Are you on holiday then?"

"None of your business."

He asked me which way I wanted to go and I said, "Pick the quickest route."

He said, "You staying a few days?"

I said, "What's that got to do with you?"

"I'm only trying to be pleasant," he said, to which I snappily replied, "Forget it."

I was being aggressive. We drew up at the Plaza Hotel and he said, "That's $33."

I said, "I'll have to get out of the cab as the money is in my back pocket."

He said, "That's not a problem."

I got out of the car, put down my gloves and my briefcase and took out the money. I gave him $100 and he drove off.

I said to the doorman, "Stop that yellow cab."

He said, "Which yellow cab? They're all yellow." It goes to show you shouldn't be that aggressive and the lesson had cost me $67.

Through Sammy Cahn, I would meet everybody at the Beverly Hills Hotel. I was very friendly with Dudley Moore and he was a real funny man who could play the piano like you wouldn't believe. Dudley said, "Let's go to the Playboy Mansion." We went up there. I kept my tie on and there I was with Hugh Hefner in his pyjamas and got to get a real Playboy photo with Heff.

I was offered my own television show in 1976 by STV (Scottish Television) but I turned it down because I wanted to be at the golf club every weekend. I reckon I could have been the Terry Wogan of Scotland as I was a big personality on the radio. Well, maybe not quite as busy as Terry but you get the idea.

I enjoyed being a guest on television programmes and I was involved in one classic moment in broadcasting history. Bill Tennant was the Terry Wogan of Scottish television and he was on every night at 5pm. He would turn up at the station at 11am and by lunchtime, he would have drunk half a bottle of Scotch. Then he would have lunch and by the time the programme came on, he would be there with his big red face, having drunk about two bottles of Scotch.

This particular day I was on the show with Rod Stewart, Denis Law and Johnnie and Fanny Craddock. They were the first TV cooks and Johnnie would sometimes wear tails and Fanny would boss him about. On that day, she was cooking us doughnuts, and at the end, Bill Tennant says, "What a wonderful show we have had today. We know that Rod Stewart is the new king of rock'n'roll, forget Elvis. We have had the prince of soccer, Denis Law, never mind Pele, and we have had wee Bill Martin writing all these Number 1s all over the world, putting that tartan everywhere with the Bay City Rollers, and we have had Fanny and Johnnie Craddock cooking us these doughnuts and Bill Tennant turned to the camera and said – "All I can say to you people in Scotland is may all your doughnuts turn out like Fanny's." We managed to stifle our mirth but I remember the cameraman falling off the camera with laughter because of that.

IV. K-Tel

In the early 70s, I met a Canadian guy, Philip Kives, who owned the marketing company, K-Tel, and he had an Australian, Don Reedman working for him. Don had a great ear so chose the songs for the compilation albums. I could see that TV-advertised compilation albums of hits could have a terrific future and that could be great for songwriters like myself. We could get our songs on there and have more sales, and I knew disc-jockeys would love these compilations: it made life easy for them.

I spent a lot of my own money flying to the Continent all the time so I knew everybody in the music business in Europe. I went to America and Canada and Australia. I could pick up the phone and they would know who it was as opposed to just a name in the paper. That is how I exploited my publishing catalogue and I still do it. A lot of people relied on their publisher or the record company to do that, but I did everything myself. That's why I deserve what I get.

Elvis Presley, the Beatles and the Rolling Stones had no control over their catalogue. RCA had Elvis. EMI had the

Beatles and Allen Klein had the Stones. They all said no to including them on compilations with K-Tel or anyone else. They wanted to keep the tracks to themselves because it didn't dilute their catalogue. It might look a bit tacky if Elvis was a compilation with some one-hit wonders, say. We weren't big enough to be bothered with anything like that so I exploited my songs to the hilt. I am on compilation albums all over the world and that doesn't bother me.

V. Francis Albert

Although I support Rangers, I enjoy watching football. Celtic were playing in the European Cup Final so I flew to the game in Milan. It was May 1970 and they were beaten by Feyenoord 2–1.

When I got back, I was due to see Frank Sinatra, Bob Hope and Grace Kelly at the Royal Festival Hall in London but my plane was delayed so it looked like I wasn't going to make it. Kenneth Wolstenholme managed to find me a place on a Celtic plane to Glasgow so being a Rangers supporter, I naturally took a lot of stick, but I can handle myself.

I arrived in Glasgow but I still had to get to London. I had a friend, James Blyth (later Lord Blyth) who was in the Ministry of Defence and I asked him to help me. He couldn't put on a plane for me, that just wasn't possible, but if I dashed to the airport, I would get on such-and-such a scheduled flight to London. I phoned Jan and asked her to get to the airport with my black tie and dress suit. She was there and I changed in the car and we went to the Royal Festival Hall.

At the time, I was out to impress Jan, my future wife, and the tickets were £100, an extortionate amount back then, but it was for charity. We went into the fourth row –saying "Excuse me" all the way – and we had two seats in the aisle outside row 4. Then came a television camera and two huge backsides in front of me and the cameramen were talking, "This is okay, but when Frank comes out, we will get him over there." When Bob Hope came out, they were nattering all the time. Bob Hope then introduced Grace Kelly and still these people were talking. I was not going to put up with this, especially after the hassle with my delayed flight.

In the interval, I went to the organiser who was there with his wife. I said, "I have paid all this money for tickets and yet I am sitting behind the camera and I am not going to see Frank Sinatra. You've got to give us better tickets or I'll kick those cameras out of the way." He said, "There is no need to do that. You take my tickets." They were in the fourth row too but they had better seats. So we sat right in the middle of the fourth row and Jan said, "This is great, fantastic."

Frank Sinatra came out, bouncing across the stage, with a long lead. He was walking the stage and prowling like a panther. He was singing 'You Make Me Feel So Young' and there was a guy in front of me with a huge mop of fuzzy hair, almost like an Afro, the largest I think I have ever seen, but he was swinging on time, I'll give him that. I wanted to say something but Jan said, "Don't you dare speak to him, we have had enough trouble. Don't poke him in the back." Frank finished the song and said, "And that's for my friend in the third row, the best set of pipes in the music business, Mr Tony Bennett.", who then stood up to acknowledge the applause. Tony Bennett wears a wig and I watched the show through the black fuzz of Tony Bennett's hair. I couldn't say 'Sit still' to Tony Bennett.

I looked across to the charity organiser and he had moved the cameras out, so now had the perfect seat, and that was Jeffrey Archer and his wife, the fragrant Mary. He took 8% of the box office so even then he was making money as the charity organiser. He knew what he was doing when he swapped the tickets - and I watched Sinatra through a black fuzz. Incidentally, Frank made an error that night. He said

"I'd like to sing the Lennon/McCartney song, "Something.".
In fact, it's the best song they've written." The problem is
that it was written by George Harrison.

We met Sinatra personally in 1977. Sammy Cahn had given
me a letter to see Sinatra in Las Vegas. It was at Caesars
Palace and I was with record producer Larry Page, formerly
the singer known as the Teenage Rage, and our wives as his
wife, Lee, was my wife's best friend. She was a tall slim
brunette and Jan's a blonde. We got a call from Jilly Rizzo, a
restaurateur who was also Frank's minder and close friend.
We were told that we could come up and see Mr Sinatra but
we were not to shake hands. Sinatra never shook hands with
people as he said that was how you caught germs. Also, you
weren't to take photographs and there must be no kissing.
We went up and he saw Jan who was very attractive and he
said, "Oh, hi" and kissed her. He said, "I am really sorry,
kids. I am not singing tonight because I have got the Desert
Throat, but I have got a great replacement and you will love
him." It was Paul Anka. I didn't like to say, "Oh, shit", but I
was ever so disappointed. Paul Anka was good but he wasn't
Sinatra.

My stockbroker was Stephen Raphael, who was very highly
regarded. He told Colgate that he could increase their
profits by 50%. He looked like Alfred Hitchcock and spoke
in a very English voice and they were so impressed that they
offered him a great deal for his secret. He said, "Make the
hole bigger" and it worked. They made the hole bigger and
you are all using more toothpaste because of him.

Another time he got two million for Errol Flynn for making
a film, another two million when they finished and then two
million when it was released. The film was supposed to be
made in six weeks and there were various tranches for
getting paid. The filming schedule was so delayed that the
movie was never made, so that they paid Errol off with
another two million, half a million he gave to Stephen.

He was a very clever man but his son Chris was not. His son turned up that night at Caesars Palace in Las Vegas to see Frank, dressed in Gucci shoes, no socks, a kilt, a black tie and a black jacket and with a paintbrush for a sporran. He thought he was being funny. Paul Anka started his act and introduced some personalities in the audience. He said, "I am starting with a Scottish guy who is a great friend of Frank's" and he is walking towards me in the booth. This idiot with the paintbrush was about to acknowledge the applause, so I pushed him to the floor and hid him under the table. Paul Anka went, "Will you stand up please, Bill Martin?" and I stood up, at the same time holding down this idiot.

Not that my behaviour has always been perfect. I went to see Anthony Newley (who was married a few times, including to Joan Collins) backstage after a show in Vegas. I had met him with lots of other people before, but I didn't really know him. I said to someone, "Please tell Mr Newley that Ron Kass has come to see him". He came out, having dried his hair, and said, "You're not Ron Kass!" I said, "I know, but I just wanted to meet you." He said, "Well, you've met me and I should say "Fuck off" because I don't like that kind of behaviour. I know who are, Bill, and don't ever pull that stunt again. Always be yourself. People gear themselves to meet someone whom they haven't seen for ages and I was looking forward to seeing Ron". We had a good conversation after that. He told me that he would have liked to have entered Eurovision but he never felt he had the right song.

Newley was an East End character trying to be a gentleman but there was always something East End about him. He was very bad with money. He lived with his mother at the end as it was all gone. He was a great actor and he loved songs. He wrote some great songs himself but I'll remember him more as a performer than a songwriter.

Chapter 15 - Golf At The RAC

I. In Britain

I was never really interested in golf as a pastime until I came back from Africa and I met Drew Neill, who was from Edinburgh, and a scratch golfer and his brother, Bobby, who was the featherweight boxing champion of Europe. He was taught golf by Ronnie Shade's father.

I got keen and through golf, I got to know so many people. I went to see Jan's father in 1970 before I married Jan and he said, "Would you like to be a member of the RAC?" I thought it was just the road organisation but he took me to this country club in Epsom and membership was £30 a year or £450 for life. To impress him, I became a life member of the town and country club and then I became captain of the golf club. When they sold the motoring services in 1998, they gave all the members £35,000. So I got that and because I was captain of the golf club, I got free golf.

Jan's father had been a golf captain at the RAC in Epsom and was very influential. As a result, Jan and I were the first people to have our wedding reception at Epsom in 1972. It was all in tails and the numbers had to be limited.

Shortly before our marriage, Jan and I were with Henry Mancini in the Mayfair Hotel and he said that he would write a tune for us to walk down the aisle and I thought that would be fantastic. Jan said, "I really appreciate that, Hank, but I have always wanted to walk down the aisle to 'A Whiter Shade Of Pale'." He said, "You mean Bach", and she said, "Well, you may call it that."

On the way to our wedding, Jan and her father passed Epsom registry office and outside was another 'B M' songwriter getting married, Barry Mason. Jan waved to Barry and his new wife Sylvan as she passed by.

When we left the RAC after our wedding reception, we drove off in our Mini, turned the corner and picked up our Rolls-Royce and driver. From there, we went straight to Barry and Sylvan's Mason's reception in Esher. I had some songwriters at mine – Mitch Murray, Peter Callander and Tony Macaulay, with Phil Coulter as one of the ushers – but he had most of the others. When we got there, after being married five hours, Barry Mason said to Ernie Wise, "And Bill and Jan have got married today as well", and Ernie said, "And they said it wouldn't last." Actually, Barry's marriage didn't last and he has been married twice since then. Ernie and Doreen Wise became good friends of ours. Strangely, Ernie was not a particularly funny man in real life and his wife is much funnier.

After we'd returned from honeymoon, we were told that there had been an accident after our wedding reception. The twin sisters Mary and Judy Downs had been there and Mary had stayed behind with some friends. She was sitting outside on the staircase and she laughed and felt backwards. She hit the floor and died a few days later from her injuries. There is now a plaque that says that it is dangerous to sit on the banister. When my own daughter got married there at the RAC in 2010, I made sure that nobody sat there.

We went to the Dorchester on our wedding night and we were going to see Jesus Christ Superstar. We were bored after the first act (sorry, Tim; sorry, Andrew). Maybe it was because we were just married and maybe it was because we knew the ending. We went back to the Dorchester and our friends, Larry and Lee Page, came to see us. We watched

Match Of The Day and we went off on our honeymoon the next day.

We had a week in St.Tropez. I saw an American songwriter reading the Financial Times, a funny paper for an American songwriter to be reading, but it was Mike Stoller, who wrote many songs for Elvis like 'Hound Dog' and 'Jailhouse Rock'. He was sitting on the beach next to me but I never spoke to him. I should have taken the opportunity and it's most unlike me not to do so. Perhaps it was the surroundings.

We collected my two little daughters from my first marriage at Nice Airport and then picked up our Rolls-Royce in London. We all took the train to Scotland, the Rolls-Royce as well as you could take cars on the train then. There was also a dog, a west highland terrier from my first marriage and we all toured around Scotland for three weeks and had a great time. I played a lot of golf too.

Jan has been a great influence on me and I needed it in those early years from 1972 to 1976. I gave up all the night clubs. I went to the golf club and Jan was fine about that as it was all guys. I became a golf fanatic but I still drank. I loved competitions so much that I created a special cup, the Golden Egg Cup, for just my brother and me. We even put the results in the Daily Mail.

My brother and I became very close after my success and although I paid for everything, I was pleased to able to share it with him especially as he was a good laugh. We played golf together and I even took him to Jack Nicklaus' Pro-Am in Ohio on Concorde and when he came to London and he met everybody through me.

The British Open is run by the Royal and Ancient Golf Club of St Andrews and their ground, Muirfield, was very snooty. Captain Paddy Hamner had a loud voice and drank port like you wouldn't believe. My brother and I were due to play golf there and his car kept breaking down when he picked me up at the airport. We had to be there for 10.02am as that was when we had to tee off. We got there just in time. When we put our bags down, Paddy asked, "Whose bags are these?"

We said, "They're ours, we're just signing in."

"Stand them to attention," he ordered. "Start at the first and I'll be watching you." He could see the first four holes. I hit the ball to the left and my brother hit the ball to the right. We both lost our balls in the rough. I said, "Pretend to have played a shot because he is watching us." We lost a few balls on the first four holes because we were that scared of him.

I vowed not to go back there but I wanted to see the Open when it was held there in 1980. You couldn't get into the club house unless you were a member of the R&A, but I had a bet with my brother and two pals that I would get in. A security man was watching everything but when he bent down to eat his sandwich, I walked into the clubhouse. I looked the part with my white hair, collar and tie and all that. I asked for a pint of bitter and a sandwich. The barman said, "Prawn sandwich, open top?" and as I didn't want to get into a conversation, I said that was fine. I was about to take my first bite and I heard this booming voice saying, "Gentlemen, I have a strong belief that there is an intruder in this room." All my prawns fell in the pint and I now had beer with prawns in it.

I sat quietly in the corner and he said, "We'll find him. Don't you worry, gentlemen." I think my white hair blended me in with the members and he didn't notice me. After a few minutes, he said, "The intruder must have gone, gentlemen." I didn't move for a while and I drank my beer, put my glass on the bar and walked out. The boys applauded me as I had managed to enter into the members' clubhouse bar.

That night we went to the local pub and we asked for four pints of bitter.

He said, "Is one of these for the guy with the white hair?"

They said, "Yeah."

He said, "Would you like me to put some prawns in it? I work at the golf club during the day "

Then he said to me, "I don't know how you escaped as we all knew where you were, but nobody would tell. Anybody else with prawns in their pint would have asked for a new one."

I was fortunate to get to know one of the world's great golfers, Jack Nicklaus, very well. He had his own Golden Bear company and in conjunction with that I made an instructional book, a training video and cassette tapes with him in 1979. His parents were German and when I met him, I said, "Jack, you know, I think one of your relations bombed our fish and chip shop." at which he laughed, taking it in the spirit intended.

I became captain of the RAC Golf Club at Epsom in June 1980 and it was the best year of my life. I was the youngest captain ever and it was such a thrill. I wasn't a particularly good player – my lowest handicap was 9 but generally it has been around 17 – but I had ideas. I inaugurated so many different things like the Dawn Patrol, which started at 4.15am on the longest day of the year, and the Past Captain's Plate and the Rosebowl, which encourages competition with other clubs. They are still being played for today. I also designed and gave to the club, for all past and future past captains, a tie which is still worn 36 years after the event.

I was about 11 stone and I got a suit made like the Duke of Norfolk with a belt in the back and plus-fours and a jacket and a tie and a cardigan. In September 1980, I hosted the Bob Hope British Classic, a pro-am event featuring golfing stars and show business celebrities including Sean Connery, Bob Newhart and Henry Cooper.

In that match, I was playing with Bob Charles, who won the British Open, a New Zealander, the first left-hander to win it, an up and coming Greg Norman and the comedian Jimmy Tarbuck.

The announcer said, "On the tee, Bob Charles". Straight down the middle.

"On the tee, Greg Norman". Straight down the middle.

"On the tee, Jimmy Tarbuck." He cracked a few jokes and hit the ball straight down the middle.

Just before it was my turn, Jimmy said, "You are not playing in that bloody jacket, are you?" I took my jacket off but kept on my cardigan and my tie.

"On the tee, Bill Martin" I could see my right elbow going up when it shouldn't go up and I hit the ball badly to the left. It struck a man in the head, a woman on the throat and another man in the eye. My ball bounced off their heads onto the walkway.

Greg Norman said, "You've got a free drop" which means I could drop it and play again. I wanted the ground to swallow me up. I hit it again and it went to the other side of the walkway and Greg said to me, "You've got another free drop." I heard people shouting "I'm okay. Save the women."

I hit the ball again and that was okay. As we were walking along, I said to Jimmy Tarbuck, "That's the first time I've ever done that." He said, "I should bloody well hope so. You've killed about three people there."

When we got onto the tee, those three golfers putted for a five and I got a five but, because of my handicap, I had a stroke deducted, so I was really the best on that hole. I shot a 76 which was a net 59 but nobody saw that. It was reported in the Daily Telegraph the next day – be aware of Captain Bill Martin if you're going to a pro-am. Nobody sued me but I did send flowers to the people I hit.

We asked Bob Hope to open the new bar at the RAC and the plaque said, "This bar was opened by Bob Hope, September 24, 1980." It was the 19th hole. Bob Hope said, "I believe, Mr Captain, that this is the only hole that you play consistently well."

Bob said to me as an aside that none of his pals would believe that he was opening a bar as he hadn't had a drink since he was 50. He only drank Coca-Cola. He had been a comedian who loved the ladies and who loved drinking. One night he did a show and lost his timing. A comedian can't lose his timing and so he stopped drinking just like that. Timing is everything in singing, in golf, in football, in telling jokes. You mustn't lose your timing.

When I was captain, I virtually took two years off . I was drinking a lot, enjoying myself and having fun. I hardly ever saw Jan, who was bringing up our children. It was all male company with no messing about, but I fell over and hit my head. They took me to Epsom Hospital: there used to be six mental hospitals in the vicinity and they had shut them with the Care In The Community policy. The remaining patients were all in Epsom Hospital.

The nurse said to the secretary of the RAC Golf Club, "This man has had too much to drink. He says he is the captain of the RAC. We'll just put him in the psychiatric ward for the moment."

Sure enough, one of the patients on the ward asked, "Who are you?"

I said, "I am Bill Martin. I am the golf captain of the RAC. Please leave me alone."

He said, "Don't worry, mate, they'll soon sort you out here. When I came in, I told them I was the Archbishop of Canterbury."

I said, "I'm sorry, I really am the captain of the RAC."

He responded, " I really am the Archbishop of Canterbury."

I discharged myself there and then as I'd had enough.

I liked joining clubs and I wanted to wear the MCC tie. Somebody approached me just because I was captain of the Golf Club and asked if I would like to be a member of the MCC. My proposers were Ken Barrington and a wicketkeeper for Sussex, Mike Griffith, whose father, Billy Griffith, ran the MCC. I thought I would be in very quickly but it took me 20 years to become a member and I only got in about 10 years ago. I go with Mike Griffith, who became MCC President in 2013 to matches and MCC dinners and he is a great companion and top man and his wife Carol has known Jan since they were small children.

The Press Club was the best place to drink in Glasgow as you could drink there all night. One of the reporters said to me, "I've got an idea for a great photo shot, Bill. It's you in the early morning, driving a ball down Sauchiehall Street." I said, "Okay, we'll do it." It was 4.30am and the longest day. We got there and I hit the ball and it was bouncing down the street for three miles. It stopped right outside where the Glasgow Empire used to be. I think I can stake a claim to having hit the longest drive ever.

II. Fighting With Oliver

There was a guy at the RAC Golf Club called Roger Cook, a businessman not the songwriter, and I had renamed him Sir Roger Cook. He was a member of Sunningdale and we were coming back from Sunningdale to the RAC at about 3pm. We were in my Rolls-Royce with my driver. In those days, the pubs were closed in the afternoon but Roger knew the Royal Oak in Leatherhead so we stopped there were greeted by the landlady, Doreen.

Roger said, "What would you like, Bill? A pint?"

I said, "We've been drinking champagne all day and we shouldn't mix our drinks, so I will buy a bottle of champagne."

The place was empty but from the back I heard a booming voice, "Do I smell a Scotsman in this establishment?"

Doreen said, "Behave yourself!" and this man got up and it was Oliver Reed. He had just woken up and had heard our voices. He said to me, "You must be the Scotsman as he looks like an English gentleman."

I said I was.

He looked at me and said, "I'm going to knock you out."

Doreen said, "Please, Oliver, we don't want any trouble."

He said, "Trouble? There won't be any, but I'll just fucking annihilate this Scottish bastard."

I had to think fast. I said, "I'll fight with you, that's no problem, but we've been driving quite a bit. Can I have a glass of champagne first?"

Oliver Reed said, "All right, but I don't drink that stuff myself. It's for poufs." Sir Roger and I had a glass of champagne while Oliver Reed tore off his shirt and displayed his massive torso. He was not tall, but he was broad.

As I was stalling for time I said, "I can't fight you on a full bladder. I'll go to the loo first and then I will come back and knock you out." Instead of the Gents, I went outside and saw my driver and I said, "Get the car running, get the door open and when I come out, I'll jump in and we're off like a rocket."

So I went back in the bar and Oliver Reed said, "Come on. Let's fight."

This time I said, "Do you mind? I'm fully clothed and you've stripped yourself off like a hooligan." He said, "What did you say?" and he lashed out and broke a chair, and Doreen said, "Oh, for god's sake, Oliver!" and he said, "Put it on my bill. I'm going to wipe him out."

I said, "I have no desire to see your body sprawling all over the floor in this lady's establishment. I'm going to take you outside and batter the living daylights out of you, and when you come back in, you'll be apologetic to Sir Roger, myself and Doreen."

He said, "I'm going to crunch you."

So we walked to the door and he was screaming and shouting, and I said, "You're supposed to be a great actor. Surely you can talk without shouting." As we opened the door, I kissed him and jumped in the car and drove off. I then sent the Rolls back for Sir Roger.

I met him some years later and he said, "You little bastard, I remember you. That was a funny act you pulled in the pub." By the way Oliver Reed, came back the following week and gave Doreen a beautiful chair.

III. In America

Bob Hope gave me his home number and he said, "If you're ever in the States, why don't you play in my golf tournament?" We had a flat in Fort Lauderdale in Florida at the time, where we had just arrived, and I phoned him. He said, "Ah, the little Scots guy from the RAC. Do you want to play in a Pro Am?" and I said, "Yes." I said to Jan, "Don't unpack our bags, we're off." We went to the airport and we went from Florida to Palm Springs, which is like going from London to Florida. We got there and there was the programme – I was to play for four days with the pros including Jack Nicklaus, Arnold Palmer, Doug Sanders and Bobby Clampett - and we got a big bag of goodies! I say 'goodies' but that is a disservice. It included a watch, clothes, whisky, crockery etc

When we went there that evening, we thought that we were going to dine with Bob Hope and his wife alone. A bus picked us as he lived up in the mountains on a private estate called Southridge. A lot of people got on this bus and then we were told to get off and transport would take us up to Bob's house. We jumped in this car and two other people got in as well. Bob Hope had invited them too and I still didn't twig. I thought it would be six of us for dinner.

His house in the mountains was the size of JFK Airport and modelled on its mushroom shape. He had invited 300 people! The big logs on the fire were really tree trunks. All the tables were laid out like pizzerias. Bob walked about, talking to everybody. We met Phil Harris, Gordon MacRae, Howard Keel, Jack Lemmon and Burt Lancaster. They were all golfers and golf has a wonderful way of levelling everything. It was like being in an auditorium and Bob Hope had a one-hole golf course in the back garden.

So I played in the Bob Hope Tournament at the Indian Wells Golf Club in Palm Springs in January 1981. He had invited Jack Nicklaus, Arnold Palmer and Seve Ballesteros as well as the entertainers, Don Rickles and Bob Newhart. I was on the first tee with Jack Nicklaus and Gordon MacRae, and Jan's father had got her a press photographer's badge and so she was inside the ropes with 35 marshals whilst 3,000 spectators watched from the other side.

Out walked Jack Nicklaus and everyone applauded. He had white shoes, brown trousers and a white shirt with a Golden Bear logo, he was the Masters and Open champion then. I was wearing the same shirt and I thought, "Oh dear, this is like me going out with the head of M&S and wearing an M&S shirt with their logo --I can't do this." So I rushed in and changed into a white shirt, pale blue trousers and white shoes and I returned to the tee.

I hit the ball to the left and moved there, and Nicklaus went, "Where's the little Scots guy?" Because it was Palm Springs, all the marshals had white hair, white shirts, pale blue trousers and white shoes. I looked like a marshal. The only thing about me that was different was a tartan hat from the Bay City Rollers' days. I put it on and I looked a pillock and I was doing everything wrong. Jan has got a picture of me with Jack and he is leaning on me, cleaning his shoes, and Jan changed the caption to, "Get off his back, Jack, he's carried you for 13 holes."

I was rubbish that day and I was walking down to the par four 18th, side by side with Jack Nicklaus having hit my one and only great drive. There were 2,000 watching at that hole and it was on CBS television. I was shooting 145, my worst game ever, and I told Jack that I had done everything wrong except a fresh air shot. Jack said, "Well, you've still got half a hole to go." Talk about pressure. I hit the ball and it wasn't a fresh air shot. It went on the green. Jack hit his ball but not as well. Jack took two putts to my one meaning I shot the hole in three and Nicklaus in four. Everyone was saying, "Who's the guy with the white hair?" and I was signing autographs. Jack was delighted for me.

The next day I was playing with the legendary Arnold Palmer, the John Wayne of golf. He never spoke to me for the first seven holes. He was standing there practising putting on the tee and I was chewing gum and he said, "My ball's gone down that hole." Nobody could get his ball and everyone was in a panic because Arnie´s ball was down a hole – Arnie was saying I like that ball. and so I stuck my chewing gum on the end of my putter, poked it down the hole and retrieved the ball. Arnie said, "Hey, that was great." That was the first time he spoke to me. He didn't speak to me again but at least he was smiling.

I didn't see Arnie for 18 years and at the time I was the chairman of Stock and Aitken's music publishing company. They asked me to see a black singer, who was part of Michael Jackson's family, as they wanted to record her. So, I flew to Los Angeles and, as usual, stayed at The Beverly Hills Hotel. Before I went to breakfast, I saw Arnold Palmer walking towards me swathed in towels and a dressing gown. He'd been in the Turkish baths. I said, "Mr Palmer." He said, "That's my name. Arnold Palmer." Real John Wayne stuff. I said that I had played golf with him at Indian Wells in 1980 and he said, "I play golf with a lot of guys."I said I was the little Scots guy, when your ball went down a hole on 7th tee at Indian Wells and he said "Ah, you were the little Scots guy with the gum who got my ball out of the hole ?" I held out my hand and said, "Bill Martin."

"Great to meet you again Bill", he said " I will never forget that day." He said he was only there until lunchtime and then he was flying back. He flew his own plane.

Later on, I was with my music people in the Beverly Hills reception and we were talking away when Arnold Palmer walked past. He said, "Great to see you again, Bill.

See you next time." They said, "That's Arnold Palmer." I said, "I know. He asked me to play golf with him today but I had to be with you as I've got to get this contract signed. I hope I get it." So I got the contract signed as they were in such awe of Arnie.

We had a weekend where Efrem Zimbalist Jr, Don Rickles, Bob Newhart and Bob Hope came as well as many professional golfers and they had an idea to repeat the celebrity fixture in America in 1982. Bob Hope said that he would get the American celebrities and so I got Bobby Charlton, Jimmy Hill, Kenneth Wolstenholme, James Hunt, Patrick Mower, Lance Percival and Kenny Lynch. Jimmy Tarbuck wouldn't come as he doesn't like flying and once again, I took my brother.

They were arguing over who was going to be captain and I said, "This is all egos, I'm going to be captain." And so I was captain. We lost that day and then I went out with my brother and my pal and took them to see my beachside apartment in Fort Lauderdale, Florida. I came back and Jimmy Hill said to me, "We've had a meeting and we've decided you're not going to be captain. I'm going to be captain." I said, "That's fine" as I couldn't be bothered to argue and the following morning, he picked the teams.

Jim Watt was a world boxing champion and Bobby Charlton was one of the world's great footballers who won 106 caps, including winning the World Cup, and was captain of Manchester United when they collected the European Cup in 1968 and Jimmy Hill said to them, "The trouble with you two is that you're not winners. You don't know how to win." Imagine saying that to Bobby Charlton. Bobby's wife said that it looked as though Bobby was going to hit him.

Jimmy Hill said, "I'm playing in the first four ball with Bill Martin and you two can go off second." We got to the first and he said, "We've got to win the first game." He hit the ball and I hit the ball. Efrem hit the ball and his partner, a big cowboy actor, whose name escapes, hit the ball. We lost the first hole because Jimmy Hill played the wrong ball. So much for being a leader. We got to the 13th and we were winning, one up, and suddenly the cowboy actor collapsed. Jimmy Hill did a very clever thing. He got out his brolly, opened it up and ran over to a well and filled it with water . It was a lost cause though as the poor chap was clearly dead. Efrem said, "We will have to get a buggy and take him in." Jimmy Hill responded, "That means you've forfeited the game. We've won."

What an idiot! Jimmy was quite adamant that we should claim the match. I said, "You claim what you like. I'm going in with them." The guy who died played in so many old western Movies, I only wish I could remember his name.

IV. Mike Stock, Matt Aitken and Pete Waterman

As I mentioned earlier, Mike Stock and Matt Aitken had invited me to become chairman of their music publishing company and I gladly accepted. They asked me to attend a meeting with a BMG record executive as the Stock/Aitken office. When he entered the room, it appeared that he took an instant dislike to me as he knew I had a good music business pedigree. It was Simon Cowell and it became apparent that he knew exactly what he wanted. It was his idea to get Stock and Aitken to record two actors, Robson Green and Jerome Flynn. It was agreed that I would receive a percentage of the music publishing while Simon chose all the songs, which were classics and included 'I Believe', 'What Becomes of The Brokenhearted' and 'Unchained Melody', all of which proved to be UK number ones.

I promised the publishers who owned the songs that if we sold one million records we get nothing but from two million and above we received 20% of the publishers' share. The album sold seven million. I knew that Simon Cowell would be a winner and Stock and Aitken were certainly winners and as Stock, Aitken and Waterman, they were the sensational songwriters of the 80s.

Pete Waterman, my old Northern Soul promotion man reputedly went on to make and lose £100m. £30m went on Ferraris as he wanted to build a Ferrari Museum in Birmingham, where he had been born, another £30m on Koi Carp and £30m on railways. Income tax and VAT took care of the rest.

Nevertheless, he's still going strong and in my opinion, Stock and Aitken were the writers and producers but they'd never have made it without Pete, who was a brilliant promotions man who had a great nose for a hit.

V. Land Deals

My stockbroker had said to me in 1976, "Now that you live in Kenwood, you should join St. George's Hill Golf Club." The golf club had a rule about no show business people. He said that his partner, Leslie Marshall, was the vice president and he would propose me. My art dealer was Bill Patterson, and he was a member too. I had a great proposer and seconder. Normally they see how you play and how you act in the dressing room and how you hold your knife and fork and what you drink during the day before they make you a member.

It was 1976 and the hottest summer for decades. I went in the bar with a dark blue suit, white shirt, blue polka-dot tie and looking more like an accountant than anybody.

The captain of the time, Peter Price, six foot eight, big blubbery wet face and covered in sweat as he had just come off the golf course.

He looked at me and said "You're Bill Martin"

"You're Peter Price, the captain of the club", I replied.

He asked me if I knew Tom Jones and I said yes, and that he was a friend of mine. He said that Tom Jones was his friend as well and asked, "Do you know the Rolling Stones?" I said, "I do know the Rolling Stones but I hope you are not insinuating that I would bring the Rolling Stones into a prestigious golf club like this." He said, "That's good enough for me. Would you like half a pint of bitter?" and just like that I was a member. I never went for ten years though, as I thought I might be thrown out!

In 1993 a guy I knew, John West, had bought some land asked me to get planning permission for him to build a health club. He said that we could make a lot of money from this and he was getting Daley Thompson to front it and the club was to be called Daley Thompson's Healthtrack. The first centre was going to be in this derelict hanger at Weybridge.

When we got planning permission, the secretary of the club at the time said, "You can't build your health club here." I said, "Why not?" He said, "We are going to object to the planning permission. You are creating another entrance and it will slow down our members in arriving."

I found out that this piece of land was attached to some tunnels during the war which were underneath the golf club. It was near Brooklands and they had to have some place for the ammunitions if Brooklands was blown up. I said, "Well, if I don't get planning permission, I will start some building in our tunnels." I explained to them what I meant and in return for them not complaining, I gave them the tunnels.

We got the planning permission and the club was sold for £28m. It now belongs to the David Lloyd Tennis Centre and is a huge success.

VI. Family matters

In 1970, I was playing golf in Portugal with my Scottish friend, Drew Neill and I spotted a great new development being built, Vale do Lobo. I showed it to Jan and she bought a house there with some money she had saved. We have had it as a holiday home ever since. It has been a good investment and we have really enjoyed our time there.

I used to give my parents the run of the houses we lived in so they had some nice holidays. Sometimes we would all go away with our four kids.

When I went to Royal Ascot for the Derby, my father always gave me tips and I usually won. He loved horses and the piano and after all, most of the old songwriters were gamblers who played the piano. I'd give him my credit card for bets and let him get into St George's Hill golf club so he that he could drink. They never wanted for anything.

Back in 1977, I had a blue Rolls-Royce and we went to Sandown Races and I had Jan with me and my brother and my son Angus, who was almost two years old. Jan's father was also there, in a box with other RAC captains and Angus loved his grandfather. He was holding the door for his grandfather but he put his hand where the door closes. It closed on his hand and nearly took his finger off. We took him to a vet on the racecourse and he said, disdainfully, "I can just chop it off." I said, "You are not chopping off my son's finger. We're going to a hospital."

We all got in the Rolls-Royce and I was driving along and I was mad and my brother said, "You're no good in a crisis. When we get to the hospital, just you be quiet." We got to the hospital at lunchtime and a young doctor came out and I said, "We don't want you. I want a proper specialist." I was like a bull in a china shop. I knew the man I wanted and he was at a rugby match.

Jan and my brother kicked me out as I was causing too much commotion. The Rolls didn't have much petrol left and Jan told me to fill it up. I drove to the petrol station and I was filling up the car when I started crying. I couldn't stop crying because I was thinking of my son but there was no way I could explain what was happening. The manager of the petrol station came out and he said, "I'm very sorry about the price of petrol but that's the way it is. I feel bad about taking your money but you'd do better with a smaller car."

While I was away, the hospital did get the specialist to look at Angus' finger. The doctor had stitched Angus' finger together and he said, "We'll see what happens. In ten days' time, it will either fall off or it will be perfect." I said, "I want him to play the piano" and he said, "You'll know in ten days' time." And in ten days' time, it was perfect. If you looked at his hand, you couldn't tell that there had been anything wrong with it.

I sent the doctor a case of white wine, Chablis, every year until Angus was 21. It just shows that you should let professionals do their business. I didn't know what to do as I wasn't a professional doctor. I shouldn't have got emotional at a time of crisis. My panic diplomacy didn't work but I learnt from this. As I get older, I know that you have to rely on doctors.

There was another dramatic incident, potentially far worse, when our second child, Melanie, was just 13 months old. She had a very old English nanny and maybe that nanny had different ways of doing things. She used to leave Melanie out in the garden at Kenwood until late, giving her a lot of air, but she contracted streptococcal pneumonia. We took her to St Peter's Hospital where the doctor didn't think that she was going to be strong enough to make it. She was in an oxygen tent where they treated her. She had tubes in everywhere and they had to drain her lungs. After three weeks of this, I said, "Can I bring in a second opinion?" I brought in a Dr Snoddy type an old-fashioned Scottish doctor who was known to us – he was like someone from Dr Finlay's Casebook. He said, "Leave me alone with her and let me get on with things."

What happened next was amazing. He pulled out all the wires and he started slapping her like you wouldn't believe. He held her upside down and all this gunge was coming out and she was black and blue. He came out of the room and he said, "She'll live but she might not do anything for two years. She might be quiet because she has had an immense shock."

We used to sit her down in Kenwood and when we had a drinks party, she was like a little roundabout with people walking around her. She was all dressed up but she wouldn't speak. One day, after a year or so, she got up and started walking and talking, and that was that.

The illness hindered her growth but not her drive and, although she is only five foot one, she is a pocket dynamo and very successful. I love all my children of course but Melanie is the one in which see I myself reincarnated. She has my determination, my street smart and probably my personality. Neither of us are academically very clever but we know how to get on with things.

In 1985, I knew my father wasn't well as I used to see him on high days and holidays. I said to my brother, "Let's all go away for the weekend as I think Pop is becoming ill." My brother, who saw him all the time and hadn't noticed the changes, said, "Don't be so stupid."

I let them have our house in Portugal in the Spring and we went over to see them. I can remember my father saying, as we said goodbye, "Isn't it great how the boys kiss me?" They were the last words that I heard him say. We had gone home and left them there.

The next morning, 1 May 1985, was Angus' tenth birthday and I gave him a card from my parents which had some money inside. He wanted to call them before he went to school but I said it was too early and he could do it when he got back home.

Back in Portugal, my father said to my mother, "I don't feel very well" and she said, "You don't look very well so go back to bed." He lay in the bed and he died.

My mother went to Miguel, the wee boy next door, and son of the couple who look after our house in Portugal, and asked for a book and he gave her the Bible. She put it under my father's jaw as when you die, your mouth opens and it can lock. They may have to break your jaw to put it back. Then the next door neighbour Carlos rang me to say he had died.I flew out the next day to bring my father home from Portugal. What a drama that was. My mother couldn't believe he was dead and she wouldn't stop talking.

They had built a morgue nearby. In Catholic countries, you are normally buried the next day. They had built this morgue because Mrs Thatcher and her cabinet were coming to Portugal and it was in case anything happened. The first person to be placed in it was my father. I asked my friend, Tony Machedo, a restauranteur, to take me to the morgue as he spoke fluent Portuguese. He said, "I don't know if I can get you in."

I said, "More importantly, you have got to get my mother in to see him."

He charmed his way in but he said that my father was lying there naked on the slab, We went back for some clothes – his blazer and his favourite shirt – and Tony dressed him and then my mother came in and she couldn't stop kissing him.

Tony said that we could get him back to Scotland and he ordered a coffin which looked like something from The Godfather. We put him in the coffin and my mother said, "We have forgotten his glasses."

I said to my brother, "The gravediggers are on strike in Scotland. You're good with unions so you sort that out and I'll get our father back. You arrange either a burial or a cremation."

I had to phone the British Consul but he was playing golf. I said, "Well, I need to get this form signed so that I can get the body out of the country." I said that I was coming out to the golf course to get it signed, which I did.

I took my mother back to the airport and as we got there, there was my father's coffin in the reception area. I turned her away and told her to have a coffee. I went to the British Airways desk and I said, "That's my father in that coffin.

Either you put him on the plane now or you put me and my mother on the plane."

We got on the plane and I saw the coffin being put on board. My mother had a wee drink, she didn't normally drink. We arrived in Scotland and when the door opened, it was freezing and my mother said, "I'm glad your father's not here. This weather would have killed him."

There were 200 people at the church and 500 came to the crematorium. I spoke at the funeral and I said, "My father was no Paul Getty but if a man's wealth is measured by the number of people who are paying their respects, he died a wealthy man. He had perfect attendance at school and he conducted his life with perfect attendance. He had this love affair with my mother and he never wavered once. He had perfect attendance. Whenever his two sons needed him, he had perfect attendance. When his grandchildren wanted him, he had perfect attendance. And he made me what I am, my old man."

I told the kids, all four of them, not to cry, especially the older two as they were very close to him. When we got to the crematorium, the coffin was there and they had draped it with a Saltire. The kids were very brave and I was proud of them as they held back the tears. The Minister pressed the button and it went down and my mother went, "Oh, he's gone".

Chapter 16 - Jukebox

When Bill and Phil broke up, I knew I had to do something and I wanted to do a musical, though I knew it was a risky business. Andrew Lloyd Webber had failed with Jeeves, so even the top people could fail although he then came back with Cats. Cats had no plot to speak of, and it was on at an unlikely venue, the New London Theatre, yet it became one of the biggest hits ever. Similarly, everyone derided Cameron Mackintosh when he put on a musical, Les Misérables (which had lyrics by my dear friend Herbie Kretzmer) at the Barbican. Everyone predicted disaster and the initial reviews weren't good. Then he took it to a more commercial theatre and his version has now been running for 37 years.

Jukebox, which opened in 1983, used a lot of the best hits of the 50s and 60s and it was the best idea that I've ever had. Even my ex-partner, Phil said that it was a brilliant idea and a brilliant title. I didn't want the show to be associated with Phil Coulter so it was ironic that I had to rely on him to take over as conductor for the opening night of Jukebox as my original choice had been taken ill. I could have found someone else but I had lost my power of positive thinking.

Everything was right about the show except for two things. One, I had no experience in the theatre. Two, an idiot named Chris Raphael was hanging around me. He had been involved when we saw Paul Anka in Las Vegas. He gave me bad advice.

Louis Benjamin who had staged many musicals, said Jukebox could be at his theatre, the Victoria Palace. That sounded good to me, but I got swayed by Chris Raphael who said that we could get a better deal at the Astoria, which was opposite Tin Pan Alley on Charing Cross Road. Years later the theatre became a Gay club and has now been demolished. It turned out to be the wrong theatre for the show.

I had thought Jukebox was perfect for me. The musical was about songs and I could manage it myself, but in reality, I was only looking after the show and not paying enough attention to the marketing.

When I was doing Jukebox, I got a phone call from Richard Branson asking me if I would be interested in selling it. I thought, "Wow, if Branson is interested, I am really on the right track." We met at a music function some weeks later and he said that the idea was fabulous, but he said he had to talk to someone else first. I was standing there for about 10 minutes and then I patted him on the back. He looked at me and never said another word. He was foolish as he would have been the perfect partner because he understood the music business and knew about marketing, so it was a chance lost. He should care with all the success he has had!

I didn't realise the importance of selling tickets long before the show is staged. I was gearing up for an opening night where everybody gets a free invite and there is a standing ovation. I hadn't appreciated that the next day you have to have bums on seats. I didn't have that and I didn't know how to do it. I should have gone with Louis Benjamin and hence, the Delfonts and the Grades. They would have taken a bigger percentage but I would got advance sales with the Keith Prowse agency and everybody else. I never had it. In essence, you have to have muscle behind you in the musical theatre and you have to pay for that muscle.

How the hell was I going to get an audience? Word of mouth helped but it wasn't enough. After six months, Louis Benjamin said to me that the show was fine but it was taking a long time to get the audience. He said, "I will put it on the Royal Variety Performance but you will have to pay for it." I said, "I can't pay for anything." I had called his bluff as he wanted the show anyway as Jukebox was a dance production that would look good in the show. I got the Royal Variety and the sales started to build.

I lost a lot of money on Jukebox and I lost a great friend. Eddie Healey, who is a brilliant businessman and now a triple billionaire. He built Meadowhall in Sheffield, a derelict steel works which became the biggest shopping centre in Great Britain, as well as developments on many other sites.. Eddie is from Hull and he was a two-thirds partner in Jukebox. He always wanted to be in the music business and he wanted to do compilation albums. He is brilliant at putting songs together. He loved songs and I didn't realise that I had found my ideal partner after Phil. I needed somebody to bounce off.

I knew that we should take it off and I said, "You're losing money and I'm losing money, and we will have to take it off." He felt that we were building up to a full theatre. I had made up my mind to take it off on December 10. His wife Carol was a director with him and they are a lovely couple.

Eddie said, "Why don't you put more money in?" and I said the worst thing I have ever said in my life, I had seen George Bush saying it, and I said, "Read my lips. I don't fucking have any." His lips were pursed as I had sworn in front of his wife. That was unforgivable and wrong of me and I had made one of the biggest mistakes of my life. I lost Eddie´s friendship and respect. We say hello when we meet but who knows what we could have achieved in the Music

Business with his business brain and my brains about songs and the music business.

Ron White, who was the chairman of EMI, thought it was one of the best shows he had seen. He was also the chairman of the Music Publishers Association and he had wanted Jukebox as their Christmas Party cabaret with my Cliff and Elvis characters. If I had done the show right, I could have been on my way to becoming the biggest publisher in the world. There could have been a whole series of K-Tel albums, Jukebox 1, Jukebox 2 and so on. As it was, I had to sell all my music publishing business to EMI.

Jukebox could have been a worldwide franchise. It would have been perfect for America but instead it became the blueprint for Buddy. The derivatives from what I did are colossal. as that's how the Buddy boys made a fortune. They went to Peer Music and they got the same deal as I had with Jukebox. It's tougher and more expensive to get the songs now, but the so-called Jukebox Musicals are everywhere. We Will Rock You, Thriller, Jersey Boys and Dreamboats and Petticoats, Mama Mia are called Jukebox Musicals. Even that term comes from my show. I was ahead of my time but I didn't know how to run a theatre.

Everything had come to a head in the 1980s. I had nearly lost my marriage. I wasn't paying any attention to Jan and I'm afraid I went off the rails. I had never been a Scotch drinker but I would come home at night and drink Scotch. I would even take a glass of Scotch to bed which was really bad.

I was even arrested for drink-driving and I lost my licence. From the end of Jukebox in 1983 to the official end of Bill and Phil in 1989, I lost that period. I came out of it when the court case with Phil was finished.

I saw Benny from Abba at MIDEM in Cannes and I said I must have two tickets for the opening night of Mamma Mia! –your new musical. He said, "I will phone Judy Craymer the producer and see that you are on the guest list." I said, "Thank you Benny", and he said, "By the way I'm Bjorn." As soon as I saw Mamma Mia!, I knew it would be a smash. Another Jukebox Musical.

We Will Rock You ran at the Dominion Theatre for 12 years, proving that what I created with the Jukebox Musicals was so right. Ben Elton has written a good book. All these things though are what I started, so I was on the right path.

In 2010, I was in the States and I saw, The Million Dollar Quartet, a marvellous show about Sam Phillips of Sun Records, and his discoveries, Elvis Presley, Johnny Cash, Jerry Lee Lewis and Carl Perkins. At the end of the show, a flashbulb goes off and the whole place goes black and then you see the four of them together in that famous picture..... Elvis Presley, Carl Perkins, Johnny Cash and Jerry Lee Lewis.

I said to Jan, "I should buy the rights and put this on in the West End" and Jan said, "Excuse me? Remember Jukebox." I said, "You're right", and somebody else put it into the West End in 2011 with only moderate success and less than I would have expected so, all in all, Jan was probably right. That said, I think The Million Dollar Quartet is a fabulous Jukebox Musical. Those that have not been a success are because the songs were not strong enough. The Spice Girls, for example, would have been better entering Eurovision, which they would have taken by storm, than agreeing to their jukebox musical Viva Forever ! which flopped.

I call the Jukebox time my blue period.

Chapter 17 - Songwriters and SODS

I. Songwriting Organisations

I do think that you should give something back to the industry you're in so I've always been happy to serve on committees. There are a lot of songwriters who haven't given back anything, an awful lot, but if you've got a lot out of it, you should give something back. That way you feel part of the community but a lot of the young guys nowadays won't make the time or don't have the inclination.

There are two key organisations for songwriters. The Performing Right Society (PRS) collects the performance royalties for radio, TV, advertising, jingles and live performances. The British Society of Songwriters, Composers and Authors (BASCA) looks after songwriters, rather like a trade union. I was a director of the PRS for 13 years and a director of BASCA for seven, and after that I was made a vice-president.

When I first started at the PRS, the directors were all old guys and some of them would fall asleep after lunch. It wasn't a good idea to have them in control of millions of pounds. I'm not ageist but there is something to be said for younger people looking after your money.

You find in America that the younger guys do make the time, but they've started paying for Director services and that is starting to happen here. That is dangerous as people might do it just because they want to get paid. You might not get someone with the right way of thinking or the right calibre of writer but I guess you can't have it both ways.

Being involved in PRS or BASCA was always very interesting for me, but the world was very different then. The technology was evolving - the CD didn't exist back then.

When a songwriter dies, the copyright remains with his or her estate for 70 years after death. I was on the board when something huge happened. George Gershwin died in the 1930s and he had written songs with his brother, Ira, and the question was, "Was the copyright to end 70 years after George's death or not?" There were 24 of us on the board so it took some time to come to a decision. We decided that the song should be considered as a whole and so the whole lot would be in copyright until 70 years after Ira's death. That is very much to the advantage of the families of deceased songwriters.

I got involved with the money received from the BBC and the commercial stations for playing records, and we have to take note of what is happening in Europe. A lot of the radio stations don't want to pay money to the PRS anymore and they have a point when they see people listening to music on the net for free.

The music business is killing itself. They should have embraced Napster, the first music internet solution, and they should have invested money to work out how the internet would function. Nobody wants to buy an album when most of the songs are rubbish. You can download the track you want and people are making up their own albums on their iPods. I can see the sense of it but I don't particularly like it. I like an album with photographs of the artist, details of the songs and the writers and perhaps some informative notes about the making of the album.

Obviously, the music business is in turmoil and it has been for years. Look at when the LP came in or when printed sheet music with piano notes and words went out of fashion but downloads is the worst crisis it has ever had and it could change the industry completely.

The days of records and CDs are numbered, and people under 35 don't buy them anymore. That's why you see so much marketing of the old stuff. I still think there was nothing better than to have an LP in my hand, but the kids of today would ask me what an LP was.

I'm sure that people still love music, but the industry has lost faith in them. It doesn't know what to do. Who is going to invest in a new band now? I know heads of companies who download stuff themselves from outrageous countries, which is ridiculous.

There is another major challenge to the record industry as, in the UK and many other countries, records go out of copyright after 50 years. The industry only started a campaign to protect copyright four years ago which was far too late: they should have seen what was happening with Frank Sinatra, Glenn Miller and Bing Crosby going out of copyright. The music business was burying its head. It is now 2017 and anyone can, for example, issue their own CD of Elvis Presley's greatest hits up to 1960.

The Beatles' records have recently started going out of copyright time and I am amazed that McCartney hasn't been fighting publicly for this. It's difficult to get the public relations right as readers might think, "What's he got to moan about? He's got millions." He would have go in on the artistic angle, that is, it would be wrong for Sgt Pepper to be in the public domain because it is intended to work as a whole and it would be wrong for some back street record label to go cherry picking the tracks.

For all that, I don't think he can make a difference now. The music executives in Europe tend to see the Beatles as a spent force, even though we don't and America doesn't, so I don't think he would make much impact there. We look on the Beatles as the Sun Gods. It would be a travesty if the law doesn't change but I don't think it will. An example to support my point is that Barry Mason, co-writer of 'Delilah', would have to have 165,000 hits on Spotify or You Tube to be able to afford a cup of coffee.

II. Publishing

American Lou Levy, who is the first person mentioned in Bob Dylan's memoir Chronicles, was a great gambler who owned Leeds Music now the giant company, Universal. He sold his company for $6m in 1964. Two million he gave to his bookie, two to his wife and two to the taxman. He was a great publisher and he advised me, "Never sell your copyrights. The minute you do, no one wants to know you." People thought he had retired when he sold Leeds Music and it was the same for me when I sold Martin- Coulter.

If you do retire, make sure the price is right. EMI talked Jimmy Phillips, my old music business publisher into retiring in 1975 and they bought his company. He should have been a very wealthy man but he sold it for next to nothing. He sold it for just one times earnings and he should have sold it for at least ten as it contained songs such as 'Smile', 'A Nightingale Sang In Berkeley Square' and two of mine, 'Puppet' and 'Congratulations.'

When I split up with Phil, I decided that I should concentrate on what I knew I was good at. I knew Paul Levinson, a brilliant businessman who is like a giant shark. He circles round and then whoosh ! He has sold three very successful businesses and made millions.

His house in England is where the Great Train Robbers went after the robbery in 1963 - before he owned it I should add. They had planned everything meticulously but somebody left their fingerprints on a can of Coca-Cola, and then they were caught. That has nothing to do with Paul, but it's an interesting aside!

Paul's son Mark was the pride of his life and Paul sent him to an American university. I was talking to Mark one day and I said, "Why don't you buy some songs?" He suggested it to his father, who knew me, and he said, "I like the idea." I was Mark's consultant and we started with Rick Wakeman but they didn't just buy the songs, they bought the records and the video rights.

I put my own songs into the company as an act of faith and I also bought them Frankie Miller's 'Darlin'' for £115,000. Mark and I were in the same branch of Barclays and someone had given the bank instructions to take £115,000 out of Mark Levinson's account to buy the song, but they took it out of mine instead. The next day I realised that they had taken it out from my account. I said, "If I don't get the money back, I am going to sue Barclays Bank for £115,000."

I told the bank that they had a fax saying that the money was to come out Mark's account, not mine, but they couldn't find it or their reply. Mark said it was nothing to do with him and so I said I would sue Barclays. This was around Bastille Day, 1998 and I had just spent a lot of money moving into Belgravia.

I told them, "You can do what you like with Mark Levinson and it will be nothing to do with me."

They said, "Can't we discuss this?", and I said, "Not without my lawyers." They said, "There's no need to bring in lawyers." I said, "I am not leaving this room until I get my money and you agree a deal with me."

Astonishingly, I both got my money back and I kept 'Darlin'', which they had effectively paid for. It was like a present!

I started Angus Publications and bought copyrights. 'Darlin'' first came out by Poacher, a country band from Warrington, and I bought it after Frankie Miller had done it. I got Tom Jones and Bonnie Tyler to record it – it's a great song for people with gruff voices. I made 'Darlin'' a phenomenal success all over again, creating a gold record for the songwriter, Oscar Blandemer.

I also bought my songs back from the Levinsons, but I stayed very friendly with them. I built the songs up for ten years and then I sold the whole operation to Sony. I have now started again and the one great thing I own is The Water Babies, the film musical with music by Bill and Phil.

I'd known Elkie Brooks for years and she had been so misplaced. She was in a rock band, Vinegar Joe and then she made 'Pearl's A Singer', which was a great record, with Jerry Leiber and Mike Stoller. I happened to be at a party with Derek Green who ran A&M then and he said, "Why not write some great songs for Elkie?" At the time, Phil and I were splitting up and I didn't feel like it. Derek said, "Well, you know all about the old songs. Do you fancy doing an album of standards with her?" As a result, Elkie and I did Screen Gems together in 1984, and it was the finest album I ever did. Instead of brass, I got a 70 piece orchestra and we did old film favourites like 'What'll I Do' and 'My Foolish Heart'.

I picked all the songs for Screen Gems and presented them to her. Some were a bit slow but there were some phenomenal songs. The conductor and arranger scored it perfectly. I love old songs, I loved her voice, and I loved the arrangements. Maybe it was a mistake not to put in the occasional sax or trumpet, but I don't think so.

All the orchestra was there in Angel Studios. Elkie Brooks arrived and it was spectacular. She had learnt her craft so well that she did every song in one take. She said, "If Frank Sinatra can record live with an orchestra, I can do it too." It was mind-blowing. She was one of the best singers I've ever heard. During my famous war with Coulter, we had a secretary who worked for both of us and she said, "Phil says that the best album you've ever done."

The album was a big success but when she went on tour, she was singing rock'n'roll songs. She did them very well but the audience wanted to hear 'Once In A While' and 'Blue Moon'. She was rocking away when she shouldn't have be doing it. If she'd walked out in a long dress with an orchestra, she would have blown the place apart.

Of course there have been plenty of albums by rock artists singing standards and it's very hard to beat Harry Nilsson's A Little Touch Of Schmillson In The Night, which he made with the old conductor and arranger, Gordon Jenkins. Linda Ronstadt did some great albums with Nelson Riddle and more recently, Rod Stewart has gone through The Great American Songbook, Robbie Williams did Swing When You're Winning and Cliff Richard has done Bold As Brass. Some were better than others.

I do feel though that the old songs could be worked much better. McCartney has this wonderful catalogue of old songs including the scores of Guys And Dolls, The Pyjama Game and Damn Yankees as well as 'Unchained Melody', 'Let There Be Love', 'Fever' and the Buddy Holly catalogue. All these songs take care of themselves. He really needs someone who knows how to work the catalogue, someone who could unearth little gems. He needs a song man like me, not an administrator.

I became involved in so many different businesses. There were two guys, Tim Massey and Alistair McKeown and they had an idea for an animated cartoon for children, The Cones. It was about the cones in the road and they paid me to be involved and we did a TV series and then the financier pulled out which was madness as they'd already made the TV pilot and recorded the song. I had written the theme tune and Bernard Cribbins was going to record it in Abbey Road. Every kid would have sung that song.

I was trying to get away from pop bands. I felt that we had been building things up in the pop world and that it could collapse. I did the theme tunes for many cartoon series, including Spider-Man and this made me want to get more involved in cartoons. I participated in a Dan Dare project where the intention was to make a Hollywood movie. Colin Frewin, the producer had built up a huge TV company, Sunset and Vine and we did a deal with Sony for the music (including the use of the Elton John song 'Dan Dare (Pilot of the Future)' but so far the film has not been made.

I got back to being friendly with EMI and the managing director, Peter Reichardt, as I bought songs for them. They wanted me to negotiate maybe buying Gilbert O'Sullivan songs but Gilbert wanted to keep his songs that he had fought so hard to get back. Peter was the Number 1 publisher for 16 years and I was his guest at a lot of key functions.

I'd known Richard Rowe since he was a wee boy as his father was Dick Rowe, the A&R manager at Decca. Dick, as legend will tell you, famously turned down The Beatles at their audition with the words "Guitar groups are on the way out, Mr Epstein." His son Richard became the head of Sony Music Publishing and he hired me to help buy some music publishing catalogues. He wanted to buy the Acuff-Rose catalogue with songs like 'Bye Bye Love and 'Singing The Blues' and I picked out 75 of their great country songs to establish the value of it. They paid me a consultancy fee, although I hate that word. A consultant is like a man who knows how to make love 50 ways but can't get a woman. I like just being called a 'music man'.

I used to play golf with Keith Turner who was Andrew Lloyd Webber's lawyer and I did once win the Andrew Lloyd Webb Silver Salver outright. In 1990, Keith told me that the music publishing for Joseph And The Amazing Technicolor Dreamcoat was for sale, but if they knew Andrew Lloyd Webber wanted to buy it, the price would jump up, I was asked to buy it for them. I asked how much I had to play with.

Keith said, "Three-quarters of a million, but try and get it for a half."

I said, "They'll want at least a million."

My commission was going to be 5% or a piece of the production. I thought that when they offered me a piece of the production that it was a scam as they wouldn't have been able to put it on the stage without Robert Stigwood's approval. What I didn't realise is that Andrew is a brilliant businessman. He went to Stigwood and he said, "You're not putting on Joseph, I am and you, Robert, will get a percentage."

Andrew's chief executive officer, Patrick McKenna, who later started his own company, Ingenious, and his in-house lawyer, Keith Turner agreed to give me a percentage of the purchase price, but I wasn't allowed to go above three-quarters of a million, but I told them that the new owners would want £1m.

I wasn't able to purchase it but about three months later, Andrew bought it for a million and never gave me anything. I always think they expected me to come back for some commission. Every time I go to a function, Andrew makes a beeline for me and talks to me, and it's like he feels guilty, although I believe Andrew knew nothing about the arrangement I had with his partners Keith Turner and

Patrick McKenna. Forget the guilt – I would rather have the cash or a piece of   Joseph And The Amazing Technicolor Dreamcoat.

I had to work hard to bring myself back into the millionaire class. I would still go to the Cannes music conference, MIDEM, and I have a great nose for songs, but I am also aware of prices. You can always pick up something at MIDEM and I met this fellow from the Continent who had ''Allo 'Allo' by DJ Idol. It was a little disco song with a good B-side. I thought if I got the record deal, I would have the publishing. So I went to EMI, and EMI said that they liked it but preferred the other side and they were going to give me £15,000 advance. They told me to come back on Monday.

Jan has great friends and one is Carol Maxwell-Lyte who is a terrific cook and is married to Mike Griffith, who became President of the MCC and proposed me for membership. One Saturday night, they were having a Valentine's Day party and we took a taxi so that we could drink what we wanted. It had been decided that food would not be served until everyone had arrived. It was getting to 10pm when the last couple arrived and we were all getting plastered. I had ordered a cab for midnight and I gave the driver a tenner at midnight and asked him to wait half an hour. We ate a heart-shaped pudding and left, but there was no taxi. Jan said, "You shouldn't have given him a tenner!"

Then this other car came for us and it was a wreck. I reckon the taxi driver had got some mate to take us home for a fiver. Jan got in the back and I was in the front. I couldn't get the seat belt to work and we were turning the corner when a car hit us and our door fell off. I went forward and hit my head on the dashboard, splitting my nose and I came down on the gear lever. I fell out of the car.

The driver said, "It wasn't my fault. It was those guys in the street playing rap and putting me off by making me swerve."

I said, "Get the police" and he said, "No", and I knew then that he had no licence.

He said that he would take us to the hospital but, at the weekend, you don't want to go to any London hospital. We came back home instead and the guy was apologetic. Jan put a plaster on my nose and my elbow was sore.

I went to the hospital early in the morning and the doctor said that it was too late for stitches. That's why I have a scar on my nose. I had cracked three of my ribs and I broken my elbow.

When I went back to EMI on Monday, I had black eyes, a plaster across my nose and my left hand in a sling. The manager said, "Bill, are you that desperate that you have to break yourself up to get a record deal?" He added, "We love the record anyway and we'll do the deal."

That night I was miserable with my broken bones and I said to Jan, "Let's go to the movies. We'll go for a pint first." She said, "No, they are too many people in the pub and you'll get bumped and shoved. We'll just go to the cinema." It was a very cold night and she had gloves on.

We were going to the cinema and Jan crossed the road, slipped and her foot stuck in the pavement and she went flying. A lovely man on a motorbike stopped and a good looking girl in a car got out. They both said, "That's a hole. Your shoe is stuck in the hole." We should have taken their names and numbers and we could have sued the council.

Jan said, "Let's not go the cinema" and so we sat in a quiet pub and had a vodka. It was coming up to 8pm and Jan could feel that something was wrong with her shoulder. We went back to the Chelsea and Westminster Hospital. It was Monday and we had been there on the Saturday morning. It was the same nurse just going off duty and she said, "Are you two beating each other up?" Jan had a Cashmere sweater and the nurse was going to cut it off, and she said, "No, no, Bill will take it off." She got X-rayed and she had fractured her shoulder in five places.

The next evening we were going to the first night of The Rat Pack, produced by Derek Nicol who is a close friend of mine and a great showbiz impresario. We looked terrible as my left arm and Jan's right were both in slings and we had to applaud together with our two good hands. I had suggested that the show should be videotaped so that they could show it to Las Vegas and hopefully sell it to them. One of the guys who had flown in from Las Vegas said, "Who are you two?" I said, "We're Scottish trapeze artists and sometimes we get it wrong."

The next day I had to meet somebody else. I always wear lace-up shoes. Jan had her arm in a plaster as did I so we couldn't tie the shoe laces. and as I walked out of the door, a swarthy guy was walking along and I said, "Excuse me, do you mind tying my shoelaces?" He was an Italian and I said there is only one line I can say in Italian, 'Quando Dico Che Ti Amo', which was the song I put into English lyrics as 'When I Tell You That I Love You'. Unsurprisingly, I never saw this fellow again.

A few days later, I had to go to Malcolm Roberts' funeral. I still had my smashed nose, my broken ribs and my broken elbow and I probably looked in a worse state than poor Malcolm in his coffin. Malcolm was a great singer in the Mario Lanza style.

Sammy Cahn told me that when Lanza sang 'Be My Love' (a song written by Sammy and Nicholas Brodsky) at Sam

Goldwyn's home, it wasn't earth shattering but glass shattering - his voice shattered the chandelier and windows.

III. Backgammon and the Beatles

When Jan and I got married, our best man was Michael Mander. He played backgammon. I didn't want to show that, coming from the tenements of Glasgow, I knew nothing about it, as I wanted to play it. You can't really read about backgammon, you have to play it. In 1970, I played with my then girlfriend, Jan, in Minorca for an engagement ring and I won so we didn't get engaged for another year.

During the 70s, Jan and I used to go to the Claremont Club in Berkeley Square and we were given some instructions in backgammon by my stockbroker, Stephen Raphael. Through him, Jan and I would play with Lord Lucan and the James Bond producers, Cubby Broccoli and Harry Saltzman.

Lord Lucan was very tall and military looking with a moustache and a ramrod back. He looked like a caricature of an aristocrat. He was plummy mouthed, he never smiled, and he had no brains. All the others liked him because he was a Lord and he was related to the Lord Lucan from the Charge of the Light Brigade. They all had millions of pounds in their bank accounts but they didn't have a history like Lucan.

Harry Saltzman was a great, old-style film producer from Hollywood and I got on better with him than Cubby Broccoli. Cubby was a keen gambler and he was more interested in gambling in the Claremont than talking. The two worked well together on the James Bond films. They hired the actor first and then they discussed the gadgets and the girls they were going to get. They could paint a picture with just a few sentences.

The first person who was going to be James Bond was Steve Reeves who had been Mr Universe. They dropped that idea because he couldn't act and then wanted Patrick McGoohan. Ian Fleming wanted David Niven but he was deemed too old by then, although he did play Bond perfectly in the John Huston spoof, Casino Royale, the only book not owned by Saltzman and Broccoli. Patrick turned it down on moral grounds because he had a young family and he didn't want to be associated with its sex and violence. Meanwhile, Cubby's wife had seen Sean Connery in the chorus of South Pacific in the West End and thought he might be right for the part. Sean had big tattoos on his arms, one said 'Scotland' and the other, 'Mum and Dad'. You can see them from time to time in the films, but normally they cover them up.

They put him in the part and he did three James Bond films for £20,000 and he had a big chip on his shoulders about that – as well as the tattoos! I must admit that I am not Sean Connery's biggest fan. I have met him 3 times in my life - in the Turkish baths at the RAC Country Club, when I was golf captain during the Bob Hope Classic and at Elton John´s White tie and Tiara Ball. He goes on about being Mr Scotland, but he lives in Nassau. He did an advert for "the finest Scotch a man could drink" and it was for Suntory Crest, a whisky made in Japan! I do, however, think he is a great actor in films like The Hill, The Anderson Tapes and The Untouchables.

Sean Connery lived in Spain after Goldfinger and whilst there, he learnt to play golf. Apparently he was playing with three guys in Spain one day and their golf buggies came up and there was a big fat guy standing on the first tee with his wife. Sean said, "There are four of us, we take precedence."

"No, no," says the fat guy, "I have been given this tee time by the starter at the hotel."

Sean said, "What do you play off?"

He said, "I play off 28"

Sean said 'You can´t be on your own, we take precedence."

Pointing some 30 yards further down the course, he added, "I'm not, I am playing with my wife. "She is down at the ladies tee and plays off 36."

Sean, now annoyed, said, "Get off the tee or I'll knock you out."

The fat guy said, "I wouldn't do that if I were you."

Sean ignored the warning, threw a punch, but this guy floored him with one jab and broke his jaw. Everyone was sworn to secrecy as it was an embarrassing incident but the guy who decked James Bond turned out to be Ingemar Johansson from Sweden, a former heavyweight champion of the world. That could even be the reason why his voice has changed from the early "My name is Bond. James Bond." to the sch, sch that we get now.

That story was told to me by ABBA's manager, Stig Andersson, who had been very friendly with Ingemar Johansson.

Sean comes across very aggressive and apparently not many people enjoy playing golf with him as, if he loses he is not too keen in coming forward with the money . He says, "I've signed your card, you've got my autograph." If he wins he apparently wants the money. I can't vouch for this as I have never played with him but people who have played with him say it is true.

Naturally, I wanted to write a James Bond theme and I dropped hints to Cubby Broccoli and Harry Saltzman but they weren't really interested. Mind you, it would be very difficult to get a James Bond song with Don Black in there, as his lyrics are always excellent.

Harry Saltzman was always full of ideas. He told me, "I am doing a film called The Meat Factory. Do you want to get involved in that?" I thought it would be an odd title for song, but I'd have had a go. The film was about the garment industry in New York and the models were the meat factory. The film never got made.

If you tell people that you play backgammon, they assume that you must be numerically clever. I am quite good but only in a Scottish way.

I got to the semi-final three times of the Junior Backgammon Championship at the Claremont Club. In the semi-final in 1973, I was playing Jan. I said, "Let me win." She said, "Why?" I said, "Because I will get to the final and I will meet Jimmy Goldsmith, and it will be good for us."

Sir James Goldsmith owned Cavenham Foods, which had Bovril and lots of other businesses. He was a giant both in stature and business. She said, "Why should I let you win?" and she beat me and got to the final. She beat Jimmy Goldsmith too.

Jan won a George Jensen silver candlestick holder and some money. We used to give dinner parties where the candlestick took pride of place on the dining table and I would regale everybody about how I won the Junior Backgammon championship trophy but I didn't realise that Jan had had it engraved and the next time I told the story, I was found out.

In 1981, Lord Grade's company, ATV, was in trouble and the Australian company, ACC, bought 26% of the shares. ACC was owned by an Australian entrepreneur born in South Africa, Robert Holmes a Court, an imposing man who was six foot four. Lord Grade and Louis Benjamin left ATV and Robert Holmes a Court let it be known that he was prepared to sell one of ATV's assets, Northern Songs.

Robert Holmes a Court never cared for the music business and the royalties were pretty static on the Beatles then. He would come into the Claremont Club and I would be mingling with him and others. I told him that I would like to buy Northern Songs, which published the Beatles' songs. Although I look the part with my white hair and nice suit and tie, he could tell that I wasn't in his league financially. He said, "Oh, that Beatles thing." They were his exact words. He wasn't interested in Northern Songs at all.

There were 210 Beatles songs, but ATV also owned Lawrence Wright Music which had standards like 'Among My Souvenirs'. Robert Holmes a Court said that he wanted to sell all that music publishing as a package and if I could come up with £25m, I could have them.

To Robert Holmes a Court, songs were not physical things like owning a television or a house or a theatre – this is a man who would end up owning half of the West End theatres. He couldn't see songs sustaining money. I told him about the royalties for 'White Christmas' but it didn't register. Another reason could be that he simply needed £25m to prop up his empire.

I said that I needed to see the books for Northern Songs – that is, the full list of the songs and their earnings - and I went round to the ATV offices in Great Cumberland Place and if I'd stayed friendly with Eddie Healey, my Jukebox partner, we might have bought them.

I was so sorry that I had let Eddie Healey down as we suited each other's company. He had four lovely kids and we were all friends. God had said that this was my new partner and I blew it. He might well have come with me into this venture to purchase Northern Songs.

I was able to raise £10m but it was difficult to get to £25m. I went to Scottish Widows and Scottish Provident and several other companies. I said that there were three reasons to buy Northern Songs: the first is that some nut may kill another Beatle and their value would soar - Scottish Widows liked that reason as they could see how profits soared after John Lennon's murder, the second is that the 210 songs are the classic pop songs of the century, and the third is that the music business is constantly evolving – cylinders, 78s, LPs. At the time, it was all cassettes and 8-track tapes, but Philips was developing the compact disc which I never knew about. The potential changes in technology could be very important to Northern Songs as the work would be reissued and sold in the new format.

I approached both EMI and Paul McCartney about buying Northern Songs and perhaps putting up £10m a piece. Brian Brolly was negotiating on Paul's behalf. Paul had two issues: he was keen to have the songs but only the Beatle songs. Odd really when he has bought so many standards like the score and songs of Guys And Dolls for MPL Publishing. He also objected to paying a huge sum of money. He felt that they were his songs because he had written them. That was a stupid argument and it doesn't work like that. It was probably the biggest mistake McCartney ever made. I said to EMI that if they put up all the money, they could own Northern Songs. If I couldn't be a co-owner, I would want to manage the catalogue which would be a fine solution for me.

Nobody wanted to put up the money and it was a year later that Michael Jackson came along. He didn't actually have the money in his hands but there was so much money from his gigantic hit album,Thriller, in the pipeline that he knew he was on solid ground. The royalties always come eventually. They had, say, $50m coming, and one way of offloading the tax would be to buy Northern Songs. Michael Jackson bought the Lawrence Wright catalogue (which contained such great songs as Among My Souvenirs) as well and he picked up all their David Gates songs as a bonus.

I said to Robert Holmes a Court, "Why don't you keep one Lennon and McCartney song before you sell ? You won't get another chance and you will regret it otherwise."

He said, "What should I keep?"

I said, "Keep 'Yesterday'." That was the obvious one and clearly the most valuable single copyright.

So, the directors of ACC were sitting round the boardroom table to sell the music publishing to Michael Jackson, and Robert Holmes a Court said, "I'm keeping one song." I think if he had asked for 'Yesterday', panic bells would have gone across the room and they would have said that that was a huge proportion of the earnings. 'Penny Lane', the one he picked, was acceptable as it wouldn't have been one of the Top 10 earners.

They had to rewrite the contracts. 'Penny Lane' seemed a bizarre choice to me but Robert said it was the one his daughter wanted. The song really belonged to ACC but he probably paid a nominal £1 for it, I don't know. 'Penny Lane' is now owned by the daughter, who lives in Australia. It's administered by Sony on her behalf, but it was all my idea.

As soon as Michael Jackson got the tracks, the Sgt Pepper album was remastered on CD for its 20th anniversary in 1987. It sold tremendously well and Michael Jackson was in profit a few months later. He had got his £25m back within a year.

When a songwriter gets into trouble, he may go to someone who can lend him the money outside of the banking circles. Michael Jackson went to his record company, Sony, and they think a long time ahead. They saw a winner in Northern Songs and so they were advancing Michael Jackson money in return for shares and eventually it became a 50/50 ownership. Northern Songs would have been owned by Sony if Michael Jackson hadn't died as he was £200m in debt to Sony. You can't pay back that kind of money if you not earning it. To borrow that kind of money is relatively easy if you have assets!

When he died, his estate was earning millions of dollars in a day, and so the whole thing is frozen again. Jackson's estate still owns half of Northern Songs, and McCartney will never get it now. Not getting Northern Songs was one of the most frustrating times of my life. It was the closest I got to being a billionaire and I would have earned it by doing something I love. Sony have now acquired Jackson's 50% and Sony EMI own the Beatles songs.

In my view, most songs are not controlled by the record companies and the music publishers anymore but by the City. Martin-Coulter Music was sold to EMI, but if I were to phone EMI, they wouldn't want to talk to me. They want new songwriters now, not the old ones, even though they own substantial catalogues by well-known writers. It's different in America where companies make money by nurturing the gems. They would listen to what an experienced songwriter like myself and fellow pros would have to say.

IV. Songwriters and SODS

In 1972, Laurence Myers, asked several very successful songwriters for lunch. He was a Music Business manager and his idea was to form a publishing company that he would run and all of us would sign to him. As a result, we would all get a piece of each other's songs. This was a non-starter as we are all egomanics. There is no way I would want Tony Macaulay, say, to have some of my royalties and he wouldn't want me to have his.

It was a good lunch and we all got on well, and as a result, Mitch Murray said, "Let's start a dining club." He also had a name for it, the Society Of Distinguished Songwriters (SODS), which was great.

Mitch Murray became King Sod The First and the inaugural members were Mitch Murray and Peter Callander, Bill Martin and Phil Coulter, Roger Greenaway and Roger Cook, Les Reed and Barry Mason, John Carter, Don Black, Tony Hatch, Norman Newell, Tony Macaulay, John Barry and Geoff Stephens.

Since then, the membership has gone up to around 60 and some of the subsequent members have been Tony Hiller, Bruce Welch, Brian Bennett, Marty Wilde, Sir Tim Rice, Mike Batt, Gary Osborne, Charles Hart, Guy Fletcher, Justin Hayward, Guy Chambers, and Gary Barlow and for a brief moment, Andrew Lloyd Webber. The latest members are Nik Kershaw, Wayne Hector, Sir Van Morrison, Gary Kemp and Marcel Stellman, who wrote 'Tulips From Amsterdam'. He is in his eighties so this is an example of new members keeping down the average age !

Other members did include Gary Glitter and Rolf Harris but they were kicked out for obvious reasons. Guy Chambers, who wrote 'Angels' and many of Robbie Williams' biggest hits was a SOD but chose to resign when Rolf Harris was convicted. I find this very disappointing as it reflects badly on all us SODS as it feels like an attempt to tar us with the same brush. It's not as if people have stopped using banks due to a few crooked bankers, dispensing with PR because of Max Clifford or stopped listening to music because of Jimmy Savile. Indeed, does he expect everyone with a gong to hand it back. His decision, in my opinion, is farcical.

Andrew Lloyd Webber was a Sod for about five minutes. He came in the room and thought, "What the hell am I doing here?" He is used to being the centre of attention. Tim Rice, on the other hand, is a great, gregarious guy – he still has a cricket team, the Heartaches, and he is mad about pop songs. He is wonderful company.

Tim Rice deserves his knighthood and he is a lovely person. He is as good as W.S. Gilbert, of Gilbert and Sullivan, the only other lyricist to be knighted. His best lyrics are from his musical Evita but he'd give that away to have written 'Bye Bye Love', 'Hound Dog', 'Blue Suede Shoes' or any rock and rock classic due to his love for the genre. I'm glad that at long last he and Andrew Lloyd Webber are working together again. They wrote a few songs for the London Palladium production of The Wizard Of Oz and I'm intrigued to know if they will follow this up.

Everybody who joins has to like good food and so far every member has been male. There's no particular reason for that but I suppose it is more uninhibited when all males are together. We have had some non-English members like the late Mort Shuman and Bjorn Ulvaeus and Benny Andersson from Abba who, although they never turn up for SODS events, faithfully pay their subscription.

Paul McCartney and Elton John have never been asked, really because they are star/songwriters. The atmosphere wouldn't suit them and anyway, we don't want knockbacks. Gary Barlow is also a star/songwriter, but he joined when Take That was finished and thought to be gone for good. He is a great songwriter, the best of his generation, and 'Back

For Good', 'Rule the World' and 'The Flood' are brilliant songs and would have liked to see more of him at SODS events but he has just resigned!

Everybody looks upon Bruce Welch as the guy we would all like to be. I certainly do! He started at 18, he played the guitar, he wrote number one hit songs, he had a good act with the Shadows. Brian Bennett joined the band two years later and people still think of him as a new Shadow. They wrote 'Summer Holiday' together and lots of good songs. Bruce is really underrated and he has a fantastic personality Both these Shads are great friends.

Another SOD who was an early starter is Justin Hayward of the Moody Blues who wrote his great song and international one,"Nights in White Satin" when he was 19. Besides, being a superb musician, Justin is one of the most popular SODS and has an air of being a diplomat. He and his wife Marie have been happily married for years and remain great friends of ours.

A lot of the older songwriters are bitter. I am never bitter about new people having success. Each generation has its time but today the records become the hits, not successful copyright songs.

With a few exceptions, there are not the songwriters today in the way that there were in the Sixties. I couldn't see someone forming a SODS dining club with just today's songwriters, although we are happy to have a few of the new guys in our membership. SODS was a great idea, a good fun thing for songwriters to meet, a good way to grow old with your mates, and we have also done little a bit for charity.

I love some of the family connections too. I like the fact that the uncle of Mike Stock of Stock-Aiken-Waterman (who were members for a year) is Johnny Worth who wrote "What Do You Want" for Adam Faith and 'Well, I Ask You' for Eden Kane, and that Gary Osborne's dad was Tony Osborne, one of EMI's best arrangers. Gary wrote the lyrics for "Forever Amber" and "The War Of The Worlds".

I admire and respect my fellow SODS. I know everyone of them has a song I wish I'd written and I am sure every SOD looks round the room and feels the same way. As a result of this friendship, some collaborations have come about. A very good early example is Andy Williams' 'Home Lovin' Man', which was written by Tony Macaulay (who wrote 'Build Me Up Buttercup' with another SOD, Mike D'Abo and 'Don't Give Up On Us', amongst others) with Roger Greenaway and Roger Cook. The two Rogers also wrote the smash hit "I'd Like To Teach The World To sing".

I want to put some words to one of Brian Bennett's melodies "The Dreaming Of The Shadows"

I've written several songs with Les Reed, who is a marvellous songwriter/musician and one of the nicest guys you could wish to meet. Our song, 'On Christmas Eve', is being recorded by Johnny Mathis and who knows, it could become my Christmas number one....one day ! Tina Turner is holding the other song we wrote, 'Can You Call This Love ?' as is Gloria Gaynor, so fingers crossed for that. Les and I also wrote a country song called 'Tina's Cantina' but I would have to go Nashville to sell it and I could end up with egg on my face as that's a hard market to crack. That said, I did go to Nashville once with a singer we had, Kimberly Clark, which was her real name. I was phoning my brother from my hotel room when an irate man barged through the door, looking for his daughter. He managed enough courtesy to knock on the door as he flew in and I was stunned to see that it was Kris Kristofferson. He thought I had got her to help me make it through the night! He looked in the bathroom and in the closets and under the bed and then he left. He was a tough guy, breathing fire rather like a cartoon character, and I'd have ended up in hospital if she had been there. It occurred to me afterwards that it might have been nice to have discussed songwriting with him (he did after all write some great songs) but I don't think he was in the mood for fireside chat !

Back to Les Reed, - in just one morning, he, along with his then writing partner, Barry Mason, wrote, 'Delilah', 'The Last Waltz', 'Les Bicyclettes de Belsize,' and 'I'm Coming Home'.

Barry then said he was leaving to play golf and Les said "Don't be mad, it's raining".

Barry replied "I'm going anyway".

As he left, Les said " I have a great song title but I won't tell you what it is unless you stay."

Barry ignored the plea and left.

Les phoned Geoff Stephens (another SOD who wrote 'Winchester Cathedral,' 'The Crying Game' and many more) who came over to Les's house and they worked on the song that afternoon. Barry missed out on a worldwide number one as the completed song was 'There's A Kind Of Hush (All Over The World)' ,

Barry Mason, a lyricist and Les Reed, a tunesmith are great talents and great friends of mine. It's a pity their songwriting team stopped. They wrote superb standard pop songs. Geoff too is very talented and another good pal.

Tony Hiller, who wrote 'Save Your Kisses For Me' and was the first person I met in Tin Pan Alley, remains a great friend to this day and although he is in his late 90's, his ability hasn't waned and he's still full of fun.

Mitch Murray ('How Do You Do It' , 'Even The Bad Times Are Good' and 'I Like it') 'stopped writing songs in favour of writing speeches. However, his former writing partner, Peter Callander, who sadly died in 2014, had continued to visit Nashville to write country songs. Mitch said, "Since we split up in 1976, we've both had the same result - nothing!" Peter would have seen the funny side of that as they were good friends.

We all like getting up and performing for a laugh. There is a clip on youtube of several of us at a SODS meeting singing 'Delilah' with Les Reed on piano. We all look pretty old but, as I mentioned earlier, the average age of SODS has hardly changed.

Roger Greenaway and Roger Cook are immensely talented together and wrote many hits such as 'Melting Pot' and 'I'd Like To Teach The World To Sing' plus they also had hit records, notably "You've Got Your Troubles," as David and Jonathan. They were so good at demonstrating their songs that if you were Gene Pitney or the New Seekers, you would find it very hard to turn them down. I'm sorry that Albert Hammond, the writer of 'When I Need You' and 'The Air That I Breathe', isn't a SOD as he lives mostly in America. He demonstrates his songs better than anyone and he is now producing Julio Iglesias for whom he wrote 'To All The Girls I've loved Before' with Hal David.

Richard Kerr really can sing - his biggest song is Mandy and when he does another hit of his, 'I'll Never Love This Way Again' at the piano, nobody can beat him.

Don Black doesn't drink but he is a great operator and he knows how to sell "Don Black" better than anybody in the world. He is a magic salesman and he could even persuade Stephen Sondheim that he, Don Black, is the greatest lyricist in the world! I joke of course as Don is an extremely clever lyricist - just listen to the words of 'Diamonds Are

Forever'. He is very witty and won an Oscar for "Born Free" and his writing credits are too extensive to list here.

He is a wonderful raconteur and maybe it comes from having started out in showbiz as a comedian. He has a way with words and his first hit was an English lyric for a Eurovision song, 'Walk Away' for Matt Monro, a very clever lyric.

I had lunch with Don Black in the RAC Club in London and we were talking over some ideas. Then he said, "I've got to go as I'm meeting God." He was going to meet Andrew Lloyd Webber!

Andrew Lloyd Webber wrote with Don Black in his house in Sydenham and he invited people to hear the new songs. When they had written Aspects Of Love, Andrew invited Mrs Thatcher, Michael Heseltine and Geoffrey Howe round, and Andrew said, "Don. I thought we'd invite them over so that we will have an idea about how ordinary people feel about the musical."

Apparently, the story about Andrew goes that he said to Alan J Lerner "Why is it people instantly dislike me ?" and Alan said " It saves time!"

At the time we were in the RAC Club, Don was writing his autobiography, and I said, "I hope I'm in your book." Don said, "If something sensational happens, I will put you in it." So we walked out of the door. I went to a meeting in Soho and Don went to meet 'God'. I looked in a TV shop window and I thought that every channel was showing The Towering Inferno but it was 9/11 and it was the Twin Towers collapsing. He still never put me in the book !

Some people call him Don But. Don is great company but he has a habit, when there is a new musical on, of saying, "It's fantastic but..." He always builds things up and then knocks them, ever so slightly. At the last SODS dinner, Don had to introduce Mike Batt who has put on a lot of weight. He gave him a good build up and then couldn't resist a "But" with "But I hope your new fitness video will sell." Don says it all with a sense of humour. I'm sure he will see the funny side of this –but – you never know!

Don is a great family man and apart from his own family, he has a great brother as well as sisters. His brother Michael Black is the last of the great Theatrical Agents. At one stage he had an office in Soho and in order to work all day without leaving the office he had an arrangement with the Deli downstairs. One tap with the foot meant a salt beef sandwich two followed by two taps meant a coffee as well. The arrangement was going great until one day a Mexican Tap Dancer came in for an audition. As he ended his tap dancing act the Deli delivered 100 salt beef sandwiches and 75 coffees!

As mentioned, Don wrote several lyrics with the late great John Barry (another SOD) for Bond movies. John also scored films such as Dances With Wolves, The Ipcress File and many, many more. Yet another SOD, David Arnold took over the mantle from John and did the score for 5 more Bond movies.

Mike Batt is a mercurial character and a rarity who can conduct, score and play the piano. I think he's wonderful. He's written 'Bright Eyes' and the hits for the Wombles, but he's a mad businessman. Mike may make £10m one year through writing and producing Katie Melua but he will spend it the next year on three tenors or two opera singers. He does this all the time. Mike has a tremendous commercial sense but instead of going off down the M1, he goes into various side roads before getting back on the M1 again. From time to time, he can't get on the highway again because he's lost most of his money but happily he tends to make it all back.

That musical he did, The Hunting Of The Snark, is his major weakness. We all write things that are not good enough, but Mike really believes in it. He has given The Hunting Of The Snark so many chances that the poor snark must be dead by now.

When Phil and I wrote that Robert Burns' musical in the Sixties, we couldn't get it staged and if we had continued to batter down the door with it, we would have been lost. Mike is an exceptional songwriter but he has the ability to shoot himself in the foot but always ends up successfully standing.

When Mike came back from Australia in 1978, he came to my home, Kenwood, and asked me to manage him. I said, "No, you are the sort of guy who would be working at the piano when the phone goes. I would go to answer it but you would grab it first and start negotiating the deal. You don't need a manager. You need a psychiatrist. You have to got to let something go." I think I said it with enough humour not to offend him.

In my opinion Paul McCartney is surrounded by yes men who wouldn't dream of criticising him, so he never receives a fair assessment of his new songs. Nobody is frightened of Mike Batt, but if someone were to tell him that one of his ideas was awful, he wouldn't listen and he'd still do it anyway. However, as I've said, he does have an amazing songwriting ability.

Herbie Kretzmer worked at the Daily mail newspaper as a journalist and became their TV Critic. In his spare time he wrote lyrics for foreign tunes. He also wrote the TV theme tunes for shows such as 'That was The Week That Was,' 'Kinky Boots,' 'Goodness Gracious Me' and the song 'She' for Charles Aznavour, but it wasn't until he was 60 years of age that he landed the dream ticket when Sir Cameron Mackintosh asked him to write the English lyrics for for

"Les Miserable" now the longest running musical of all time. Herbie is now 92, a multi millionaire and a great wit. Herbie wrote a lyric in Les Mis ," I Dreamed a Dream" -well, Herbie sure did and his dream came true.

Dear reader - May you dream and when your dream comes true we will sing "Congratulations"

I saw Pete Waterman in a restaurant in London 1982 and he was staring into space. The restaurant was above his league and I said, "Pete, how are you doing?" He used to work for me but I had to sack him due to a dispute over expenses. I had sent him to New York for a disco convention. I told him where to stay but he chose to stay elsewhere. Holding up the hotel bill, I said "Pete, what does this say ?" He said "I don't know because I can't read or write." I was amazed. Apparently he has now taught himself but back then because we, Bill and Phil, were very hot writers, he said 'You can't sack me because I want to be a songwriter.

I said "Pete, the only way you'll be a songwriter, is to go into the studio with an actual songwriter and cough and put your name on the song".

However, in this restaurant in 1982, he was very serene and told me that he was partners with two unknown songwriters, Stock and Aitken, and that he was building a recording studio. They had no money, but Pete kept writing cheques and got the studio built before the financiers could start taking the money back as the banks had been on strike. He is so street smart and once the studio was built, they were making hits and he was able to repay the bank.

He is great at picking songs but not much of a songwriter himself. When he worked for me, he said, "You have got to buy this" and I thought it was terrible. It was 'Gordon Is A Moron' and, of course, he was right. It was a hit. Pete doesn't know where he is these days – is he a record man, a promotions man, a songwriter or a TV railway personality? I would say that first and foremost, he is a promotions man, a really great one. What he created with Stock, Aitken and Waterman was the £100m songwriting success story of the 80s.

One of our SODS, Marty Wilde was as big as Cliff Richard in the late 50s with hits like 'Teenager In Love' and 'Donna.' However, Marty married Joyce, one of the Vernon Girls and, believe it or not, that was taboo in the rock and roll industry back then and it unfortunately diminished his career somewhat.. His daughter Kim was a big star in the 80's having hits with songs like 'Chequered Love' and the international smash 'Kids in America', both written by Marty and his son Ricki, who is also, yes you've guessed it, a SOD. Ricki also wrote, this time with Kim, 'You Came' , another of her hits. Jan and I are great friends with the Wilde family which includes their other children, Marty Jr and Roxanne.

Marty's group in his heyday was called Marty Wilde and the Wildcats. A young boy, aged 16 auditioned for them but Marty thought he was too good looking and too good a guitarist and singer but he still gave him a shot. The young lad didn't hang around long and joined a group called the Moody Blues and at just 19 years of age wrote the classic song, 'Nights in White Satin' . He is of course SOD Justin Hayward but sadly for Justin, Lonnie Donegan owned the publishing rights and, to this day, he is fighting to get them back.

The next SOD, Tony Hatch of 'Downtown' and 'Don't Sleep In The Subway' fame was Chief Barker of the Variety Club of Great Britain, which raises money for charity. I am proud to say that only 3 SODS - Tony, Nicky Chinn and myself have been awarded Silver Hearts which are presented to people who have raised a tremendous amount for good causes. For my part, I raised £168,000 at a music business banquet in 1979. I hope this doesn't sound like self promotion but I am conscious about giving something back to society, but I prefer to do it quietly and in my own way, hence I always ask for my speaking fee to be given to charity. It guess it was sufficient as I was awarded the MBE for services to the music business and charity.

Of the above, Tony Hatch was probably the first SOD to be internationally successful with his songs being sung by Petula Clark in particular.

Tony has a great sense of humour as shown when we discussed whether we should open the SODS to ladies and, due to his acrimonious divorce from singer/songwriter Jackie Trent, he said "No, they should have their own organisation and call it 'Confederation of Woman Songwriters" (COWS).

Nicky Chinn, with his Australian partner Mike Chapman had 19 hits in the UK top 40, including 5 numbers ones from 1973-1974. When they met, Mike was a penniless waiter whilst Nicky was from a wealthy background and you could live on his 21st birthday presents alone. Incidentally, when they split up, Mike went on to co-write one of Tina Turner's biggest hits, '(Simply) The Best'. Unfortunately, due to jealousy from a couple of SODS, they were invited to join years later than they should have been. Mike saw it as a sleight and declined but I am delighted to say that Nicky remains a prominent SOD.

Another SOD, who'd be considered more of a performer than a songwriter, was Errol Brown, lead singer of Hot Chocolate and who wrote songs like 'It Started With A Kiss', 'Every 1's A Winner' and 'You Sexy Thing'. He wrote the latter when he went to the famous Tramp discotheque in London and saw his future wife, a beautiful Mauritian girl named Ginette. Errol was a great pal of mine but rarely attended SODS events as he lived in the Bahamas which provides delicious irony as Johnny Gold, who sold Tramp to a Scottish friend of mine, Kevin Doyle, lives up the road from Errol in the Caribbean. When I bought Kenwood, we used to have dinner parties and our two youngest children, Angus and Melanie acted as 'door openers' and took our guests' coats. The doorbell rang and the kids did their job and we heard the door slam. They rushed up to us and said 'Daddy, there's two dark people outside". I knew it would be Errol and Ginette so I accompanied the kids back to the door and opened it to see Errol dressed in a full length white coat and a white fedora and apologised profusely and he replied "Don't worry Bill, we're used it". This would obviously be construed racist today but remember this was the mid 8os and the kids had never seen a black person. Sadly, Errol died of cancer last year at his home in the Bahamas.

We always keep a memory on our gavel of the former King SODS and the SODS who have died. One of the latter was a great lyricist called Norman Newell who wrote the Matt Monro hit 'The Portrait Of My Love'. However, we embrace the new blood and I am pleased that Gary Kemp is a very active SOD. For those who were asleep in the 8os, Gary wrote, amongst others, the terrific songs 'Gold' and 'True' for his band, Spandau Ballet.

We had only one honorary SOD, Lionel Bart, who wrote 'Oliver!', 'Fings Ain't What They Used To Be', 'Living Doll' and many more. Towards the end of his life, he had no money and as King Sod in 1975, I took the decision to make him an honorary member. He was an inspiration to all songwriters as he'd been successful in the 50's, before us all. Another SOD I would like to mention is Guy Fletcher, writer of 'Power to All Our Friends.' When Phil Coulter and I had our first publishing contract in Tin Pan Alley, the young lad who sang our demos was a slim blond, angelic looking young boy - Guy. He is no longer that blond, no angel and I'm afraid there's a few less pies on the shelf. However, Guy is one of the SODS who has really given back to the music industry as Chairman of BASCA, Chairman of The Ivor Novello Awards and a past Chairman of the PRS and did a great job. A nice little postscript is that Guy, along with his long term songwriting partner, Doug Flett (yet another SOD), has a song, 'Fallen Angel' which was never a huge success first time round but is included in the smash musical 'Jersey Boys'. This means that the song receives the same percentage as every song in the show which makes it a well deserved pension for Guy and Doug.

King Sod in 2014, was Frank Musker who along with his then writing partner and fellow SOD, Dominic King, wrote 'My Simple Heart' for the Three Degrees, whose lead singer at the time, Sheila Ferguson caught the eye of a young Prince Charles. I hope he enjoyed his 'reign' (Frank, that is, not Charles!) as much as I did when I was King Sod number 4 in 1975 and King Sod Number 35 in 2007. Sir Tim Rice was our King in 2015 and in 2016 it was Roger Greenaway and now me again in 2017.

The SODS has provided me with much pleasure in my life. Some of these friendships go back to my first days in Tin Pan Alley in 1962 and I am delighted to have met so many other friends on the way. Thanks boys !

Chapter 18 - Showbiz Snippets

I. - SONGS

Elsewhere in the book, I have told stories about certain songs where it was relevant or appropriate but I thought I'd share a few more interesting snippets .

'WITCHCRAFT'

Cy Coleman wrote the music but it was a woman, Carolyn Leigh, who wrote the lyrics, as she did for their other big hit, 'The Best Is Yet To Come' (which is also the epithet on Frank Sinatra's gravestone).When Elvis came out of the army in 1960, Sammy Cahn produced a TV show for ABC called The Frank Sinatra Timex Show. He employed a young writer named Neil Simon who went on to write many famous plays and scripts, winning copious awards on the way, and Bob Fosse as choreographer who famously went on to win an Oscar for directing Cabaret. Elvis wore a tuxedo for the first time in his life and sang 'Witchcraft', whilst Sinatra sang the Presley hit 'Love Me Tender' proving that Frank couldn't sing silly pop songs.

'SOME ENCHANTED EVENING'

Cole Porter was with his musical publisher in Sardi's restaurant in New York when he heard a tune playing. He said to the publisher "This is a lovely tune, who wrote it ?" The publisher replied "Rodgers and Hammerstein". Cole replied "It took two of them to write that?" This was perhaps a little unfair as the song is considered by some to be the single biggest popular hit to come out of any Rogers and Hammerstein show.

'ALEXANDER'S RAGTIME BAND'

Irving Berlin changed music law in America where this song is concerned, During his lifetime, 'Alexander's Ragtime Band' was taken from him and put into the public domain as laws in the U.S. at that time meant that ownership only lasted 50 years (Berlin lived till 101). President Reagan changed the law, saying "It'll never happen again".

Speaking of Irving Berlin, he wrote a song where every line was a question – some achievement.

HOW MUCH DO I LOVE YOU
How much do I love you I tell you no lie,
How deep is the ocean how high is the sky,
How many times a day do I think of you,
How many roses are sprinkled with dew,
How far would I travel to be where you are,
How far is the journey from here to a star,
And if I ever lost you how much would I cry,
How deep is the ocean how high is the sky ?

'QUE SERA SERA'

Cole Porter never won an Academy Award for songwriting but in 1956 he was convinced he'd win for 'True Love' from the movie High Society but it was beaten by 'Que Sera Sera', sung by Doris Day in the Hitchcock film, The Man Who Knew Too Much and one that is probably treated more as a football song nowadays in England.

'ME AND MY SHADOW'

Al Jolson never wrote a song in his life and he used to get off the train from Los Angeles to New York and he'd be met in the Big Apple by the impresario Billy Rose and he would say

"What did we write last night, Billy ?"

Billy replied "You wrote a great song called 'Me And My Shadow', And that's how Jolson got his songwriting credits. Jolson was the first giant singer, then, Bing, Sinatra, Elvis and The Beatles. The rest were all derivatives.

'THANKS FOR THE MEMORY'

'Thanks For The Memory' first appeared in the 1938 movie, The Big Broadcast of 1938 and was sung by Bob Hope and Shirley Ross. It won the Academy Award in 1938, the same year I was born. The song's writers were Ralph Rainger and Leo Robin, the latter of whom went on to write Gentlemen Prefer Blondes, the 1949 film, starring Marilyn Monroe and Jane Russell.

The song is often regarded as a companion piece to 'Two Sleepy People', written later in 1938 by Hoagy Carmichael and Frank Loesser, also performed by Bob Hope and Shirley Ross in the 1939 movie 'Thanks For The Memory', which took its title from the success of the song. Bob hosted the Academy Awards a record 18 times and on each occasion, his entrance was heralded with the band striking up 'Thanks For The Memory'.

'FLY ME TO THE MOON'

Everybody has heard of Irving Berlin and Richard Rodgers but very few people outside the music business have heard of Bart Howard. From 1945 until 1955 he played the piano every night at the Algonquin Hotel in New York. Every night people, including many famous names would say "What a great night Bart but what is that obscure song you play? It's great but I only ever hear it here." When Frank Sinatra asked the question, Bart said "That is my song, Frank. I wrote it." Nothing really happened until Peggy Lee sang the song on The Ed Sullivan Show in 1960, increasing its popularity. As a result of that appearance, it started to become better known as 'Fly Me To The Moon' and in 1963 Peggy persuaded Bart Howard to make the name change official. Bart had been reluctant arguing that 'Fly Me To The Moon' only appears once where as 'In Other Words' appears seven times. Peggy was right though and once the title was changed, the song made one million dollars a year prompting Peggy to say, "No need to thank me Bart, just go to the bank and check your balance."

'I'VE GOT YOU UNDER MY SKIN'

Cole Porter's great song 'I've Got You Under My Skin' was, in my opinion, Nelson Riddle`s best arrangement and Sinatra´s finest hour. After a recording session, Frank never said "How did I sound?" He knew he was great and when a recording had been spot on. All he ever said after a take was "Let's hear it." When he knew he had nailed a great recording , he would often say "Guys, thanks but I am off for the day." Although the musicians would have been paid for the day they would have to leave but if Frank left the studio and said "I'll be back." everybody panicked as it meant something was wrong and that he wasn't happy. After the recording of 'I've Got You Under My Skin', Frank did just that and left the studio. In his absence, Nelson Riddle was checking the score to find the mistake and all the musicians were listening to the play back but they could not find anything wrong. Frank then came bouncing back into the studio with his driver carry a full box of oranges and went straight to the trombone player, Milt Bernhart, and said "Milt, you're the star of this record so when it comes to your solo, stand on the box. Now I'm off for the day". So there it was - they took just one take to record the masterpiece. Imagine that nowadays - and without all the current technology.

'LET THERE BE LOVE'

Noel Coward had been asked to go to New York to discuss plans to write a new musical but he didn't want to go. So he sent another, sophisticated, urbane Englishman named Ian Grant. On the way to the theatre, Grant asked his taxi driver if he had anything to read but all the cabby had was The Bible. Grant took it, opened the book and started reading Genesis. There he saw the line 'Let there be light' which inspired him to write the lyrics to 'Let There Be Love' during the 20 minute cab ride. He rushed into the theatre with the words but the composer of the new musical wasn't there so he asked a session musician, Lionel Rand to write the tune and the rest is history.

'CALL ME IRRESPONSIBLE'

Written by Sammy Cahn and Jimmy Van Heusen, Sammy was desperate for it to win an Oscar but a song can't be nominated if it has been released before the film. Therefore, when Frank Sinatra asked for the song, he refused because it was scheduled to be   in the film 'Papa's Delicate Condition' starring Fred Astaire. When Sammy sang it to Fred, as he always did when promoting his songs, Fred stopped him halfway through and said, "Sammy that's the best song I have ever heard." Sammy replied "Excuse me Mr Astaire, but that's the best half song you've ever heard. May I finish please."

Fred who had a habit of winning Oscars for many songwriters said "Please don't give that song to anyone else."

However, Astaire's contractual obligations prevented him from accepting the role but still Sammy held on to the song. The role eventually went to Jackie Gleason who introduced it, much to Sinatra's annoyance, and it promptly won the 1963 Academy Award for best song.

'MISS OTIS REGRETS'

Cole Porter was in the Algonquin Hotel in New York with his old school friend, the actor, Monty Woolley. Dorothy Parker, the writer, was due to join them for lunch and Monty said "Cole, I bet you can't write a song based on the next words the waiter says."

Cole replied 'Monty, you purport to be a gentleman but come along now, the next words the waiter says will be "Gentlemen, can I get you a drink" or, "It's lovely to see you again Mr Porter" or something of that ilk. Once he's said the obvious, I'll write a song based on what he says after that.'

The waiter came up and, after the predicted pleasantries, said "Mr Porter, Miss Otis regrets that she'll be unable to dine today"

Miss Otis was a friend of Dorothy Parker who was also joining them for lunch Dorothy arrived and Monty said "You won't believe this but Cole has just written a song on demand, can you do that ?"

Dorothy replied, "Monty, I am a journalist not a song writer." Wooley laughed and offered her a drink and then she said the famous line:

"I don't drink very much, one or two at the most,
 Three or four if I'm able, five I'm under the host."

'MOON RIVER'

Henry Mancini wrote a lot of his great songs in the Mayfair hotel in London but 'Moon River', which was to be included in the movie Breakfast at Tiffany's, nearly never saw the light of day because the wife of the film's producer objected to Johnny Mercer's lyric "my huckleberry friend". Hank Mancini and lyricist Johnny Mercer convinced them that it was right, Audrey Hepburn sung it in the film and sure enough, 'Moon River' won the Oscar. Andy Williams recorded it in 1961 and sang it at the Academy Award ceremony in 1962 and it became his theme song. He even named his Production Company and theatre in Branson, Missouri after it. However, he never released it as a single. Purely by coincidence, the singer who had the biggest chart success was Danny Williams, who had a UK no.1 with the song in 1961.

'SMILE'

It is pretty common knowledge that the music for 'Smile' was written by Charlie Chaplin but the lyrics came from Geoffrey Parsons and   Jimmy Phillips (although he wrote under the pseudonym John Turner). One morning Jimmy was taking his son, Peter, to school and the lad was upset as he didn't want to go so Jimmy started singing:

" Smile though your heart is breaking,
  Smile, even though it's aching."

Jimmy promptly took it to Parsons who completed the lyric and a classic song was born.

'AS TIME GOES BY'

School teacher Herman Hupfeld wrote 'As Time Goes By' for the 1931 Broadway musical Everybody's Welcome but it was only a modest hit. When he came back from entertaining troops during WW2, he was delighted to find that it had been re-introduced in the movie Casablanca. Although Doolcy Wilson sung it in the film, he was unable to record it due to a musicians' strike so Victor swiftly re-issued Rudy Vallee's earlier recording and it gave him a number one hit in 1942.

The famous opening line, 'You must remember this..." is actually the start of the chorus as the song was originally written and performed but because the prior verse was omitted by Wilson, hardly anyone knows it and no-one sings it today.

The song was voted 2nd in the AFI top 100 songs in cinema, behind 'Over The Rainbow'.

As an aside, if there is anyone out there who doesn't know this: in Casablanca Humphrey Bogart never said "Play It again Sam." His actual words were "You played it for her, you can play it for me."

'OVER THE RAINBOW'

This was the song that made and killed Judy Garland as it launched her to superstardom, a mantle that never sat comfortably.

Harold Arlen had written the music but lyricist Yip Harburg couldn't come up with the words. One day, his wife was driving him across Brooklyn Bridge when he suddenly shouted at her to stop the car. She protested that she couldn't as it was illegal but Yip insisted. He leaped out and there was the sight that had inspired him - a rainbow over New York. He managed to scribble enough words down before the police moved them on.

'FOOLS RUSH IN/DAY IN DAY OUT'

Johnny Mercer told me the story of how Rube Bloom came to meet him and played him two tunes. Johnny said, "I love the tunes, Rube but you'll have to wait two weeks before I can write the lyrics as I am just too busy but if you play it to anyone else, I'll never talk to you again." So Rube waited the two weeks and Johnny wrote the lyrics to both his tunes which ended up being the standards 'Fools Rush In' and 'Day In, Day Out.'

'I WANNA BE AROUND'

I was so chuffed to have the great Johnny Mercer on my Radio Clyde show as he very rarely gave interviews and, by the time we recorded our interview, he was very ill and was sporting a beard to hide the scars from various operations that he'd had to try and cure the cancer that ultimately killed him. He was great company and very forthcoming and told the story of 'I Wanna Be Around.'

316

"Well Bill, it was a big song for me but an even bigger one for the lady I wrote it with, Sadie Vimmerstedt. She worked on a cosmetics counter in Youngstown, Ohio and she was ten years older than me and she sent me this title with a note that said "I want to you dedicate this to Nancy Sinatra as I'm sure someday he'll come back to her." I paid no attention to that but I loved the title and said that if you can wait a month or two, I'll write it. Tony Bennett was looking for a follow up to 'I Left My Heart In San Francisco' so I took it to him and he recorded it and made it an instantaneous hit. This made Sadie famous and kinda rich and she quit her job at the cosmetics store and went on radio shows and went to New York to be on TV and she wrote me a letter. It said. Johnny, it's wearing me out, I've gotta get out of show business."

'EV'RY TIME WE SAY GOODBYE'

Of all Cole Porter's songs, this was his wife's favourite and Cole's favourite version of the song was by Ella Fitzgerald. Cleverly, in the line "change from major to minor" Porter begins with an A♭ major and ends with an A♭ minor thereby matching the lyrics.

'BE MY LOVE'

Sammy Cahn told me the story of how he and the Hungarian Nicholas Brodszky wrote 'Be My Love' for the Mario Lanza movie, The Toast Of New Orleans. Brodszky was, in Sammy's words "The Irving Berlin of Hungary" but he could really sing so, when the lyrics were ready, he sang every word so that Sammy could get the best idea possible of what it would sound like when Mario Lanza finally sung it. When I asked Sammy if he was pleased with Lanza, he said "No mechanical reproduction can capture the brilliance, the tonality of his voice. He frightened you, he was animalistic. I was watching him singing 'Be My Love' and he sung a note that wasn't even in the song." Although it was Oscar nominated for best song in 1950, it missed out to 'Mona Lisa.'

Sammy also told me how Brodszky had escaped the Nazi machine that was rumbling across Europe in the 1930s and arrived in England. However, he was deemed an alien during the war and was interned in a camp on The Isle of Man. Whilst there, a movie he was associated with (if memory serves me correctly it was A Matter of Life and Death or Stairway To Heaven as it was known in the States) was to be the Royal Command Performance. Normally, Brodszky would have been in the receiving line to meet the King and Queen but he was in this camp. So, he was called into the commandant's office and the commanding officer said "Mr Brodszky, what are your politics ?"

Brodszky replied "What politics ? I'm a composer, I don't have politics."

The C.O. said "How would you like to become a British subject ?"

Brodszky said "In an instant."

So, they flew him down to London to the Foreign Office and he was sworn in as a British citizen and that night he stood in the receiving line and did indeed meet the monarch.

'COME FLY WITH ME'

Sammy Cahn wrote 'Come Fly With Me' with Jimmy Van Heusen for Frank Sinatra's new album and Sammy told me, "I love this song because it was written to order. When people ask me which comes first, the music or the lyrics, I always say "the phone call." And in this instance, the phone call came from Frank and he said "I am going to do an album about flying." The original second line was 'If you could use some exotic views, there's a bar in far Bombay.' I said to Van Heusen, you know, the line I really want to use is 'If you could use some exotic booze....' but in those days I was afraid that the use of the word 'booze' would restrict it being played on the radio. So, when Sinatra was singing the song on the record date, I said to him, "You know, Frank, when you sing this in the nightclubs and the cabarets, you can say '...some exotic booze...'. Frank said "Whaddya mean in nightclubs ? I'll do it on the record"...and he did !"

'THE SECOND TIME AROUND'

Another Sammy Cahn story here as told to me: he and Jimmy Van Heusen originally wrote 'The Second Time Around' for a Bing Crosby movie where a widow meets a widower and, as Sammy said, "What kind of love song do you write for a widower to sing to a widow? So I said to Van Heusen one day, "What do you think about the title 'The Second Time Around' and he said "how do you mean it ?" This is how we worked. I would give him a title and he would always ask me how I meant it so he could think it through. Jimmy was also a bit of a lyric man and this time, he stood up and went to the piano and started playing and sang,

 "Love is lovelier, the second time around, just as wonderful with both feet on the ground."

Sammy said, "When people walk up to me and say "You wrote the best song, I know they mean 'Second Time Around' because it has become a kind of a hymn of hope for people who have lost a loved one or gone through a divorce or trying a new romance and I'm very proud to have written that song." He also told me that Sinatra begged him to let him sing it before it was released in the film but Sammy was aiming to win an Oscar. Although it was nominated, it didn't win, being beaten by 'Never On Sunday.'

'IT'S IMPOSSIBLE'

Singer Perry Como (who'd started out as a barber at the age of 13) decided to retire from singing to relax and concentrate on playing golf. RCA called and asked him to do one more song and he said "If you bring a mobile recording studio to me, I'll sing it, thinking they'd refuse. They agreed and the result was 'It's Impossible' and it gave Como his first U.S. top ten in 12 years. It was also enough to bring him out of retirement for a further two years which was a bonus as he had hits in that time with 'And I Love You So' and 'For The Good Times,' two great songs.

'THREE COINS IN A FOUNTAIN'

Frank Sinatra was supposed to do a movie with Marilyn Monroe but she never turned up so he was free. The producer of another film came to see Sammy Cahn and Jule Styne and asked them to write the title for it. Sammy asked what the film was called and the producer said "We Believe In Love." Sammy replied "That's rather boring and easy, I can do that in 5 minutes, tell me the plot. The plot was about three women who go to Rome seeking love and throw a coin each into The Trevi Fountain. Both the movie and song became 'Three Coins In The Fountain.'

When Jule Styne heard Sammy's repeated line, 'Which one will the fountain bless, which one will the fountain bless', he complained that it didn't rhyme so Sammy said "Well do something about it then" and Styne decided to make the second line a higher note. Simple eh ! 'Three Coins' was the last song Sammy and Jule wrote together as Frank Sinatra told Cahn to stop writing with Styne after he'd spoken to journalists about Frank and Ava Gardner so they wrote not knowing they were splitting up. Sammy knew that the orchestra were around for the Frank and Marilyn movie so they persuaded Frank to record it there and then and it won the 1954 Oscar for best song.

'FOR ONCE IN MY LIFE'

Two white guys, Orlando Murden and Ronald Miller, used to sit in Tamla Motown's offices, standing out like a sore thumb, waiting for Berry Gordy. Everyone from Diana Ross to Marvin Gaye asked Berry who the two 'honkies' were. Berry replied that they were his Broadway writers and had written 'For Once In My Life', a song that most people think was written by Stevie Wonder, although Wonder duetted with Tony Bennett in 2007 and their version won a Grammy.

'AMERICAN PIE'

At the start of 1959, Buddy Holly was touring the States as part of The Winter Dance Party with J.P. Richardson (The Big Bopper), Richie Valens and Dion and The Belmonts.

After appearing in Clear Lake, Iowa, Holly chartered a small plane to take him and two others to Moorhead, Minnesota for the next stop on the tour. The pilot took off in a snowstorm and, shortly after take off, in the early hours of February 3rd, crashed, killing Holly, Richardson, Valens and the pilot.

Waylon Jennings, the bass player in the tour's backing band, had given up his seat on the flight to The Big Bopper as the latter struggled to fit in the tour bus seats. This caused Buddy to jokingly say to Jennings "I hope your ol' bus freezes up." Waylon shot back laughingly, "Well I hope your ol' plane crashes." Although obviously banter between friends, it was a line that would haunt Jennings for decades.

The first song to commemorate the musicians was 'Three Stars' by Tommy Dee, and whilst it was a hit, winning a gold disc, it was the 1971 Don Mclean hit 'American Pie' that was the worldwide smash. Contrary to popular myth, the name of Holly's plane was not 'American Pie' and in 1999, Mclean himself stated that he made up the song title. When asked what 'American Pie' meant, Mclean jokingly replied "It means I never have to work again."

The song was number one all over the world but not in the UK, where it was kept off the top spot by 'Without You' although Madonna's version did make number one in 2000.

The Recording Industry of America (RIIA) produced their songs of the century and 'American Pie' was voted 5th. Once again, 'Over the Rainbow' was number 1.

'TUTTI FRUTTI'

There was a lyricist named Dorothy LaBostrie who was so so skinny, with no curves at all, that her nickname was '6 o'clock.' i.e. straight up and down. She would frequently turn up at recording studios and try and get someone to listen to her lyrics and add music to them but didn't have a lot of joy. One day, Little Richard couldn't translate the sound he made live into the studio surroundings and, every time he got frustrated, he started swearing so they had a break and Dorothy came in and the producers said to her "6 o'clock, can you write something for Richard ?" He started with "A whop bopa-a-lu a whop bam boo", and she immediately replied "Tutti frutti oh Rudy"and they were on their way to a hit.

In those days, black singers didn't get played on white radio so the angelic Pat Boone used to get away with covering Little Richard songs and at the end of the session, Richard said "Let's see Pat Boone get his mouth round that." If you listen to both versions, I think you'll agree that Pat didn't !

'LONG TALL SALLY'

Producer 'Bumps' Blackwell was introduced to a poor black girl by Honey Chile, who was a popular disc jockey at the time. The story goes that the little girl wanted Little Richard to record the song so that she could pay for her ailing Aunt Mary's medical treatment. The song, which was actually just a few lines on a piece of scrap paper went like this:

Saw Uncle John with Long Tall Sally
They saw Aunt Mary comin'
So they ducked back in the alley."

Not wishing to upset an influential disc-jockey, Blackwell "accepted" the offer and took the idea to Richard, who was reluctant at first but he liked the line "ducked back in the alley" as that was exactly what they were looking for and Richard kept practicing until he could sing it as fast as possible, once again in order to make it difficult for Pat Boone to copy They ended up with the song they wanted and it turned out to be the best selling 45 in the history of Speciality Records.

A woman named Enotris Johnson was also given a writing credit on the song, probably as an act of benevolence, as Johnson and his wife Ann, a white couple, had taken

Richard in after he had been kicked out of his home. Little Richard might not have liked Pat Boone singing his songs and 'sterilising' them but the fact that many artists covered his tunes, made him rich. In fact, Elvis covered so many of Richard's songs that he got up every day and thanked the Lord for giving Elvis to the world. In turn, when Richard retired to become a preacher, Presley sent him a signed gold Bible.

'BAND OF GOLD'

The superb songwriting team Holland-Dozier-Holland was made up of Lamont Dozier and brothers Brian and Eddie Holland. They were Motown's premiere songwriters and also arranged and produced many songs that helped define the sound of Motown in the 60s for the likes of The Supremes, Marvin Gaye and The Four Tops. However, by the end of the decade they were in dispute with Motown, having left in 1967, so, in order to avoid a lawsuit, wrote 'Band Of Gold' under the pseudonym, 'Edythe Wayne'.

It was a number one smash for Freda Payne. The lead guitarist on the single was Ray Parker Jr of Ghostbusters fame.

'BAKER STREET'

Even though we were both Scottish, I never really hit it off with Gerry Rafferty. I had known him from his time in The Humblebums with Billy Connolly and when he went on to success with Stealer's Wheel. After his first solo album flopped commercially, he was down on his luck again and, much as I would happily help up and coming singer/songwriters, Gerry was a bit of a pest. Before I had my famous Alembic premises, I had an office in Baker Street and Gerry paid a visit to try and flog me is latest song for

£1,000. However, when he got there, he couldn't bring himself to knock on my door due to his pride. The resultant song was 'Baker Street' and if you listen to the line ' you think that it was so easy, ..., you're trying now', that was aimed at me. Fair play to Gerry, the song was brilliant and deservedly won the 1978 Ivor Novello Award for best song. What really made the song was the opening sax solo, played by Rav Ravenscroft (and not by Countdown presenter Bob Holness as urban legend has often claimed). He was paid just £20 and the cheque bounced so I guess Gerry's money skills hadn't improved. Sadly, his alcoholism got the better of him and he died of liver failure aged just 63.

'PEACE ON EARTH'/ 'LITTLE DRUMMER BOY'

It really was a little bit of magic when Bing Crosby and David Bowie came together in 1977 to record 'Little Drummer Boy' for Bing's forthcoming TV special. However, Bowie hated the song so the writers came up with 'Peace On Earth' which he sang as a juxtaposition to Bing's 'Little Drummer Boy.' Bowie later claimed that he only appeared on Crosby's show "Because I knew my mother liked him " but I think that is unfair as everyone knew who Bing was, especially as Bowie was trying to 'normalise' his career after the Ziggy Stardust and Aladdin Sane periods and the curiosity surrounding his sexuality, and there was little more mainstream or normal than Bing Crosby.

During rehearsals (which took under an hour) for the song, Bowie was clearly nervous and he became scared saying "I don't know if I can do this song. It's not in the right key." Bing said "Just take a shot David, I'll get in there somewhere." Now, that's class. Let's put it another way - Bowie benefitted far more by duetting with Bing than vice versa.

Sadly, Bing died aged 74 just over a month after recording the track when he walked off a Spanish golf course and suffered a massive heart attack.

'THE JAMES BOND THEME'

For many years, James Bond movies have had a 'Bond song' but in the first film of the franchise, Dr No, there was no such song. However, the iconic 'James Bond Theme' did appear, as it has in Bond movies ever since. It was written by Monty Norman and arranged by John Barry. This has caused many people to erroneously think that Barry wrote it, including John himself who twice went to court to claim as much, losing on both occasions. Norman has also successfully sued publishers for libel for claiming that Barry wrote it so it has been an emotive tune. John may have lost both cases and plenty of money into the bargain but he did compose the soundtracks for eleven Bond movies so didn't do too badly.

There was one song in Dr No. It was 'Underneath The Mango Tree' and sung by Ursula Andress's character, Honey Ryder. However, Miss Andress's thick Swiss accent meant that she was dubbed for the whole movie and this included the song, which was actually sung by Monty Norman's then wife, Diana Coupland who is better known as the actress who played Sid James's wife in the sit-com Bless This House.

OTIS BLACKWELL

Otis Blackwell was a diminutive New York African-American songwriter who used to sell his songs for $25. He wrote great rock 'n' roll songs like 'Great Balls Of Fire' but more importantly, several songs for Elvis, including 'Don't

Be Cruel,' 'All Shook Up' and 'Return To Sender'. However, Otis was hustled by Elvis's manager Col. Tom Parker who made him add the singer's name to the songwriting credits. This should surprise no-one who recognises that Parker was an odious man who stilted Elvis's career for his own cnds.

When Elvis found out that he was being given unwarranted credits to the detriment of Blackwell, he put a stop to it. However, in certain cases, this wasn't followed through which is why you still sometimes see Elvis credited and sometimes you don't.

II. MUSICALS

CAMELOT

Alan J Lerner and Fredrick (Fritz) Loewe were sensational Broadway Musical writers with titles such as My Fair Lady, Gigi, Paint Your Wagon and Brigadoon. They had just the hottest musical in London and Broadway with My Fair Lady and they were dining in the Guinea Pub in Bruton Place, just off Berkeley Square in London's Mayfair district. As they left lunch, Alan was trying to persuade Fritz to write one more musical, Camelot. Fritz who was recently divorced, said that he would not write another musical and that he was going to buy a big yacht, fill it full of gorgeous blondes, brunettes and redheads and enjoy life and divide his time between the South of France and Palm Springs. As they were walking round Berkeley Square, they passed the Jack Barclay Rolls Royce showroom.

Fritz said "Alan look at the cars. I am going to buy that green Rolls for you and I shall have the yellow one and have them shipped back to the States."

Alan replied "No Fritz, I will buy them as you bought lunch and now, what about Camelot ?"

They did eventually write Camelot together and Fritz did retire until his death in 1988.

HELLO DOLLY!

The great Jewish theatrical impresario, David Merrick was a genius at putting on shows. and he was staging 'Hello Dolly' by Jerry Herman . The great Hal David of Bacharach and David, had an older brother named Mack, who was an excellent lyricist in his own right and was nominated 8 times for Best Song Oscar. Mack David went to see David Merrick but was told he was too busy.   David insisted, saying "I really think he'd like to see me so I suggest you get him." It turned out that Mack David had written a song in 1948 called 'Sunflower' which had been a hit for Dean Martin and Frank Sinatra amongst others. Jerry Herman's theme tune for Hello Dolly! used the same melody line as 'Sunflower'. Mack David said to Merrick, "You've got $6m in this show and I suggest you listen to my song. Having done so, Merrick said to Mack,

"What are you doing for lunch ?"

Mack replied, "Five minutes ago you wouldn't agree to see me and now you're offering me lunch."

Merrick left the room and returned with an attache case, handed it to David and said "Here's your lunch."

The case was reputed to contain $250,000. The two men shook hands, verbally agreed terms which included that Mack had to sign that he had no alleged claim now, or in the future. Mack consented but said "Where's the salad to go with my lunch ?". Mack replied that he could have two tickets to the opening night instead.

Herman always claimed he had never heard David's 'Sunflower' prior to working on Hello Dolly! and I believe him.

WEST SIDE STORY

Leonard Bernstein was asked to do a musical based on Romeo and Juliet and it was to be called West Side Story. The main trouble in those days in New York was between Puerto Ricans and whites. They hired a young, exceptionally tall, lyricist half the age of Bernstein, named Stephen Sondheim, whose mentor was Oscar Hammerstein II. Sondheim and Bernstein took an instant dislike to one another, perhaps because they were both gay at a time when it was still considered taboo. Sondheim's parents came home to their apartment overlooking Central Park and found their son on the floor crying. His wealthy father, who was prepared to help fund the show was furious and wanted to know what was wrong and ranted about pulling his philanthropy.

Stephen said "They've given me the lyrics to write." "Well that's terrific", said his Dad, "Why the tears ?" "I could have written the music as well" replied Stephen. He was that confident and arrogant about his own ability.

Bernstein's score for West Side Story was magnificent and he told Sondheim, when discussing the song 'Maria', that he didn't want him to use the words "I love you". He said that anyone can do that. The aggrieved Sondheim retaliated by putting the word 'Maria' in the lyric 48 times. Bernstein then gave him the music to 'America' which was so fast that Sondheim had to cram the lyrics in but the result was magnificent. Sondheim was a brilliant lyricist - just listen to another song from the show -'Gee Officer Krupke', not to mention 'Tonight". West Side Story became the must see show on Broadway in 1957, running for 732 performances before becoming a box office movie in 1961.

HIGH SOCIETY

High Society was the musical based on Philip Barry's play The Philadelphia Story. Frank Sinatra wanted to get the co-lead role of Mike Connor, which he did. He also duetted on two cracking Cole Porter numbers, 'Who Wants To Be A Millionaire' (with Celeste Holm) and 'Well Did You Evah' (with Bing Crosby) but he failed to get the duet he really wanted, with Louis Armstrong. This was the first time Bing and Frank had collaborated but, for some reason, Crosby remained professional and a little distant from Sinatra and, to rub salt into the wound, Bing and 'Satchmo' sang 'Now You Has Jazz' together and the Bing and Grace Kelly duet of 'True Love' received an Oscar nomination. It was, incidentally, Grace Kelly's last film before she became Princess Grace of Monaco and, if you look at the film closely, you'll see she's wearing the engagement ring given to her by Prince Rainier.

HOLIDAY INN

Holiday Inn was being filmed at Paramount in 1941 and it was felt that something was still missing but the studio was short on money so they called Joe Schenck, who was a close friend of Irving Berlin and asked him to help. Various stories have been told as to the origins of the song 'White Christmas.' One suggests that it was written in La Quinta, a warm desert town in California near Palm Springs, whilst The Arizona Biltmore claims that it was written there.

However, this is what Irving told me when I met him. He was staying in The Beverly Hills Hotel when he was asked to write a song for Holiday Inn. He had a tune that he'd proffered for Top Hat but it had been rejected so he dug that out and added the words. The oft forgotten first verse supports Irving's version of the song's source.

It goes:

The sun is shining, the grass is green,
The orange and palm trees sway,
There's never been such a day
In Beverly Hills, LA.
But it's December the 24th,
And I'm longing to be up north.

The result, 'White Christmas' is the biggest selling song of all time.

TOP HAT

Irving Berlin had a long running feud with fellow songwriter, Harry Warren. When Warren went to see Berlin's musical Top Hat during the Second World War, he was heard to exclaim that "They bombed the wrong Berlin." Warren actually had more number ones than Berlin in the 40s (although none of them of course was 'White Christmas'), including 'Chattanooga Choo-Choo and 'On the Atchison, Topeka and Santa Fe' and when Berlin wrote 'Freedom Train', he included the line "It's a song about a train/ Not the Atchison, Topeka/ Or the Chattanooga choo-choo..." They may not have got along but they certainly wrote some amazing songs.

GUYS AND DOLLS

Guys and Dolls was written by Frank Loesser, a real heavy drinking, chain smoking New Yorker. The show had been such a great success on Broadway that Sam Goldwyn wanted to make the film and he did so in 1955. Although three numbers had been added from the Broadway show specifically for Frank Sinatra, the song he really wanted, 'Luck Be A Lady Tonight' was given to his co-star Marlon Brando, who played the role of Sky. Sinatra had wanted Brando's role and relations between the two were strained, especially as Sinatra had originally been considered for the role of Terry Molloy in the previous year's On The Waterfront which gave Brando a best actor Oscar. Gene Kelly too was seriously considered for the role of Sky Masterson but Goldwyn insisted on Brando as he was the biggest box office draw at the time. Loesser offered to fly to LA to try and help but Sinatra had the hump and told him not to bother. Sinatra was known for only ever doing one take so his frustration with method actor Brando merely inflamed the situation. One day he said to director Joe Mankiewicz, 'When Mumbles is through rehearsing, I'll come out."

A few years later, Frank Loesser married his second wife, Jo. She was a tall Hollywood girl who hated his drinking, smoking and carousing and she banned him from seeing his pals, including Groucho Marx, who dubbed her 'The Loesser of Two Evils.'

SINGIN' IN THE RAIN

Considered by many to be the greatest musical of all time, Singin' In The Rain was directed and choreographed by Gene Kelly and Stanley Donen, the pair having been asked by producer, Arthur Freed to put it together. Between them, they chose almost entirely old songs to give the movie the right feeling of 'age'. The famous 'Singin' In The Rain' number was originally intended to be sung by Kelly and co-stars, Donald O'Connor and Debbie Reynolds but ended up as a solo. Despite Hollywood lore, Kelly did not complete the song in one take as it was filmed over two days. However, the dance sequence was filmed in a temperature of 103 degrees and his wool suit shrunk in the wet.

Kelly worked Debbie Reynolds so hard that her feet bled when filming 'Good Morning' and she was so upset with it all that Fred Astaire offered to help her with her dancing. Even Kelly admitted that he'd been tough on her. However, Debbie told me that it was all worth it as it launched her career and said "If you look at the clip from 'Good Morning' when we're coming down the the stairs, we are all looking straight ahead. We didn't look down at our feet."

Years later, Jan and I met Gene Kelly at a drinks party in Hollywood, following a 3 Tenors concert. He was stocky and muscular. When we'd finished talking, I patted him on the shoulder and it was like touching concrete even though he was in his 70s by then. Whereas Fred Astaire was slim, Gene was very much more the gymnast build.

CATS

Before Cats opened, Andrew Lloyd-Webber couldn't raise enough money for the show to open. Showbusiness entrepreneur Brian Brolly, who was MD of Lloyd Webber's Really Useful Group came to see me and explained that they were £80,000 short. He asked me for £50,000 to inject into the show and said he'd give me the music and poetry publishing for the other £30,000. I said "Get Tim Rice to write a song and I'll do it. Tim agreed as long as Lloyd Webber agreed to replace Judi Dench as lead with his then girlfriend, Elaine Paige. Andrew played the tune to Tim and he came up with the lyrics and entitled it 'Memory'. Tim went to the studio only to discover that his lyrics had been replaced by those of Lloyd-Webber and Trevor Nunn but the title remained (you can't copyright a song title). 'Memory', as written by Andrew-Lloyd Webber and Trevor Nunn went on to be the climax and best known song from Cats and won the 1981 Ivor Novello for Best Song. Tim and Andrew didn't speak for years.

Similarly, I missed out on the publishing to what is the second longest running show in Broadway history as Andrew Lloyd-Webber declined my offer and re-mortgaged his house in order to raise the money, such was his belief in Cats and his talent, a decision for which I have nothing but admiration.

BENNY GREEN

Although not a direct connection to musicals, Benny Green was well versed in the musical world. Shortly before the 1967 Eurovision I was invited, along with some of the other songwriters, to appear on the BBC to discuss the contest itself and music in general. The resulting programme is very interesting for a number of reasons and represents a snapshot in time. I am sure it is on Youtube somewhere and worth a look.

Along with Mitch Murray, Chris Andrews, Roger Webb and Jimmy Stewart, we comprised the writers or co-songwriters of the proposed songs for the UK entry. Benny was a jazz saxophonist and BBC regular who didn't pull any punches when claiming that there had been no decent songs written since the Great American Songbook and that none of the songs of the intervening years would ever be considered classics.

The debate was reasonably heated but what the viewers didn't know was that Green was a bitter man and a failed songwriter who, accordingly, didn't have any time for the likes of us. Looking at the footage today, we are all in suit and tie and all smoking. If you do manage to see it, you'll notice that, being someone who didn't smoke cigarettes, I don't know how to hold the fag, let alone exhale! Also anachronistic was the debate as Green was incredibly rude and insulting to the 5 songwriters sitting in front of him. Never mind Grace Jones clipping Russell Harty round the ear years later, if this was a debate today, I think one of us would have chinned Green.

III. COMEDIANS

TOMMY COOPER

When I was playing in the Showbiz XI football team, Tommy Cooper used to pick me up and he had a different car every week. When I asked him why, he told me that the local garage was so desperate for him to buy one that they kept lending them. I think the garage cottoned on because one day he turned up in an open top MG Midget which was a very tiny car for a big chap like Tommy. He sat there, head above the windscreen in a Biggles hat and goggles. We were running late but Tommy put his foot down and we made up the time......until we passed a thatched pub and Tommy stopped and said "That's the best sign I've ever seen," pointing to 'A pie, a pint and a friendly word'. Ignoring the fact that we were going to be late, he led me in the pub, sat at the bar, and said to the landlord, "Two pies and two pints please." We were halfway through our pies when Tommy said, 'Landlord, what about the friendly word?" The landlord shot back, "Don't eat the pies."Tommy laughed so hard he fell off his stool.

JOHN LAURIE

John was best known for his role as Private Frasier in Dad's Army but he was actually a prolific Shakespearean actor not to mention appearing in films such as The 39 Steps and Fanny By Gaslight. I made an album with him because he loved the Scottish poet William McGonagall (who I thought was shit!) Well, he fulfilled his ambition of the album and we had two great days recording it. I think it sold about 10 copies - thanks to HIS Mum this time !

Incidentally, commenting on Dad's Army, he said "I've played every part in Shakespeare, I was considered to be the finest Hamlet of the twenties and I had retired, and now I'm famous for doing this crap."

GALTON AND SIMPSON

Prior to Kenwood, I lived in Sunbury and frequented a pub there. One day, a couple of chaps who drank there regularly were sitting, writing at a table and they kept laughing. After a few days of this, I was intrigued so I went over and introduced myself. It was Ray Galton and Alan Simpson, famous for writing Hancock's Half Hour. They showed me what they were now writing and had been laughing at - it was the script for Steptoe and Son! After that we met regularly and they were very nice and funny guys.

RODNEY DANGERFIELD

I was staying at The Sherry Netherland Hotel in New York and Rodney Dangerfield was at the bar every evening. He was larger than life and exactly as he appeared on TV and film. He never stopped telling jokes and all his contemporaries like Bob Newhart and Bill Cosby thought he was the funniest. His mind was so active that he couldn't remember people's names but, because of my striking white hair and Scottish accent, he always remembered me. He is the only man I've enjoyed or allowed to call me 'Jock', a term I, like most Scots, don't like.

DUDLEY MOORE

Dudley Moore was a good friend of mine – I used to meet him at The Beverly Hills Hotel, where he was allowed to play the house piano because he was such an accomplished pianist. He couldn't understand how I could write pop songs whereas he couldn't but I'd rather have played piano like him. One night he asked me to wait with him as his ex-wife, Tuesday, was coming to see him with Bobby Darin's ex wife Sandra Dee. The four of us sat in the Polo Lounge having a drink and Tuesday said "I'd like you to be the first to know that I'm getting married .

Dudley said 'Who to?" and Tuesday replied "Fredric March. Dud exclaimed " No, he's far too old !"

"No," said Tuesday, "I'm not marrying the actor. It's his grandson, Fredric March III."

Quick as a flash, Dudley said "You can't do that. You'll be known as Tuesday, March 3rd."

She never did marry March.

JAMES HUNT

Maybe James shouldn't be in the 'Comedian's' section but this story seems to fit rather well.

I was on a celebrity golf trip to Florida and, in our group was James Hunt, the Formula 1 racing driver and an ex-

Public School Boy who never wore a tie. He would always be dressed in a jacket, open necked white shirt, jeans and frequently no socks.

I told him that it was great that he came along on the trip and about the big names who had arrived. I said to James "We are here to promote Great Britain so have a good time but, at the opening dinner, please wear black tie and socks." "Of course I shall old boy" he replied.

Well, he arrived at the dinner looking more like James Bond than James Hunt. He was wearing a green velvet jacket, black tie, shoes AND socks and with his blond hair he stood out! I was so pleased. After the initial cocktail party gathering, we were all sitting in our various places having the formal dinner and I look round to see James - jacket off, white shirt open, no tie and somehow he had managed to get his Jeans! What could I say? He was a major player in the Formula One world and soon after he would become World Champion.

PATRICK MOWER & SUZANNE DANIELLE

On the same Florida trip, Patrick Mower (at the time a top TV actor in the UK) along with Jim Watt, ex boxing Middleweight Champion, World Cup winner Bobby Charlton and the The Duke & Duchess of Roxburghe were to present the Prizes.

I had known Patrick from his acting and when we both opened The Pennyhill Golf and Country Club for owners Ian & Pam Hayton (who went on to buy Foxhills and transform it into a beautiful Golf & Country Club), I got to know him and particularly his girlfriend, Suzanne Danielle, very well.

Suzanne was, and still is, stunning but somehow her and Patrick didn't quite gel as a couple. I said to her "I'm not sure he's right for you," and her response showed that she was aware of this. "Someday my man will come along" she said. I am sure she never realised that was the line from a well known Gershwin song called 'The Man I Love.'

She did get the man she loves, marrying golfer Sam Torrance, the ex Ryder Cup winning captain and a fabulous guy. They now have four kids and live in Sunningdale where Sam plays golf.

Incidentally, Sam's father, Bob, was one the best golf teachers in the world but he sadly died at the 2014 Open Golf championship. There were accolades galore from the golf fraternity, not only about his teaching of many golfing champions, but also for his wit. I once asked Sam if his father would give me a lesson. Sam said "When I tell him that you are Scotland's number one Songwriter he will give you a lesson."

I'd only ever had one lesson - from a Mr John Shade whose son was a Scots Lad Ronnie Shade, a top amateur player who even beat Jack Nicklaus in the 1966 Eisenhower Trophy but died too young to make a further impact. Ronnie's initials were RDBM or 'right down the bloody middle' as he became known.

I went for my lesson with old Bob Torrance and he made me swing the club four or five times before stopping me and asking where I got that swing. Feeling rather pleased with myself I said it was from Ronnie Shade's father. Bob said "That's not a swing from old John Shade."

I replied "I didn't like it so I thought I would change it, hence my seeing you. "

Bob said "Come here, son." and put his arm round me. "Stick to songwriting, son. Your swing will last long enough for the level of people you play with !"

Lesson deemed over, we went to the Pub and I asked him who was the best person he ever taught and, as quick as a flash he said, "My boy Sam, but he never listened."

Sam played at the Pro Am at the RAC with comedian Jerry Stevens, my pal Wally Ball and me in 1979, the year before I became captain. We won that day. Jerry and Wally are great competitors but it was Sam who won it for us that day, shooting a masterful 62 - a new course record.

IV. HOLLYWOOD

GORDON MACRAE

Each year at The Bob Hope Classic, every team had to put on a short show. In 1981, the actor and singer Gordon Macrae, star of musicals such as Oklahoma! and Carousel, represented our team. Bob Hope had put on a little weight and Gordon stood up and parodied his hit song from Oklahoma, singing "Bob is busting out all over." It went down a storm and Bob took it all in great humour. The comedians got up and told jokes, whilst the singers sang. I am confident but no way did I have the nerve to stand on the same stage as those greats.

At the time, we owned an apartment in Fort Lauderdale, Florida and Gordon, who was a recovering alcoholic, stayed there for 6 months. We didn't charge him rent as he was such a lovely chap and he wrote us the most beautiful thank you letter and I was pleasantly surprised to see that his notepaper letter head was a tam o'shanter. Although

Gordon was born in New Jersey, his father was Scottish, hence the letter head.

CHARLTON HESTON

I had been to New York to sign Martin-Coulter to a contract with Famous Music, the worldwide music publishing division of Paramount Pictures and was flying back on the red eye to London in business class. This was when business class was upstairs and there was a bar in 'the bubble' of the Boeing 747s. I sat in my seat and a tall American gentleman sat next to me and immediately started talking. "Do you want to sleep ?" he said "Cos I don't." I looked up and it was Charlton Heston. As soon as the seat belt sign went off, we went to the bar where we stayed for virtually the whole flight. You won't be surprised to learn that he talked passionately and at length about firearms and his pro-gun stance. What did surprise me though was that, for most of his life, he had been a Democrat, and a liberal one at that, joining a picket line in the early 60s when his movie El Cid was being shown in a segregated cinema.

He was fascinated about the music industry and publishing in particular and we talked through the flight, downing large scotches, something I rarely drink despite my roots. In turn, I asked him about the movies and all the gossip - who slept with who rumours. He said that Hollywood was like any other village where people slept with one another. That is such a simple, yet succinct response. I asked why he kept doing epics and he said "Because that's where the big pay is." He said that one of the most popular actors in Hollywood was David Niven, with whom he'd starred in 55 Days At Peking and that he was just "the best raconteur of them all" and that he enthralled everyone. We landed in London and walked off the plane, pissed and the rest is history.

As an aside, I only saw the aforementioned David Niven once. I was in Annabel's nightclub in Berkeley Square and he was in there with some friends. Unfortunately, it was late in his life when he was suffering from Motor Neurone Disease and he was having to be fed. Obviously, I did not approach him as it would have been wholly inappropriate but it did remind me of what Charlton Heston had said and it made me sad to think that this was the man who'd been so vibrant and "the best raconteur of them all." Illness can be very cruel.

CARY GRANT

I met many people through dear old Sammy Cahn and one day he said "Bill, you have to come and meet George Barrie." George owned Faberge and created Brut, the famous cologne. In addition, he and Sammy were Oscar nominated twice for Best Original Song, in 1973 and 1975 and I had lobbied on their behalf so George was happy to meet me. Anyway, we walked into George's New York office and there he was, with Cary Grant, who was a director of Faberge. As soon as he found out that I was British, Cary said, in that wonderful voice with which we are all so familiar, "How is the old place?" He was immaculately dressed as you'd expect and even though he was in his seventies, still very handsome and with white hair like mine.

After some time just shooting the breeze, George pressed a button and one of the office walls slid back to reveal a full recording studio with instruments, microphones, mixing desk, the works. Cary said "You know George got an Oscar nomination?" I said that I did know as Sammy had told me.

Cary then said "I only got an honorary one," and paused before adding, "but maybe I didn't deserve anything more."

VIC DAMONE

Despite Cary Grant's elegance, I would say that Vic Damone was the best dressed man I ever met. When I was doing my interview series which was broadcast on Radio Clyde, Vic was one of my guests. We were both going to a BBC party that was being held in his honour so I met him at his hotel room and we talked about his career and golf as, like me, he was a keen golfer. I still believe that his version of 'On The Street Where You Live' is the best ever recorded and I told him that, which he much appreciated. However, he was much surprised when I brought up Pier Angeli, the actress who was his first wife. I asked him whether it was true that James Dean really loved her and he said "Well I don't know about love because Jimmy Dean was gay but what I can tell you is, that when Pier and I were married, he turned up outside the church and sat there on his motorbike before roaring off, as we walked out."

DAME JOAN COLLINS

Jan and I were in New York and decided to go to the 21 Club which, at the time, was the City's top night club. My white hair stands out and Ron Kass, a Warner music executive, spotted me and we started talking to him and his then-wife, Joan Collins who was, and still is, beautiful. The four of us has a lovely time chatting and drinking and Ron told Joan that I was a songwriter and music publisher. She said that I couldn't possibly be as good a songwriter as her previous husband, Anthony Newley and when Ron pointed out that I was also a music publisher she joked "He's got nice hair but that's about all." See, my hair again !

LIBERACE and LANA TURNER

On another occasion, it was Anthony Newley who invited Jan and I to a party at Liberace's house in Las Vegas. If you've seen the biopic about Liberace, Behind The Candelabra, then you'll have a pretty good idea of what the decor was like. "Lee" as he insisted on being called, greeted us heartily, with a broad white smile, as he did all his guests, worked the room and then just disappeared leaving everyone to have a good time but without our host. During the evening I looked across the room and saw what could have been a scene from a Hollywood movie. There, on a stool by the piano, dressed in a tight white polo necked jumper was a woman who I guessed was middle aged but who had obviously once been a great beauty and who, even now, was still quite something.

I said to Jan "Am I seeing things or.....," and she interrupted me saying, "No Bill that IS Lana Turner."

Well, this was an opportunity not to be spurned so I approached Miss Turner and told her how much I enjoyed her work, naming some specific films such as 'The Postman Always Rings Twice', 'Peyton Place' and many many more. I asked her what it was like being such a big star in the golden age of Hollywood and she said "I miss the Hollywood days. You're built up, put on a pedestal but, unless you're Bette (Davis), you're just stuck on the back burner once your youth is gone. But I still miss how it was." A little sad I felt, certainly wistful, but for me to have met the original 'Sweater Girl', as Lana was known, was quite a thrill. Oh, if only mobile phones and their built in cameras were around in those days.

AVA GARDNER

In the 1974, during my golf-mad period, I was running late to play a round at the RAC Club with the captain and the pro. I jumped in my mini with the number plate WEE11, which I still have, and sped off to the golf club. In my haste, I misjudged a crossroads and hit a Volvo, which turned upside down in the impact. I jumped out of the car and helped the chap out of what was left of his Volvo and said to him, "I'm really sorry, it was totally my fault." Handing him my card, I added "Here are my details. Give me a call and I'll pay for the damage to your car but I am late for a game of golf so really have to rush." I think the poor chap must have been utterly stunned as he never did contact me, let alone charge me for the repairs.

It turned out that I had broken three ribs when the seat belt pulled me in so I decided to take myself off to Forest Mere, an alcohol free health farm in order to relax and aid my recuperation. I noticed one day that outside the door opposite my room there were two empty vodka bottles but didn't think much more of it. However, the next morning, as I left my room at about 8 am, the door to the room opposite opened and there stood Ava Gardner, clad in nothing more than a flimsy negligee. I must have stopped dead in my tracks as she said to me "Is there something wrong, honey ?" I was so amazed that I just about managed to utter "No." She asked me, "Why don't you come in for a drink ?" and for reasons that I cannot now fathom out, I declined. I never saw her again but I'll never forget that she had the most amazing green eyes and I could certainly see why she was the love of Frank Sinatra's life.

Purely by coincidence, a guy at my golf club named Alan Burgess worked on Ava's autobiography with her. Alan did well as a later book by Peter Evans was never published as Sinatra persuaded Ava that it was a bad idea. That may sound controlling but Frank paid for Ava when she fell on harder times until the day she died.

ROBERT STACK

The house we rented in Beverly Hills was on Maple Drive and we had some illustrious neighbours. On one side lived Diana Ross and on the other, Robert Stack. We didn't see much of Diana although I can tell you that she she was beautiful, if somewhat enigmatic, whereas Robert was just a super guy and still very handsome, something to which Jan will attest. He loved to power walk and one morning I asked if I could join him, a suggestion which delighted him. We became good friends for a while and chatted openly during our morning excursions. I remember asking about The Untouchables, the movie starring Kevin Costner and Sean Connery as Robert had starred in the TV series of the same name, playing Eliot Ness. He said that he enjoyed the movie but that he felt the TV series was a more realistic portrayal. As I write this I look back fondly on the time I spent power walking with Robert in the early morning warmth of the California sun.

ELIZABETH TAYLOR

I was in the Beverly Hills Hotel when Elizabeth Taylor walked out of the lift and into the foyer. As you can imagine, she was the sort of star who turned heads and sure enough, everyone stopped when she entered. I thought this was an opportunity not to be missed so I walked up and introduced myself. Being English, she was pleased to discover that I too was British and we were soon chatting away. She particularly liked my hair and I got the impression that she was quite taken with me. However, before I was able to find out if my hunch was correct, I came out with the most stupid line ever, saying "Miss Taylor, you're my mother's favourite actress." As I heard myself say it, my brain was trying to tell my mouth to stop but too late. The warm smile disappeared and the beautiful violet eyes of one of Hollywood's great beauties narrowed as Miss Taylor said "Goodbye Mr Martin." and she turned on her heel and disappeared in the direction of the car park and her driver.

A couple of days later I was telling a friend of mine Tony Shipp, an English vet who lives in Bel Air, how I had met and chatted with Elizabeth Taylor and he said "Oh I know her well. I look after her dogs. I am due to see her next week so come along if you like." A second chance which I, once again, managed to scupper when I told the vet the whole story, to which he replied "Ah, probably not a good idea then."

Maybe I am deluded that I had a shot with Elizabeth Taylor, but seeing as I'll never know for sure, I'm happy to stay that way.

V. THE BRILL BUILDING

The Brill Building is an office building located at 1619 Broadway on 49th Street in Manhattan, New York and is famous for housing music industry offices and studios where some of the most popular American music tunes were written. The Brill Building housed many famous songwriters, producers and performers although, ironically many of these writers came to prominence while under contract to Aldon Music, a publishing company founded by my hero Don Kirshner and Al Nevins and which was actually located a block away at 1650 Broadway.

347

The most prolific writers from the Aldon stable were probably Neil Sedaka, Howard Greenfield, Carole King, Gerry Goffin, Neil Diamond, Paul Simon, Phil Spector, Barry Mann, Cynthia Weil and Jack Keller. However, even this esteemed group were probably eclipsed by Burt Bacharach and Hal David who met at The Brill Building and whose first two songs, 'The Story Of My Life' and 'Magic Moments' both made number one in the UK charts. Not a bad start but their catalogue is as good as any writers in the business.

'ANYONE WHO HAD A HEART'

'Anyone Who Had A Heart' was the first pop song to use polyrhythm, meaning that it changes time signature constantly, 4/4 to 5/4, and a 7/8 bar at the end of the song on the turnaround. When I met tall, skinny Burt Bacharach, we talked nothing but songs and he told me of this polyrhythm, "I didn't plan it that way, it just came naturally as, that's the way I felt it." Hal David had not completed the lyric and wasn't happy with the sixth line of the first stanza, "And know I dream of you", feeling the stress on 'of' as opposed to being on 'dream' didn't feel right. He never did reconcile the problem and said, "I tried to find a way to make the 'you' do something and I could never do it...I had to let it go."

In those days (this was 1964) it was common for a song that was successful in America to be recorded by British artists and when the Beatles' producer George Martin heard 'Anyone Who Had A Heart' he decided to record it with Cilla Black. Cilla's version hit the UK charts the week before Dionne Warwick's original and ended up reaching the number one spot whilst Dionne's floundered. Indeed, a few years ago BBC 2 revealed that "Anyone Who Had a Heart" by Cilla Black was the biggest female UK chart hit of the 1960s

348

This rankled with Dionne Warwick for many years and, despite the international success and recognition of her original version, the fact that Cilla Black's version fared better in the UK has long been a sore point with Warwick. In the mid 90s, she said that Black's version of "Anyone Who Had a Heart" replicated Warwick's to the point where had Warwick coughed while recording her vocal for the original track or had that track's organist hit a wrong note, those features would have been present on Black's cover. As an aside, Bacharach and David failed to win an Oscar despite having been nominated for such great songs as 'Alfie', 'The Look Of Love' and 'What's New Pussycat' but finally won in 1969 for 'Raindrops Keep Falling On My Head.'

In September 2013, I was talking to Hal David in London and asked him, of all the lyrics he'd written, which was his favourite. His reply was "Alfie." Hal died in 2012, aged 91.

'HOUND DOG'

Elvis's favourite songwriters were Jerry Leiber and Mike Stoller, another duo who worked out of the Brill Building. Mike was on holiday in the South of France and when his liner pulled into New York harbour, Jerry was jumping up and down and waving from the dock. Unfortunately, the captain made of mess of manoeuvring the ship and it crashed into the dock, triggering the release of life boats and an emergency evacuation. When Mike came ashore, Jerry gave him a big hug and said,

"You'll never believe it - Elvis has recorded 'Hound Dog.' Mike replied "I nearly drowned and all you can talk about is a song."

"Well, it is Elvis !" shrugged Jerry.

Elvis never really understood the words to 'Hound Dog' and changed one line to 'You ain't never caught a rabbit' but Lieber and Stoller said just leave it.

In fact, Freddie Bell of Freddie Bell and the Bell Boys, who had recorded the song prior to Elvis tried to sue to get some of the composer royalties as he had changed some of the lyrics but he lost as he had done so without the permission of Leiber & Stoller. Who'd have thought a song comprising just one verse would cause so much aggro!

'STUPID CUPID'

Don Kirshner wanted to find a song for Connie Francis so he took Neil Sedaka and Howard Greenfield, another top Aldon duo, to her house. Neil is a very talented pianist but Connie kept thinking that the songs were too ordinary but, just as it looked as though the day was going to draw a blank, Don said to Neil, "Play that little song you played me this morning." Neil was reluctant but Don insisted and when Connie heard it, she loved it and the resultant recording was a worldwide smash, 'Stupid Cupid.'

'YOU'VE LOST THAT LOVIN' FEELING'

Another Brill Building partnership, both personal and professional, was Barry Mann and Cynthia Weill who wrote some fabulous tunes, including one of the greatest pop songs ever , 'You've Lost That Lovin' Feeling.' The Barry and Cynthia wrote it with Phil Spector and the song is one of the best examples of Spector's 'Wall Of Sound.' When the Righteous Brothers recorded the song, Bobby Hatfield was disgruntled that he would have to wait until the chorus to join in with Bill Medley's vocals and said to Spector, "What am I supposed to do in the meantime ?"

Spector replied: "You can go straight to the fucking bank and collect your money." as he was that confident that the song would be a hit. It's easy to say now with the benefit of hindsight but, at the time, there were fears that it was too slow and too long. It ran for nearly four minutes which was very long for contemporary songs; so much so that Spector even listed the song on the label where the time is printed, as 3:05", instead of the track's actual running time of 3:45". He got it right though as, in 1999, the performing-rights organisation BMI, ranked the song as having had more radio and television play in the United States than any other song during the 20th century.

A little bit of trivia - when the original recording of 'You've Lost That Lovin' Feeling' was made, Cher was one of the backing singers and Glen Campbell a guitarist.

'RIVER DEEP MOUNTAIN HIGH'

Phil Spector's aforementioned 'Wall Of Sound' was just that - he would use more instruments than had been employed before to create a dense, layered, reverberant sound that came across well on radio stations and jukeboxes that were popular in the era. He employed it again when it came to recording the Ellie Greenwich/Jeff Barry (another Brill Building duo) song, 'River Deep Mountain High.' It was credited to Ike and Tina Turner as singers but sung solo by Tina as Phil Spector knew that Ike was a control freak in the studio so paid him $20,000 to stay away. With the Wall Of Sound employing over 60 musicians and backing vocalists, the studio was rammed and very hot and after take number 30, Tina Turner was perspiring and stripped to her bra (and some say her knickers) but Phil was a bit of a voyeur, so wasn't bothered. The song flopped in the U.S. and Spector

351

said "I'm never going to make another record." He stuck to this pledge for 2 years. Of course, Phil is in prison now for shooting and killing a young actress so maybe he was more than a voyeur after all !

Chapter 19 - The Water Babies

With Martin and Coulter, I had created a songwriting team like Leiber and Stoller, Bacharach and David, Goffin and King, Reed and Mason, Chinn and Chapman and Greenaway and Cook. We weren't as good as them but we were good. Phil never realised how hard it was to create a team, and it upset me when it went wrong. I was clinging to the wreckage of trying to keep a team together. In the 1980s, we spent five years fighting and wasting money and arguing with lawyers.

Phil wanted to be a film composer in America. He never got a single film. He didn't know how to knock on doors in the States and take rejection. In the meantime, as mentioned earlier, I had also signed Sky, a group consisting of superb musicians: Herbie Flowers, John Williams, Kevin Peek, Tristan Fry and Francis Monkman and instead of keeping them for myself, I put the whole lot into our joint company. When Phil came back to me, I got The Water Babies film, but we could have done so many other things.

Whenever I had a bit of success, I would always buy myself something, a painting or whatever, and I would always buy Jan some clothes. I am no good at sizes and I went to little places that would take them back. In 1976, I bought a beautiful dress from this shop in Knightsbridge and this girl who took my order was in the McAlpine family. She was the wife of a film producer, Peter Shaw, and Peter had got McAlpines and his bank to put up the money for a film of The Water Babies. He asked me through a mutual friend, Guy Collins, if I wanted to do the music. I met the bank executive, Nigel Galliers-Pratt, who was putting up the money and I secured the record deal. He thought it was easy, but I said, "What do you mean? Do you know how hard it is to get a record deal on a musical ?" And walked out.

There were only a few songs in the production but they worked fine, and the cast included Billie Whitelaw, James Mason, Bernard Cribbins and David Tomlinson, but Lionel Jeffries was the director. That was a bad mistake as he drank too much and was always inebriated. His direction wasn't that good and the animation could have been better.

Phil and I had written the score for The Water Babies in 1978 and it was a great film success. We flew out to see an American publisher, Billy Meshel, and our lawyer was Michael Sukin, whose Step Father was Lou Levy, the great music publisher. We had gone across just after Christmas and we would be back in England for New Year. We couldn't get a hotel and so our lawyer took us to the St Regis Hotel in New York. William Paley, the man who built CBS, had an apartment there. Everywhere was fully booked except the Bronfman suite as the Bronfmans had gone skiing in Aspen. Samuel Bronfman, who owned Seagrams, died a few years later and his son Edgar took over this great booze company: he then sold it and went into the music business. He was the chairman of Warners and they should have merged with EMI. It's all too late now. Anyway, we got the Bronfman suite for next to nothing and there was a grand piano in the main room.

As we made our way along the hall to our suite, we saw an elderly man walking towards us with a dressing gown draped over his shoulders and he wore a singlet, boxer shorts, suspenders and stockings. He had the largest cigarette holder I have ever seen and a big twirly moustache and it was Salvador Dali. I recognised him and said his name and he turned round imperiously and he said something in Spanish, and fortunately Phil could speak Spanish. We told him who we were and he knew 'Puppet On A String' and 'Congratulations'.

We told him about The Water Babies and we invited him to hear one of the songs. We went into the suite and we played 'High Cockalorum'. While we were doing that, he picked up a piece of paper and he started drawing. He drew a grand piano but all the notes were coming out of the piano, they weren't on the keyboards. He had Phil with tails on sitting at the piano as though he were playing Tchaikovsky and he drew my big eyes and my cigar and my white hair. He signed it, 'Dali'.

When he'd gone I said to Phil, "Salvador Dali has just given us a drawing. We'll have to take it with us." "No," said Phil, "We'll only get pissed and we might lose it." We left it on the piano. We went out for dinner and we came back and the cleaners had been in and they had thrown it away – an original Salvador Dali. The Water Babies was released and nothing much happened, but 'High Cockalorum' was a very popular song. Terry Wogan kept playing it on Radio 2. In the UK, it is on a video called Showbox, and it has been released in several other countries around the world but you wouldn't believe how difficult it is to get the royalties from films. This was a new field for me.

Jan said, "What are you going to do if you sell all your publishing?" My son Angus had just been born and so I started Angus Publications and I put songs in there like 'Darlin'', and I, very fortunately, kept The Water Babies.

A couple of years ago Peter Shaw decided to make The Water Babies into a stage musical. He invited me onto the initial board as musical director but he then got two other people involved who wanted to write their own songs. Instead of using the original songs Phil and I had written they wrote 'musical songs' and it opened for one night in Leicester and sank without a trace.

Chapter 20 - And in the end

I. The Lincoln Memorial

In 1961, my brother Ian moved to East Kilbride when he got a job with their Development Corporation. He helped to build one of the best new towns in Great Britain. In 1968 my parents moved to East Kilbride, living on the main street opposite South Lanarkshire College. My mother took a job at the new Bruce Hotel as a sewing mistress but she didn't tell me for a couple of years as she knew I didn't want her to work anymore and would have paid for everything. She liked her independence.

My brother knew Lord Wallace and it was working with him that led to his being awarded the MBE way back in the 70s. Ian has been very meticulous in his work and has had an illustrious career in construction and, although I don't begrudge him his MBE, I did feel at times that I had been ignored. Sanguine as I was, my mother was very bitter about it, especially as a lot of my peers and contemporaries had been honoured.

As it turns out, I had been ignored but Phil Coulter hadn't. He was offered an MBE in the early 80s but he turned it down because he is a staunch Irish Republican. I have never had an honorary doctorate from a university but Phil gets them all the time. Maybe I should have kept the family name. Someone may have been looking for Wylie Macpherson without realising that I am really Bill Martin.

I was at a dinner with Sir Georg Solti's wife. She said, "You look so distinguished." I said, "Yes, but I have no honours, nothing at all." She said, "Georg was always being given things. I'll give you one of his medals", and she gave me the Lincoln Memorial Medal. I thought I am going to wear this with white tie and tails.

My brother has been president of nearly everything in Scotland, he likes being on committees and being president. One particular event was for the stonemasons and at this Glasgow dinner, some of the top people were very snooty. The accountants and the doctors dress up, and so I arrived in white tie with my medal. My brother had his MBE on display and others paraded theirs. We were in the Trades Hall in Glasgow and round the wall there are wooden panels which tell you that so-and-so left so much to the Trades Hall.

Anyway, that evening in Scotland, I was a guest speaker and having mingled with people, I found myself seated next to the head of Touche Ross. He said, "I don't recognise your medal." I said, "I'm surprised. You're a senior partner in Touche Ross and you don't recognise the Lincoln Memorial Medal." He said, "You get that for...." and I said, "You're not sure, are you ?" I said, "Very few people have this medal and you get it for winning the Eurovision Song Contest." Everyone was very impressed and kept coming up saying, "I hear that you have the Lincoln Memorial Medal."

I was speaking after the interval and Jimmy Reid, The Clydeside Firebrand, ex head of the shop stewards, was due to be speaking before me but had not turned up yet. He was meant to be sitting on the other side of the chap from Touche Ross. It was decided that I may have to speak before

Jimmy Reid but it was all a bit ad hoc and confused the toastmaster.

Just before the interval, the President, who was my brother, said, "I would like you all to be upstanding for the toast." As I was getting up, the toastmaster was pushing me down. He said, "You stay there as you are speaking next." He thought I was being introduced but it wasn't my turn to speak and they were toasting the society. I continued to try to stand and the more I tried, the angrier the toastmaster got and, in his annoyance, he hit the gavel so hard that it bounced up and went straight through a priceless stained glass window that had been there since the 16th century.

I ended up speaking next and it was difficult but I did it. When I sat down, the accountant said, "Did you give a speech when you got the Lincoln Memorial Medal" I said, "You don't give a speech. It's infra dig to do so. You accept the Lincoln at a presentation." Again all rubbish.

Jimmy Reid finally arrived, apparently preferring the racing at Ayr and, although he wore a tuxedo, his shirt was hanging out. He talked about Glasgow, the shipyards and Socialism but for 25 minutes as opposed to the 5 minutes he'd been allotted. We met after our speeches and I asked for a wee Saint George but he said, "No, you'll have a big Saint George because your a top man." I had actually asked for a Nuit Saint-Georges, which is a French wine, but I was not sure if he was trying to be clever or had never heard of the wine.

I am delighted to say that, in June 2014, I was awarded the MBE in the Queen's Birthday Honours list, something of which I am very proud. Princess Anne presented me with the medal at Buckingham Palace and yes the band played 'Congratulations'!

II. All In The Family

As my mother reached her eighties, I used to do things to keep her brain working over so I said, "These are my lottery numbers. We're going to Portugal and we're going away for eight weeks, but every week I will ask you about the lottery."

One Sunday morning, I called her up and asked her to tell me about the lottery and the winning numbers. She read out the six numbers and they were the same as our six numbers so I said, "Are you sure? We may have won £32m." I said that I'd call her back. I told Jan what she had said and Jan said that we should check it, but first she wanted a large vodka! We phoned my mother again and we got the same numbers. I said, "And those are the winning numbers for last night?" "Oh no," she said, "Those are your numbers."

As my mother got through her nineties, we were quite excited as we thought she might make it to 100 but it didn't happen. She was in her 99th year when she passed away.

My mother had a stroke in the summer of 2003 and from then on lived in Abbey Lodge in East Kilbride.

However, when I went up to see her in Abbey Lodge when she was 99, she said, "You've got to get me out of here, son."

I said to the nurses, "I am going to take my mother away."

They said, "No, she is too old. You're not allowed to do that."

I argued with my brother and he said, "No, she will be all right."

I said to the nurses the next day, "Please have her dressed. I don't want her sitting in old clothes."

They dressed her and I knew she was tired and I said, "Take her to bed and I will come in and see her."

I kissed her and she just said, "I love you, son."

A few hours later, she died.

My mother died on 18 December 2003 and she was survived by two sons, six grandchildren and five great-grandchildren. I have strong memories of her and her strength of character. She was my guiding light and I did everything for her. When I've failed, I felt that I was failing my mother. That made me hoist myself up and I was back to the level that she was accustomed to.

I hadn't spoken to my brother since the funeral. We are both strong characters. He thinks he made the right decision and I know he didn't. To my mind, he made wrong decisions and said things that are incorrect. We should all be very close and we were, but that's life. Then, whilst Jan and I were in Glasgow one weekend in the Autumn of 2014, we bumped into him. After 11 years of non communication, it was like putting on an old shirt and I'm delighted that we are back being pals.

Jan is the rock of my life. She not only looked after my first two kids but she brought all four kids up as a family. She has thrown some of the best parties and dinner parties that a man could ever have in both Kenwood, Belgravia and at Wylie's Cottage in Portugal. She is a wonderful hostess and an excellent horse rider until I made her stop. She was riding a horse for a friend and it was a bit frisky and it bolted through the trees and her head hit a branch. When I saw her, the hat was smashed in. If she hadn't worn the hat, she would have been dead. I said, "We have got all these little kids and I can't bring them up." Then she started breaking legs and breaking shoulders and yet she has not got bad bones. She has not got a bad bone in her body! They just keep breaking!

She has been an incredible and beautiful wife and a great home-maker. Everybody loves her and we are a great team. It is an honour to go to one of her dinner parties as she is a great cook and you would never know that she had been working so hard. People would think that there was a team of people in the kitchen. She is always serene. We had up to 200 people at times in Kenwood - the whole golf club might be there.

A couple of years ago, I told Jan to have a colonoscopy which she did and they found she had bowel cancer. They caught it quickly, operated and removed the cancer. Seven years ago now but it was a worrying time.

I'm delighted that all my children are great friends but I had to work hard to make it happen. I spent a lot of money flying them to see each other as Meran and Alison lived in Brussels with their mother.

I love my children. Much like the row of pubs outside the Govan shipyards, I often refer to my kids by number.

Number 1, Meran, has a brilliant brain. She graduated from Bristol University and lives in Brussels with Jessica, her daughter. She has worked within the European Union in various departments and is currently EA to the Vice-Chairman. She has been married three times so I think she likes wedding cake or dressing up. She is currently happily married to Wilf Moore.

Number 2, Alison, graduated from Glasgow University and became a successful international property broker. She is living in Oxford and is enjoying a different career in literary editing. She, too, is exceptionally clever and has an inmate sense of style, which I like to think she inherited from me. She is very beautiful and has a great sense of humour.We were delighted when she married John McClure in 2014.

Number 3, Angus, works in hospitality in London running pubs for The Urban Pub Company. He also DJ's parties and clubs when he has time. He can create the best atmosphere at a party, no matter what the age group is. He knows what to put on at the right time. I see my own father in him as he is very laid back and he takes after him with a musical ear and plays the piano and saxophone well. He has a lovely character, is very honest and never wants to hurt anybody.

Number 4, Melanie worked at MTV Networks Europe. Foster + Partners, and Starbucks Coffee Company. She has my drive and Jan's organising skills and is a real pocket dynamo. She married an Englishman, Rupert Townsend, at the RAC Club in Epsom in May 2010. He is a civil engineer building tunnels and bridges in Australia. She worked at Hill + Knowlton for a few years and now they are parents to 3 beautiful children, Poppy, Huxley and Barnaby. They have just moved to their 'forever home' in Bilgola Plateau on The Northern Beaches North of Sydney.

None of my kids has ever told me that they have written a song. My son is the only musical one but even he has never given me anything he's written, if indeed he has written anything.

The worst trait that I have given my kids is that I spend. I do save but I spend. If I give a party, I want everybody to have a great time.

III. Don't You Wear Black

Over the years, I have been to many funerals. As you get older, there are more funerals and fewer weddings. Every funeral to me is a little bit different and tells you something about the person.

I knew Paul Raymond quite well but I didn't go to his funeral as it was private. He made a fortune through porn and he put a lot of it into property and he practically owned Soho including of course, the Windmill Theatre. A lot of people said that he didn't haven't a sense of humour but I thought he had a great sense of humour. At his funeral, they played David Rose's 'The Stripper', at his request, to send him on his way. That is really giving two fingers to the world.

In 2002, some of us were drinking with Richard Harris in The Coal-Hole in The Strand. He was very skinny and he said, "I'm dying Bill' and he said, "Don't be silly." He had a suite in The Savoy and the next night the ambulance came to take him away on a stretcher and they were going to use the back entrance. He said, "You take me out through the front. I'm a star. I must have top billing." They took him out while people were going into the restaurant. Richard used all his strength to shout from his stretcher, "It was the food, I tell you, it was the food!"

Adam Faith was a strange character, very individual, and as befits his personality, he was buried in a wicker basket. His final words can hardly be bettered: he was flicking through the TV channels in a hotel room and he turned to his girlfriend and said, "Channel 5 is crap, isn't it," and promptly had a heart attack and died. Adam was a terrific fellow.

My great friend, Ian Wooldridge, the brilliant journalist at the Daily Mail told me this story:Mark McCormack, who managed the golf stars like Arnold Palmer, Jack Nicklaus and others, had a lined face like parchment. He left his wife and kids and married a tennis player, Betsy Nagelsen, and had a kid with her. IMG was a huge company, and he decided to have a facelift and he died on the operating table. He left everything to his little girl. She was about seven. When you see golf, it is like seeing peacocks as there is a lot of vanity there, but the biggest vanity of all is when you lose your life by trying to change your face.

A couple of years ago, I was talking to my old friend Tam White from the Boston Dexters and he said "Are in the mood for writing songs?" I guess I was as we wrote 'Don't You Wear Black' shortly before he died and I think it is an incredible song. I thought it would have been great for Joe Cocker and I was going to mention it to him when we next met but he sadly passed away from cancer in December 2014.

Don't You Wear Black

Don't You Wear Black
If you come from miles around
Life hasn't been so bad, I'll testify that's what I found.
I travelled many highways meeting up with folks like you
So please don't wear black, maybe pink or bright bright blue.

Now Don't You Wear Black
'Cause that was never where I was at
Broken down on a flight would make the beer and the party fall flat
So I have a dram or two as sure as hell I would do
So please don't wear black, maybe pink or bright bright blue.
Yeah, don't you wear black, maybe pink or bright bright blue.

Don't You Wear Black
When they lay me out to rest
You know I had a good time and I believe I did my best
So goodbye and fond farewell

I must bid you all adieu

But please don't wear black, maybe pink or bright bright blue.

Yeah, don't you wear black, maybe pink or bright bright blue.

c Bill Martin

I went to the funeral service for the American songwriter, Mort Shuman, famous for so many hits, at Golders Green Crematorium. When Kenny Lynch sang Mort's song, 'Save The Last Dance For Me', it was extremely poignant. Mort's wife and his daughters were visibly moved and there was not a dry eye in the congregation. Tim Rice was sat next to me and he dug me in the ribs and said, "You'd better write a decent song fast, Bill, otherwise you're going to get 'Congratulations' at your funeral." That's okay, but for me, Sammy Cahn's 'Call Me Irresponsible' would be more suitable.

Chapter 21 - What's Next?

I. Life in Belgravia

In 1976 Michael Caine put up some money for Langan's Brasserie with Richard Shepherd and Peter Langan. The first year they made three times the money that they had put up and years later, Michael sold his share to Richard.. Then, tragically, Peter Langan, a heavy drinker, died aged 47 after a fire at his home in Essex, which he is alleged to have accidentally started himself. Richard secured his shares and Langan's remains a great establishment, although I am unsure as to his current involvement.

I have only met Michael Caine through Langan's as he still goes there. I was once in the cigar shop in Mount Street in Mayfair I said to him, "Are you off to the canteen?", meaning Langan's . Next thing I hear is that he opened a restaurant in Chelsea called The Canteen.

Richard once had an overweight guy who worked for him called Michael, his maitre D, who wore an ill-fitting black suit. Michael went up to three ladies one day and asked what they would like to drink, and one was very portly. They asked for gin and tonics but the big one said, "I'll have a gin and tonic but with a slimline tonic." Michael said, "It's a bit late for that, isn't it, love?" Michael quietly left the company.

There is a famous restaurant in London's Mount Street called Scotts and it is owned by Richard Caring, who also owns Annabel's and the Ivy. My friend Philip Lawless started his career in Scotts in 1958 and it was during the Troubles in 1975 when the IRA decided to bomb prestige establishments around Mayfair. They picked Purdey's, which sold the famous Purdey guns, and opposite Purdey's was an Italian restaurant, both of them in Mount Street. That night the IRA blew up the restaurant, not Purdey's: they'd made a mistake.

Philip had been in Scotts, very immaculately dressed as always, and he had seen a patron signalling him to the front door. As he walked to the door, a bomb came through the window of Scotts restaurant and the place was blown up. Fortunately, there was only one fatality, a man at the bar, as it was only just open. Philip decided that he would go to Belgravia and build his own restaurant. He said, "If I'm going to die, I'm going to die in my own restaurant." In 1982, he bought and then built up Motcombs, a very successful wine bar and restaurant where I meet pals like Terry Venables, Frank McGrath, Russell Spence and others.

Twice a year I play golf with Richard Shepherd and Philip Lawless and we go to my golf club at St George's Hill. After the game, we either go to Motcombs or Langan's and it is a great day out.

II. Philosophy of Life

My philosophy of life is simple: you don't get what you want by saying, 'If only...' You make up your mind whether or not to do it. If you do it and you fail, you've still tried and you've had the experience. If you don't do it, then that's what you've decided and you shouldn't complain.

As my mother used to say to me, "You should cherish the past, adore the present and create the future." She was full of little gems. She also told me that I should keep my own counsel and that I was too busy talking to people when I should have been listening as that's how you learn.

I was very sorry that I split up with Phil Coulter and although I wish I had written more songs since then, the split has given the opportunity to say 'If only...' a few times and to try things that I hadn't done before.

I've enjoyed my property negotiations and buying song catalogues, but most of all I'm enjoying my career as an after-dinner speaker. Since 2006, I have been talking on cruise shops, and I've worked with Cunard, P&O, Fred Olsen, Page and Moy, and Saga. On the cruises, I can talk about The Rat Pack, James Bond Songs, The Golden Age Of Musicals, Song Secrets and the Best Country Songs. Whatever you want on songs really. Naturally, I'm happy to talk about my own songs! I have 30 different shows all with song stories

I am hopeful that these shows will lead to having my own TV show and interviewing musicians and sportsmen I admire.

I have always wanted to write a theme for a show like Coronation Street, something that would go round the world. I have never written a Christmas Number 1, so there are two more ambitions for a start. I would also love to write with Gary Barlow one day.

My mother used to say, "Age only matters if you're a wine or a cheese." She was right, but lots of people in the music industry wouldn't agree with her. If a record company knows that a big old style songwriter has written something, they don't want to know. I, or any of my fellow SODS, could write songs for Robbie Williams. I could write songs for the likes of Duffy and Adele but the record industry chiefs don't want the older songwriters. Every one who has heard my ballad, 'Clearly Invisible,' loves it. I would like to get it to Simon Cowell as it would be perfect for someone like Susan Boyle, but so far no luck. So you keep trying no matter how much success you've had.

In 2007, Sandie Shaw recorded this new slow version of 'Puppet On A String' that has been arranged by Howard Jones, and the song had a new lease of life. There is a clip on youtube of her performing the song with Jools Holland who said how he thinks the lyrics are great. I could imagine Susan Boyle doing 'Puppet' that way too. After all Sandie's derogatory comments about the song, would you believe she asked for my help in promoting it !

Fortunately, the old songs continue to be used. I know that some songwriters don't allow adverts but I regard it as the icing on the cake. You don't think when you're writing a song that this could lead to an advert.

I might as well enjoy them as there is little I could do about it. The publisher will send me a letter out of courtesy and say, "This is going to be used on such-and-such an ad." Even if Phil or I said no, the publisher would overrule us. Phil and I would never discuss it together as too much of a divide has come between us.

I'm very lucky as I know so many people. I don't need to buy football tickets as I know the right people. I can go to Manchester United because I know Sir Alex Ferguson. I am not an every week, do-me-a-favour kind of guy. I don't phone up every record company every time they put out a record but occasionally I ask for something. Use but never abuse, which was another of my mother's sayings. That way I can always go back.

In one respect, I prefer watching the game on the terraces as it is hard to show your emotions if you are in the directors' box. You're supposed to be more reserved, but if you are a Rangers supporter and Rangers are playing Celtic, the atmosphere is quite fantastic on the terraces at Ibrox Park. If Rangers score a goal, it is an unbelievable feeling. If you're in the directors' box and Celtic scores a goal, the directors will go, "What did you do last night, Bill?" They will ignore it. There is no sportsmanship: no one would say it was a good goal.

A few years back I bumped into Bernie Ecclestone and I said, "Bernie, I have a big birthday next year, I'm 65, I've never asked you before. Can I go to a Grand Prix?"

He said, "Which one do you want to go to? Brazil, Australia? Monte Carlo?"

I said, "Which one would you recommend for a first timer?"

He said, "Monte Carlo."

"I'll go for that."

"Okay, but you may have trouble with accommodation as it is very difficult, but everything else will be taken care of."

My aforementioned pal, Justin Hayward, lives in Monte Carlo. He has two flats there so he let me use one. He was going to be on tour at the time which is not surprising because Justin is always on tour but his wife Marie showed us great hospitality.

We got our badges and we entered by all the big mobile homes in the drivers' paddock away from the thronging crowds. While Jan went to freshen up, I was standing around and Sir Jackie Stewart came up to me. He was wearing tartan trousers and had a tartan hat and we got on well together. He asked me if I had met Brad Pitt and George Clooney and I said no. They were making a film about a Jaguar car with a diamond in it, that was racing in Monte Carlo. I was talking to them all, and they left me. Jan came out and I said, "I've been talking to Brad Pitt and George Clooney." She said, "Bill, have you been drinking already." George Clooney is the love of her life!!

If you go to a Grand Prix, there is something like a trailer park by the pits with the big buses owned by the key players. Bernie Ecclestone had a big brown bus with tinted windows. It was set apart from the others and you couldn't see in. He could see everybody who was milling about and he could come out when he wanted to. He must have seen Jan and I as he came out and greeted us. We thanked him for the tickets. He couldn't have been nicer but then we do go back a long way.

The race took place and I met Max Mosley who was a charming man. I said that I admired his father as you have to have guts to show your convictions in those days even if I didn't agree with his views. He never picked up on that so he clearly didn't want to discuss it which was understandable.

The Monaco Grand Prix finished and the Jaguar entry crashed in the underpass and the jewel 'disappeared'. It was supposed to be for the film but it was stolen.

In April 2011, I received a Great Scot Award for lifetime achievement, an event sponsored by Johnnie Walker. This was at the Boisdale Wine Bar in front of 300 hundred prominent Scots people, and I received my award from Sir Jackie Stewart.

Lorraine Kelly said, "Oh, oh, I'm not expecting this award" and didn't know what to say. She is very bright and nice but she's either shy when it comes to accepting an award or maybe she just needs cue cards. The golfer Sam Torrance said that he liked Johnnie Walker as it had helped him through his career. Another Great Scot, Sir Tom Hunter once said he was going to give everything away like Andrew Carnegie but he keeps getting richer and I'm not sure what he has given away yet! Annie Lennox spoke about nothing but her AIDS projects. This is all very commendable but it's not the right subject for a night like that. People are there for a laugh. I got up in my multi-coloured tartan jacket and I said that it was my trying-not-to-be-noticed jacket. I told the Spindonna story which brought the house down and the BBC political presenter, Andrew Neil, gave me a big hug and thanked me for giving a funny speech.

At the moment I am hopefully planning a TV show with Scottish Television. Their Chief Executive, Alan Clements, is married to Kirsty Wark, and they certainly heard my speech that night – so who knows.

III. Looking Back

I hope you've enjoyed this book as much I've enjoyed living it. It has been a very colourful life, certainly for someone who was born in a tenement in Glasgow.

I miss Saturday nights in Govan when my father was playing the piano when I was small.

I miss Friday nights in Priesthill when I was a teenager getting ready to go to the Boy's Brigade with my brother.

I miss Tin Pan Alley and the excitement of writing a hit song and the magic of writing a global Number 1.

I miss the thrill of being Number 1 as a Music Publisher, as a Songwriter and as a Record producer as I was in 1976.

I miss my golf captaincy at the Royal Automobile Club and especially the Bob Hope Pro-Am.

I love that I played golf with great players like Jack Nicklaus, Arnold Palmer, Severiano Ballesteros, Greg Norman, Sam Snead Sam Torrance etc as well as personalities like Jimmy Tarbuck, Bob Hope, Henry Cooper, Graham Hill, James Hunt and many more.

I love the thrill of my four children being born in perfect condition.

I loved meeting 5 prime ministers - Harold Wilson, Ted Heath, Margaret Thatcher, John Major and Gordon Brown and above all being introduced to Queen Elizabeth II when a segment of my musical Jukebox was chosen to be on The Royal Variety Performance and then again last year at The Windsor Cricket Ground during a Saints & Sinners lunch and cricket match.

I miss my Mother and Father but I am happy knowing I did everything for them.

I miss my pals who have died and I miss the fact that I created a songwriting team 'Bill Martin and Phil Coulter', 'Bill & Phil', 'Martin & Coulter' knowing we could have gone on together to greater heights with more songs and musicals for the West End and Broadway.

It's been quite a journey from the shipyard tenements in Glasgow to Belgravia in London.

And having said all that, as Louis Armstrong sang, 'What A Wonderful World'.......and of course, I have to sign off by

telling you who wrote it - Bob Thiele and George Weiss, not
SODS but I wouldn't have minded writing that myself.

BILL MARTIN -AWARDS

Ivor Novello – 'Puppet On A String', Most Performed Song of 1967

Ivor Novello – 'Congratulations', Most Performed Song of 1968

Ivor Novello - Songwriter Of The Year, 1974/5

Grand Prix RTL National Song Contest, Luxembourg – 'My Boy', songwriter 1971

ASCAP (3 awards – one each for 'My Boy', 'Thanks' and 'Saturday Night')

Rio de Janeiro Song Festival Award of Excellence, 1967, 1969

Antibes Song Festival Award, The Palme D'Or for Best Song, 1971

Yamaha Best Song Award, Japan, 1978

Eurovision Song Contest, first place as writer, 'Puppet on A String', 1967

Eurovision Song Contest, second place as writer, 'Congratulations', 1968

Eurovision Song Contest, first place as a Music Publisher, 'All Kinds of Everything', 1970

Freeman of the City of London

Freeman of the City of Glasgow

Variety Club Silver Heart, 1979

Golf captain, RAC Country Club, 1980/81

Scotland's Songwriter of the Decade, 1980

British Academy of Songwriters, Composers and Authors (BASCA), Gold Badge 2009

Govan High School – Inaugural member of Hall Of Fame along with Sir Alex Ferguson, 2011

Johnnie Walker Blue Label Great Scot Award, 2011

Tartan Clefs Living Legend Award 2012
and many gold, silver and platinum discs!

In 2014 I was awarded The MBE (Member of the British Empire) in The Queens Birthday Honours list

BILL MARTIN - SONGS
as compiled by Spencer Leigh

AIRPORT PEOPLE (Bill Martin – Phil Coulter)
Mindbenders (1967)
Roulettes (1967)

ALL NIGHT LONG (Bill Martin – Phil Coulter)
Back Street Band (1979)
Geraldine (1979)

ALL OF ME LOVES ALL OF YOU (Bill Martin – Phil Coulter)
Bay City Rollers (1974) UK 4

ARE YOU READY FOR THAT ROCK & ROLL (Bill Martin – Phil Coulter)
Bay City Rollers (1974)

BABY, I LOVE YOU, OK! (Bill Martin – Phil Coulter)
Kenny (1975) UK 12

BACK HOME (Bill Martin - Phil Coulter)
England World Cup Squad (1970) UK 1
Martin-Coulter Marching Band (1970)
Scotland World Cup Squad (1974)
Royal Marine Band of HMS Ark Royal ()

BAD MAGIC (Bill Martin – Phil Coulter)
Geraldine (1979)

BALLAD OF RONNIE'S MARE, THE (Bill Martin – Phil Coulter)
The Dubliners (1973)

BANG (Bill Martin – Phil Coulter)
Dave Dee, Dozy, Beaky, Mick & Tich (1966)

BARBARELLA (Bill Martin – Phil Coulter)
Vince Everett (1968)

BENEATH THE WILLOW TREE (Bill Martin – Tommy Scott)
Bachelors (1964)

BIG BASS BOOGIE (Bill Martin – Phil Coulter)

BIG MOODY (Bill Martin – Phil Coulter)

BOOGIEST BAND IN TOWN, THE (Bill Martin – Phil Coulter)
Slik (1975) Film, Never Too Young To Rock
Arrows (1976)

BREATHALYSER (Bill Martin – Phil Coulter)
Cocktail Cabinet (1967)

BREMNER'S VOLUNTEERS (Bill Martin – Phil Coulter)
Scotland World Cup Squad (1974)
That was for Billy Bremner.

BRING BACK THE GOOD OLD MELODIES (Bill Martin – Phil Coulter)
Christian (1978)

BRINGING BACK THE GOOD TIMES (Bill Martin – Phil Coulter)
Bay City Rollers (1974)

BUMP, THE (Bill Martin – Phil Coulter)
Bay City Rollers (1974)
Kenny (1974) UK 3

CAN A BUTTERFLY CRY (Bill Martin – Phil Coulter)
Mirelle Mathieu (1971)

CASABLANCA (Bill Martin – Phil Coulter)
Geraldine (1979)

CELEBRATION (Bill Martin – Phil Coulter)
Georgie Fame (1967)

CHARLIE ANDERSON (Bill Martin – Phil Coulter)
The Herd (1966)

CINNAMON STICK (Bill Martin – Phil Coulter)
England World Cup Squad (1970)
227

CLEARLY INVISIBLE (Bill Martin)

CONCENTRATION (Bill Martin – Phil Coulter)
Scotch (1979)

CONGRATULATIONS (Bill Martin - Phil Coulter)
Cliff Richard (1968) UK 1
Phil Coulter Orchestra (1968)
England World Cup Squad (1970)
George Harrison (as 'It's Johnny's Birthday') (1970)

DANCE DANCE (Bill Martin – Phil Coulter)
Dick Emery (1970)

DANCERAMA (Bill Martin – Phil Coulter)
Slik (1976)

DEAD MAN'S POOL (Bill Martin – Phil Coulter)
From The Water Babies.

DEATH OF LEOPOLD, THE (Bill Martin – Phil Coulter)

DO AS YOU WOULD BE DONE BY (Bill Martin – Phil Coulter)
Now known as 'DWBDY'
From The Water Babies (1978)

DON'T LOSE YOUR HEAD (Bill Martin – Phil Coulter)
Mike Sammes Singers (1967) Film theme

DREAMS (Bill Martin – Phil Coulter)
Ken Dodd (1966)

EASY EASY (Bill Martin – Phil Coulter)
Scotland World Cup Squad (1974) UK 20

EVERYBODY WANTS TO LEND A HELPING HAND
(Bill Martin – Phil Coulter)
Scotland World Cup Squad (1974)

EVIL FOREST (Bill Martin – Phil Coulter)
From The Water Babies

FACE IN THE CROWD (Bill Martin – Tommy Scott)
The Bachelors (1965)

FANCY PANTS (Bill Martin – Phil Coulter)
Kenny (1975) UK 4

FOREVER AND EVER (Bill Martin – Phil Coulter)
Kenny (1975)
Slik (1976) UK 1

FORGET THE JANES, THE JEANS AND THE MIGHT HAVE BEENS (Bill Martin – Phil Coulter)
Bill Anderson
Kenny (1974)
Bryan Chalker (1975)

GIVE IT TO ME NOW (Bill Martin – Phil Coulter)
Kenny (1973) Irish vocalist, not the group
Bay City Rollers (1974)

GLASGOW RANGERS (NINE IN A ROW) (Bill Martin,
Mike Stock, Matt Aitken)
Ally McCoist (1997)

GOLDRUSH (Bill Martin – Phil Coulter)
Phil Coulter Orchestra (1968)

GOOD THING GOIN' (Bill Martin – Phil Coulter)
Butch Moore (1968)
Phil Coulter (1979)

GOTTA BE NEAR YOU (Bill Martin – Phil Coulter)
Geraldine (1976)
Arrows (1976)

GREEN LIGHT (Bill Martin – Phil Coulter)
Tony Blackburn (1966)

GUITAR'D AND FEATHER'D (Bill Martin – Phil Coulter)
Disco Kid (1975)

HEART OF STONE (Bill Martin – Phil Coulter)
Kenny (1973) UK 11, Ireland 4. Irish singer Tony Kenny, not the group
229

HIGH COCKALORUM (Bill Martin – Phil Coulter)
From The Water Babies (1978)

HI HI HAZEL (Bill Martin – Phil Coulter)
Geno Washington (1966) UK 45
Troggs (1967) UK 42

HOLY MOSES (Bill Martin – Phil Coulter)
Christian (1971, reissued 1978)
Pumpkinhead (1974)

HOME (Bill Martin – Phil Coulter)
Christian (1971, reissued 1978)

I CAN DREAM (Bill Martin – Phil Coulter)
Geraldine (1975)

I WANNA GO BACK (Bill Martin – Phil Coulter)
New Seekers (1976)

I WAS LORD KITCHENER'S VALET (Bill Martin – Phil Coulter)
Peter Fenton (1967)

I'M A WINNER (Bill Martin – Phil Coulter)
Kenny (1975)

I'M CUTTIN' OUT (Bill Martin – Phil Coulter)
Los Bravos ()

I'VE GOT NO CHOICE (Bill Martin – Phil Coulter)
Dream Police (1970)

I'VE GOT SOMETHING TO TELL YOU (Bill Martin – Tommy Scott)
Boston Dexters (1965)

INCREDIBLE MISS BROWN, THE (Bill Martin – Phil Coulter)
Herbie Goins (1966)

IN MY CALENDAR (Bill Martin – Phil Coulter)
Helen Shapiro (1966)

ISN'T IT A SHAME (Bill Martin – Phil Coulter)
Billy Connolly (1977)

IT'S ALL FOR YOU (Bill Martin – Phil Coulter – Pierre Cour)
Geraldine (1975)

IT'S ALL OVER (Bill Martin – Phil Coulter)
J. Vincent Edwards (1970)

IT'S SO NICE (Bill Martin – Phil Coulter)
Soft Pedalling (1970) For Commonwealth Games

I'VE GOT NO CHOICE (Bill Martin – Phil Coulter)
Dream Police (1970)

JENNY GOTTA DANCE (Bill Martin – Phil Coulter)
John Kincade (1973) (Germany, 45, 1975)
Bay City Rollers (1974)

JULIE ANNE (Bill Martin – Phil Coulter)
Kenny (1975) UK 10
James Last (1975)
Sylvie Vartan (1975)

KID'S A PUNK, THE (Bill Martin – Phil Coulter)
Slik (1976)

KISS ME NOW (Bill Martin)
Tommy Quickly (1963)

LET ME LOVE YOU (Bill Martin – Phil Coulter)
Arrows (1976)

LONELY SINGING DOLL, A (Bill Martin – Tommy Scott – Serge Gainsbourg)
'Poupée De Cire, Poupée De Son' (France Gallo (1965 original)
Twinkle (1965)

LULI LU LI (Bill Martin – Phil Coulter)
From The Water Babies (1978)

ME AND MY MINISKIRT (Bill Martin – Phil Coulter)
X Y Zee (1966)

MESSRS LINSEY, PARKER AND FLYNN ()
Lee Drummond (1966)

MR. DISAPPOINTED (Bill Martin)
The Beatstalkers (1966)

MOLLY MAGUIRES, THE (Bill Martin – Phil Coulter)
Dubliners (1969)

MONEY-GO-ROUND (Bill Martin – Phil Coulter)
Koobas (1967)

MY BOY (Bill Martin – Phil Coulter – Claude Francois – Jean-Pierre Bourtayre – Yves Lavot)
'Parce Que Je T'Aime Mon Enfant' (Claude Francois) (1970 original)
Richard Harris (1971) US 41 (13, Easy Listening)
Elvis Presley (1974) UK 5, US 20 (1, Adult Contemporary)

MY LIFE (Bill Martin – Phil Coulter)
Ken Dodd (1968)

NICE TO HAVE YOU HOME (Bill Martin – Phil Coulter)
Kenny (1975)
New Seekers (1976)

NINE TIMES IN A ROW (Bill Martin – Mike Stock – Matt Aitken)

NO MEAN CITY (Bill Martin)
Written 1982 after being asked by Lord Provost of Glasgow for song.

OH! BABUSHKA (Bill Martin – Phil Coulter)
Fureys & Davey Arthur ()

OH SAMUEL DON'T DIE (Bill Martin – Tommy Scott)
Bachelors (1964) B-side of 'No Arms Can Ever Hold You'.

OLD FRIENDS (Bill Martin – Phil Coulter)
From The Water Babies

OLD WISHING WELL (Bill Martin – Tommy Scott – Mueller)
Bachelors (1965) B-side of 'In The Chapel In The Moonlight'

ONCE UPON A TIME (Bill Martin – Phil Coulter)
Arrows (1976)

ON TO HARTHOVER HALL (Bill Martin – Phil Coulter)
From The Water Babies (1978)

OTHER MEN'S GOLD (Bill Martin – Phil Coulter – Giovanni Ferri)
Song from Italian western, A Man Called Sledge (1970), starring James Garner and Dennis Weaver

PEPPERMINTS AND POLKA DOTS (Bill Martin – Phil Coulter)
Written for Lulu but not recorded (1970)

PRIVATE SCOTTY GRANT (Bill Martin – Phil Coulter)
Private Scotty Grant (Bill Martin)

PROPOSAL (Bill Martin – Phil Coulter)
Richard Harris (1971)

PUPPET ON A STRING (Bill Martin - Phil Coulter)
Sandie Shaw (1967) UK 1, plus foreign language versions
Cocktail Cabinet (1967)
Pinky & Perky (1967)
England World Cup Squad (1970)

Scores of orchestral versions including Mantovani, Joe Loss, Tony Osborne, Paul Mauriat, Sounds Orchestral and James Last.

RELY ON ME (Bill Martin – Phil Coulter)
J. Vincent Edwards ()

REMEMBER (SHA LA LA LA) (Bill Martin – Phil Coulter)
Bay City Rollers (1974) UK 6
Scotland World Cup Squad (1974)

REQUIEM (Bill Martin – Phil Coulter)
Slik (1976) UK 24

ROLLER COASTER (Bill Martin – Phil Coulter - Moretti)
Disco Kid (1975) TV theme for Noel Edmonds

RUNAWAY BUNION, THE (Bill Martin – Phil Coulter)
Phil Coulter Orchestra (1966)

SATURDAY NIGHT (Bill Martin – Phil Coulter)
Bay City Rollers (1975) US 1
Ned's Atomic Dustbin (1993) US modern rock chart 26

SCORN NOT HIS SIMPLICITY (Bill Martin – Phil Coulter)
The Dubliners (vocal, Luke Kelly) (1970)
Sinead O'Connor (1994)
Three Irish Tenors (2000)
The Dubliners (vocal, Paddy Reilly) (2002)

SCOTLAND SCOTLAND (Bill Martin – Phil Coulter)
Scotland World Cup Squad (1974)

SHANG-A-LANG (Bill Martin – Phil Coulter)
Bay City Rollers (1974) UK 2

SHINE IT ON (Bill Martin – Phil Coulter)
Christian (1978)

SOUND OF SUPER K, THE (Bill Martin – Phil Coulter)
Kenny (1975)

SPANISH FLY (Theme) (Bill Martin – Phil Coulter)
Film music (1976)

SPIDER-MAN (Bill Martin – Phil Coulter)
Music for TV cartoon series

SUMMERLOVE SENSATION (Bill Martin – Phil Coulter)
Bay City Rollers (1974) UK 3
Bobby Vinton (1974)
Sylvie Vartan (1974)

SURROUND YOURSELF WITH SORROW (Bill Martin – Phil Coulter)
Cilla Black (1969) UK 3 n

SWEETHEART (Bill Martin – Phil Coulter)
D'Arcy (1973)

TAKE A GIRL LIKE YOU (Bill Martin – Phil Coulter)
Foundations (1970)

TAKE ME BACK (Bill Martin – Phil Coulter – Natil – Ramoino - Polizzi)
Geraldine (1981)

THANKS (Bill Martin – Phil Coulter)
J. Vincent Edwards (1969) (prod M/C) France 25
Bill Anderson (1975) US country 24

THAT'S THE ONLY WAY (Bill Martin)

Adam Faith (1962) never released – first song accepted.

THEME FOR SMART ALECS (Bill Martin)
TV theme by Busted.

THIS IS OUR CHILD (Bill Martin – Phil Coulter)
Richard Harris (1971)

TOI (Bill Martin – Phil Coulter - Pierre Cour)
Geraldine (1975) Luxembourg's entry for Eurovision, came fifth.

TOM (Bill Martin – Phil Coulter)
From The Water Babies (1978)

TONIGHT IN TOKYO (Bill Martin – Phil Coulter)
Sandie Shaw (1967) UK 21

TRAPPED (Bill Martin – Phil Coulter)
Los Bravos ()

TRY A LITTLE HARDER (Bill Martin – Phil Coulter)
From The Water Babies (1978)

WATER BABIES, THE (Bill Martin – Phil Coulter)
Bernard Cribbins (1978)

WHAT'S THE MATTER WITH THE MATADOR (Bill Martin – Phil Coulter)
Deano (1967)

WHEN I TELL YOU THAT I LOVE YOU (British lyrics: Bill Martin – Phil Coulter)
Originally 'Quando Dico Che Ti Amo'
Al Hirt (1967)

YOU ARE AWFUL BUT I LIKE YOU (Bill Martin – Phil Coulter)
Dick Emery (1970)

YOU'RE DISAPPEARING FAST (Bill Martin – Phil Coulter) For Sandie Shaw but not recorded (1968)

ZARA (Bill Martin – Phil Coulter)

INDEX